EXPRESSIONS OF
FAITH

EXPRESSIONS OF
FAITH

TESTIMONIES OF
LATTER-DAY SAINT SCHOLARS

EDITED BY

SUSAN EASTON BLACK

DESERET BOOK COMPANY
SALT LAKE CITY, UTAH
AND
FOUNDATION FOR ANCIENT RESEARCH AND MORMON STUDIES
PROVO, UTAH

Library of Congress Cataloging-in-Publication Data

Expressions of faith : testimonies of Latter-day Saint scholars /
  edited by Susan Easton Black.
    p.   cm.
  Includes bibliographical references and index.
  ISBN 1-57345-091-X
    1. Church of Jesus Christ of Latter-day Saints—Apologetic works.
  2. Mormon scholars—United States—Biography. 3. Church of Jesus
Christ of Latter-day Saints—Biography. 4. Mormon Church—
Apologetic works. 5. Mormon Church—United States—Biography.
  I. Black, Susan Easton.
  BX8635.5.W58   1996
  230'.9332—dc20   95-51330
                                        CIP

Printed in the United States of America

10 9 8 7 6 5 4 3 2 1

CONTENTS

PART 3: *Faith and the Book of Mormon*

PREFACE

Noel B. Reynolds
Professor of Political Science, Brigham Young University
President, Foundation for Ancient Research and Mormon Studies

From THE DAY Joseph Smith first shared the marvelous revelations that God was pouring out upon him, detractors began to gather. Today, as during his own lifetime, small groups of Christian antagonists and Mormon dissidents attack Joseph's revelations and the testimony of believers with endless repetitions and reformulations of arguments invented in the first years of the Restoration. In spite of the wide acclaim for the positive achievements of the Church and the way in which its critics have been overwhelmingly refuted, the negative spirit of anti-Mormonism lives on, surviving its retired or expired standard-bearers. Each generation recruits new champions, mostly from a relatively small number of dissidents on the fringes of Mormon society.

In our own generation many in the news media who are drawn mindlessly to controversy have given the detractors new status and power, christening them "Mormon intellectuals" and presenting them to the world as the thinking Mormons who know the inside story about the Church. In their rush to produce controversial news, many journalists have overlooked the obvious truth—the LDS intellectual and academic communities are composed of strong believers in Joseph

Smith's revelations and solid supporters of the Church leadership. Only at the fringes is there noticeable dissent. The overwhelming majority of LDS academics and intellectuals are active, faithful Latter-day Saints who find these detractors to be driven by a secret hate for a goodness they cannot understand or enjoy on their own terms.

In spite of occasional eruptions of anti-intellectualism in the LDS community, the long-term reality has been that Mormons, perhaps more than any other religious group, seek and respect learning. Joseph Smith set the example himself, establishing schools for adults and studying biblical languages. The LDS community has always produced far more than its share of highly educated people. And the Church has always taken advantage of the education of its members by calling well-educated Saints to positions of authority and responsibility at every level of Church organization. The media's errors might be excused to the extent that they are relying on a received common knowledge: in almost all religious communities the more educated groups are the most likely to exhibit reduced religious belief and commitment.

But why should this ignorance be excused among those who specialize in Mormon news when it has long been established by sociological research that educated Mormons show exactly the opposite tendency? The simple truth is that higher levels of religiosity among Latter-day Saints—as measured by devotion to private prayer, scripture study, tithe paying, church attendance, and other forms of religious observance—are directly correlated with higher levels of education. It may be an anomaly, but it is true of the LDS community that the more educated a person is, the more likely he or she is to be fully observant and faithful.[1]

There may be good reasons for this surprising characteristic of the Latter-day Saints. Mormonism is a religion of both the spirit and the intellect. Mormon missionaries tell their investigators that they have answers to the great human questions. Conversion stories are always stories of learning and inspiration. Converts feel the spirit of the divine, and the gospel helps them receive answers to their questions about life and about themselves. Mormonism is not a religion that tells its members they have no right to know the divine mysteries. Rather, it tells them to seek knowledge of all things. There is nothing that God is not willing to reveal to his children, even to the point of showing himself to them on special occasions.

Nor are Mormons taught to be irrational or to despise logic in their understanding of the divine. From Joseph Smith to the present prophets, the Saints have always been urged to grasp a grand and coherent vision of themselves and their relationship to God. They are urged to acknowledge contradictions in their own lives and beliefs and to reconcile themselves to the full set of gospel truths. Latter-day Saints learn early that the Spirit can be their most valuable asset in this great quest, and that there is no true opposition between mind and spirit. The two must function harmoniously together to reach fully satisfying truth.

It would be fair to say that Latter-day Saints see themselves as both prophets and intellectuals. They depend daily on spiritual guidance, and they treasure deeply the understanding of God and his world that they have been given. They feel responsible to search the scriptures as a means of strengthening their spirits and their understandings simultaneously. They are suspicious of people who seem to emphasize one of these sources of knowledge to the neglect of the other. Both are God-given, and both are necessary for a fullness of life.

The testimony that individual Latter-day Saints bear of the truthfulness of the Church and the Book of Mormon, as well as the other revelations of Joseph Smith, is highly personal. The mind and spirit of a man or woman are finally quite private in their innermost workings. Each person must come to that mix of understanding and spiritual assurance that he or she finds adequate. There is nothing that others can hand you off a shelf that will do the job. It requires personal inquiry, reflection, prayer, and openness to God's revelations.

Though all believing Latter-day Saints find great commonality in the testimonies they hear from others, differences of personality and experience also stand out. Testimonies are multidimensional. They involve personal insights, spiritual witnesses, other people, miracles, personal experiences, and struggles with sin. Different individuals may emphasize different dimensions in their own understanding of their testimonies. I have always appreciated the fact that in Joseph Smith's first written account of his 1820 vision, it was the forgiveness of sins that most impressed him.

My experience is the same. For as we become aware of our sinfulness, we also begin to know of our distance from God and his high expectations—which becomes the most important problem in our life. And once we have experienced God's grace—the baptism of fire by which sins are purged and the desire to do evil is cleansed away—we've had an experience to which none other can compare. When one has been so directly touched and benefited by God's love, one will treasure and protect that gift at all costs. It is a form of knowledge that only a fool would deny or compromise.

The message of the gospel of Jesus Christ is that God offers this experience to every human being born into this world. The personal nature of such experiences renders them inaccessible to scientific investigation or to external examination and evaluation. The believer cannot fall back on science or the opinions of others to make decisions about spiritual experience. Each person must learn to recognize the voice of God in his or her own life and to honestly distinguish between experiences with that voice and other internal experiences of emotion or imagination. Our salvation depends on our personal integrity. And only we and God can know. The opinions of others do not count much, except as they are useful in helping us to learn to recognize the Spirit.

As a young professor I had a pointed experience that helped me understand this more clearly. In 1978 I spent a week in a small conference with other philosophers and economists, discussing basic issues of human life and social organization. The question of religious knowledge emerged and was dismissed by some as a product of wishful thinking. A distinguished economist in the group (later to receive a Nobel prize) looked across the room and said, "Reynolds, you Mormons believe in personal revelation. How do you know it's not just psychological?" The answer that came to me then was simple, but adequate for me and the group that day. I know from experience what it means to come to believe something out of wishful thinking. And I know what it means to receive guidance from the Spirit. And the two are very different experiences. For one thing, the Lord has his own agenda and is as likely to direct against my own wishes as to support them. Wishful thinking never does that!

When Susan and Steven Booras first suggested in 1992 that a

compilation of scholars' testimonies might be a useful response to the news media's lionizing of dissidents, it seemed like a project that might be worth trying. Little did we realize what a powerful and varied battery of personal witnesses we would receive. As I have read through the individual contributions to this volume, I have repeatedly been touched, enlightened, and inspired. Many of the writers open the most personal corners of their hearts to share priceless treasures. They offer significant insights into the process by which the Lord helps honest seekers to find the truth. Many report how personal failings or sins interfere with spiritual knowledge, and how repentance leads the way to enlightenment and sure knowledge of God's love.

When the leadership of the Foundation for Ancient Research and Mormon Studies (FARMS) determined to produce this volume, we thought immediately of Susan Easton Black, professor of Church History and Doctrine at Brigham Young University, as someone ideally suited to pull these testimonies together in a way that would be most useful to the Latter-day Saint community. Backed by the interest and participation of thousands of faithful Latter-day Saints, FARMS promotes the efforts of LDS scholars in numerous academic disciplines to expand and develop our understanding of the scriptures that have come to us through revelation to Joseph Smith. While these scholars occasionally engage in religious apologetics, refuting critics and dissidents, their primary efforts are directed to expansion of our understanding of the scriptures themselves. In the process, however, they demonstrate to the faithful that these precious scriptures can be reasonably defended by educated professionals using the highest scholarly standards. Such demonstrations can provide important shelter for fledgling testimonies that may be exposed to the fiery darts of the adversary.

Above all, the application of faithful scholarship to the LDS scriptures is another way of rejoicing in the great expansion of God's revelations to man in this day of restoration. While it is clearly the exclusive right of the Church leadership to pronounce official interpretations of scripture and doctrine, there is much in the background and literary character of these sacred texts that scholars can help us to see.

Readers of this volume will discover a marvelous and uncoached unity in these testimonies. The invitation to participate in this volume contained only minimal instructions—to share testimony; to discuss, if they desired, the interaction between their faith and their scholarly endeavors; and, if applicable, to reflect on their research into topics related to the Book of Mormon—yet the resulting testimonies share a number of attributes. Although most contributors are persons of substantial learning, none base their beliefs in scholarly insights. Rather, all point to an inner conviction that has come through life experience and God's gift. As they explain, these testimonies enlighten their entire lives, including their scholarly endeavors. None feel conflict between the canons of scholarship and of religious belief, but rather find the two mutually reinforcing and even necessary. But the reader will also notice a distinctive variation between these testimonies as each writer reveals the inner thoughts of a unique individual. The processes and events that each finds pivotal in the formation of his or her personal testimony reveal an authentic effort to rise to fuller understanding of the truth.

Our hope and prayer in publishing this volume is that it can strengthen others by precept and example as they pursue their own efforts to know the Lord and to understand his love and dealings with men. We do thank Susan Easton Black for the wonderful job she has done in soliciting and assembling these personal statements. We also thank Susan and Steven Booras for the original suggestion and Stephanie Terry of the FARMS editorial staff for her excellent editorial work. We thank especially all who have so unselfishly given of themselves in contributing to the volume. This volume contains the combined work and effort of many people, and it is better for each contributor. Finally, we wish to thank each reader who will find something of value here for taking the effort to seek truth, and we express the hope that he or she will share it with someone else who can benefit. The spirit of the book is that of sharing that which is most precious. We hope it will motivate and assist others who wish to do the same.

....

NOTE

1. See Stan L. Albrecht and Tim B. Heaton, "Secularization, Higher Education, and Religiosity," in *Review of Religious Research* 26, no. 1 (September 1984): 43–59.

PART 1

PERSONAL ODYSSEYS OF FAITH

CHAPTER 1

LIFE AND TESTIMONY OF AN
ACADEMIC CLINICAL PSYCHOLOGIST

ALLEN E. BERGIN
Professor of Psychology, Brigham Young University

IN 1955, at the age of twenty, I became a Mormon.[1] Now, in 1995, at the age of sixty, I have been honored by a request to reflect upon my life and testimony. Nineteen fifty-five seems like yesterday. My decision then was difficult because I loved the scientific method and believed that observation, experimentation, and reason were the most useful avenues to truth. My high school academic training in Spokane, Washington, was devoted especially to science and mathematics. The arts, humanities, and other intuitive disciplines seemed "soft" and unimportant. Religion seemed chaotic and confusing, though intriguing.

My freshman scholarship at the Massachusetts Institute of Technology (MIT) was a dream come true. The trip to Cambridge was a pilgrimage. There I was, a poor boy from an uneducated family, the first to finish high school, putting my luggage down on the sidewalk outside the MIT rotunda, pausing to absorb the drama of the moment. That memorable pause marked an epochal transition for me as I entered the high-powered world of the secular intelligentsia.

Our studies ranged from Thucydides to Einstein. Our exposure included daily contact with famous scientific contemporaries. Modern microwave radar had been developed there during World War II; Norbert Wiener was discussing cybernetics; my chemistry teacher had worked on the first nuclear fission reaction at the University of Chicago; and my ingenious roommate was working on one of the first modern computers, a giant three-story machine that we could walk around in. (It literally had bugs in it!) Our informal contacts spread to Harvard and the myriad centers of learning in the Boston area. There was intellectual excitement in 1952—virtually more than a down-home boy could absorb.

Oddly, the MIT experience was so thorough an immersion in hard science that I gradually became saturated with it and found myself surprisingly unhappy with its inadequate attention to the human dimension. I was puzzled by the purpose of it all and spent time with a research psychiatrist who was studying group dynamics, a campus rabbi, and a Catholic roommate who seemed very clear about his beliefs.

As the year drew on I found myself searching harder to redefine myself, my purposes, and the meaning of life. I dipped into psychology and philosophy books. Once I prayed the agnostic's prayer: "Dear God, if you are there, let me know what this is all about." When I discovered that MIT had joint programs with some outstanding liberal arts colleges, where I could concurrently obtain a B.S. from MIT and a B.A. from the designated college, I decided to enroll. Reed College in Portland, Oregon, was my choice. I knew Portland and had been admitted to Reed the previous year.

Though it seemed impossible, the year in Portland was even more dramatically transforming than the one in Cambridge had been. Intellectual debate on the major issues of human history and contemporary life was endemic and epidemic. Radical dissection of every belief, value, and cultural norm was our daily bread. Some vulnerable people became suicidal over it; others thrived and won Rhodes Scholarships. I wavered between depression and exhilaration. It remains the single most intellectually stimulating year of my life—a year of intensive philosophy and psychology courses, in addition to my standard fare of math and science. Reed brought me past the scientific method to a level of logical and philosophical analysis that soared beyond the technical wizardry of MIT. I came to love analysis of ideas as much as science, and the idea of God seemed even more remote. Now I had both science and philosophy—the keys to knowledge. But another drama unexpectedly intervened, and nothing has been the same since.

I met a young woman at Reed by the name of Marian Shafer. A Mormon from Alberta, Canada, who had just finished high school in Utah, she was on a creative writing scholarship. She was seventeen and had won an award for a short story that was to be published in *Seventeen* magazine. She seemed to have everything—intelligence, good looks, a vivacious personality, and clear religious convictions. She was an anomaly at Reed, having only the first of these traits (intelligence) in common with most of the students.

Our relationship started at a dance just before school began and gradually developed through fall semester. Her Mormon habits were different, but her theology was out of this world. Certainly, I had been searching for a frame of reference, but the disjuncture between modern revelation and secular empiricism was dramatic.

Though I had grown up in a family mixture of nominal Protestantism and Catholicism, my Christian convictions had been learned largely by osmosis and then had gradually faded away, although the Bible continued to resonate faintly in my mind. Mormonism suddenly put new light upon religious history and upon my sense of the world. My knowledge of this new faith slowly grew while my relationship with Marian continued to evolve. Both of these objects of interest provoked approach-avoidance tendencies, but by the end of the year I was hopelessly entangled in both theology and romance. Could I ever disentangle the two?

My opportunity came with summer and an offer from my father, a construction superintendent, to join him on a project in Alaska. I collected a box of books on Mormonism, evolution, philosophy, and eastern religion and headed north. Before leaving Reed, I read every anti-Mormon critique I could find in the library, of which there were many. I also found a used 1920 edition of the Book of Mormon in the Reed Bookstore, which I purchased for fifty cents and packed with my other items. I still have this little volume, with notations I wrote in the margins during the summer of 1954.

One of these notes was written in response to 2 Nephi 33:5, which says "no man will be angry at the words which I have written save he shall be of the spirit of the devil." I had written beneath this: "Then, I am." The dogmatic certainty of Nephi's words flew in the face of my scholarly devotion to tentativeness and care in making strong assertions. But, ironically, I later found Nephi's testimony powerfully convincing, and eventually I wrote a tribute to him.[2] It surprised me later to find that Marian possessed an identical 1920 edition of the Book of Mormon given to her by her aunt, Marjorie Wight, in February 1946. In the back of the book Marian had written: "Started July 21, 1946. Finished reading it December 21, 1946." She was ten years old.

That summer in Alaska I read the Book of Mormon thoroughly, along with the Bible, the other LDS scriptures, and several volumes of speeches and writings by Church leaders. This intensive effort was spiced by a great variety of other, contrary readings. However, the key events of this time concerned my efforts to pray. This activity was new to me, but I went alone into the Alaskan wilderness on many occasions and prayed with youthful energy that God would reveal to me the truth about these matters and his will for me. There, on the banks of the Tanana River, my heart and mind were opened to a new way of experiencing the world. I felt things I had never felt before. The spirit of God came upon me undeniably. At moments, my awareness of spiritual realities became transcendent. Sense perception and reason were no longer the only sources of light and wisdom. My heart overflowed with a sense of goodness and warmth. My test of God, the Prophet Joseph Smith, and the Book of Mormon (Moroni 10:3–5) yielded far more than I had anticipated.

Despite such powerful manifestations of the sacred world, I was so steeped in a secular way of looking at things that I frequently reverted to it and questioned everything I had experienced. Conversion, for me, would eventually require a thousand checks and double checks on whether I was engaging in wish-fulfilling self-deception, which I believed most of humanity was duped by. My year of psychology and philosophy had crystallized an already skeptical nature.

Equally important, I missed Marian and we corresponded frequently and in depth. Toward the end of the summer she made the surprise move to transfer from Reed to Brigham Young University, a school about which I knew nothing. So I traveled to Utah for a visit with her and to see BYU. The university and its setting had a magnetic effect upon me, and Marian's presence there cemented my motivation to transfer too. Fortunately, I was able to gain immediate admission, go back to Portland and Spokane for my belongings, and make the switch.

The fall of 1954 was tempestuous. I began to love Utah and the new gospel as much as I loved Marian; then, however, we had personal and emotional differences and split up. Our friend and mentor, Robert K. Thomas, became our counselor. (A young English professor, he later founded the BYU Honors Program and ultimately became academic vice-president.) He was a Reed College alumnus, and we felt immediate rapport with this man of prodigious intelligence, great human warmth, and an unwavering faith in the restored gospel. His Book of Mormon class became a weekly challenge to my views. It was difficult to maintain skepticism in the face of one who was simultaneously so spiritual and so intellectual. His advanced training at Columbia University combined with his degree from Reed had equipped him with a formidable spectrum of secular knowledge. I had to ask myself: "How does he contain both of these in the same mind?" I also had to ask: "If he can do it, can I?"

It was during this turbulent fall semester that I first attended BYU devotionals and the LDS Church general conference. I was also studying, praying, and testing the LDS lifestyle. My mind was open to the messages and the witnesses of General Authorities. I listened intently and felt things that took me beyond the earlier experiences along the Tanana River.

At the same time my study of psychology intensified and I immersed myself totally in Robert Howell's History of Experimental Psychology course. History shows that psychology as a discipline arose out of a marriage between philosophy and science. So I was back again reviewing the history of philosophy and the rise of modern science, but this time with the focus on human behavior. I loved this course, as many dimensions of my recent experience came together.

During this period when I was deeply exploring psychology and the gospel on two separate tracks, my relationship with Marian was on hold on a third track and mostly out of mind. Later I realized that this turn of events allowed me to grapple profoundly with my whole life—intellectual, spiritual, and emotional—without the distractions and disturbances of romance. It also provided an acid test of the sincerity and objectivity of my conversion process, disentangled from the biasing effect of loving a person who was identified with the beliefs I was assessing. My deep interest in her had focused my attention upon God and his will. Now I had to face him alone on his terms.

Doing so was a struggle. I already held perspectives that made religious belief difficult, if not impossible. The conversion process became a self-study, a jockeying between opinions—all in my own head. What was I to do with the Book of Mormon, the testimonies of the authorities, the faith of Bob Thomas? What about the secular searchers for truth whom I had studied and respected who had chosen a life of uncertain open-endedness blended with positive human valuing?

The decisive moment came when I realized that I had not given God a full and complete test. I had never totally given myself, entirely and consistently, to spiritual inquiry comparable to my intellectual devotion. I scanned again the numerous invitations and bold challenges throughout the scriptures and in the words of contemporaries that specified, like an experiment, how to approach God. Once again, the Book of Mormon set forth a provocative and powerful recipe (see Alma 32; Moroni 10; 2 Nephi 9; 33).

As I began to sincerely pursue this, a tremendous feeling of peace came over me. My being began to settle into the orthodox Mormon frame of reference. I began to know God and to walk in his ways and feel his Spirit. The scales of secularism fell daily from my eyes. A whole new way of seeing the world was being grafted into my intellect. Unlike my previously analytical outlook, this one was accompanied by warmth and hope, and it colored all relationships and aspects of life.

Coincidentally, Marian came to visit and we began to talk and to review our feelings for each other. Also, psychology was gripping my soul as well, since its blend of both the deeply personal and the objectively scientific seemed congruent with my changing orientation to life.

Thus it was, as the fall semester drew to a close in December of 1954, that a momentous transformation occurred. I accepted Mormonism as a faith, chose psychology as a discipline, and asked Marian to be my eternal companion. The rest were details: plans for baptism in March 1955 by Bob Thomas, marriage in June to Marian, and a doubling-up of psychology courses in order to catch up on this new major by the end of my junior year.

All of the preceding context is important because it shows that spiritual knowing is multidimensional. It touches everything and is touched by everything. Detached intellectual knowing is one-dimensional and incomplete: such inquiry cannot reach into the godly realm, and its effects upon relationships, lifestyle, and values are often negative. The eternal principles of living and the values that guide their application are learned by a composite of studious examination, careful life testing, critical ratiocination, and opening of self to the intuitive free-flow of spiritual communion. There is a balance among these ingredients that leads to the good, the true, and the beautiful. Omitting one of these factors from (or entering too much or too little of a given factor into) the equation for one's life orientation results in a failure to equate.

Another two and a half years at BYU seasoned and strengthened my formulation of what life and truth were all about. It also resulted in a master's degree in psychology, our first two children, a marriage anchored in the restored gospel and its associated lifestyle, and an invitation to work on a Ph.D. in clinical psychology at Stanford. Thus, I recycled into the powerful world of the secular intelligentsia but with an entirely new and vibrant perspective. The next fifteen years became a profound odyssey.

I had spent so much time evaluating Mormonism and scrutinizing it with the Reedian blend of scientific objectivity, philosophical analysis, and skepticism that no challenge from secularized Stanford professors or naturalistic psychological theories came close to undermining my new faith. On the contrary, I began slowly then, and continue to the present day, to turn my mental and spiritual skills upon psychology—dissecting and reorienting it for myself, hopefully improving its capacity to reach the broad spectrum of human phenomena, including the spiritual. Psychology had abandoned religion at the turn of the century. Unfettered by superstition, the discipline was supposed to become the wave of an enlightened secular future. Colleagues wondered why I wanted to return to the "myths of the past."

My view was very different. I did not consider it necessary to include the erroneous baggage of religious history in order to restore a spiritual dimension to behavioral science. Indeed, I agreed with many of the criticisms of religious traditions. The restored gospel provided abundant advantages in such an effort. Nevertheless, my efforts to include spirituality in psychology were muted by consistent rejection from many prominent and powerful professors I encountered as a graduate student at Stanford, a postdoctoral fellow at the University of Wisconsin's Psychiatric Institute, and a junior faculty member at Teachers College, Columbia University. Though there was mutual respect, virtually all expressed skepticism toward my views.

Thus, for fifteen years—three at Stanford, one at Wisconsin, and eleven at Columbia—I found some of my keen interests difficult to express. Clearly I, and everyone like me, was boxed in by a coercive ideology that pervaded the great universities of western civilization— an ideology that was laced with mechanistic, naturalistic, humanistic, and secular themes.[3] I understood this very well and could even sympathize with it because the yoke of ancient religions and myths had so often stifled freedom and the search for truth. To a degree, I thrived in the modernist atmosphere because I had the right tools of analysis and method. Indeed, I thoroughly enjoyed and became well-known for my psychotherapy research on understanding and changing psychological disorders.[4] Although I was unable to bring my deep interest in moral values and a spiritual perspective to fruition, I was able to achieve some satisfaction by including material on the topic within my own classes at Columbia. Still, it was frustrating to regularly face the undercurrent of opposition from students and faculty. In addition, there was little literature or research to draw upon from the mainstream of professional scholarship. It is true that there were voices of support over the decades, such as those of William James, Carl Jung, Gordon Allport, Viktor Frankl, and others, but the core direction of modern psychology was essentially unaffected by them.

I did have many deep discussions with faculty members and some of their families over the years about my faith and its basis. These discussions were penetrating and mutually respectful. I often identified the Book of Mormon as a powerful evidence in support of the restored gospel. It is a tangible object, observable by the senses. Where did it come from? Was Joseph Smith a prophet? Some were intrigued and investigated to a degree. Very few were convinced. Most were honest enough to acknowledge that they had no answer for the book. These were brilliant and sincere individuals who made their peace with this evidence by choosing an honest course of benign avoidance. When I read contemporary critiques of the Book of Mormon, I am amazed by their inadequacies. Many of the more sophisticated doubters tend to leave it alone lest they risk their reputations against a document inspired by the mind of God.

Although I became a tenured full professor at Columbia and received offers from many universities to further pursue psychotherapy research, I chose to accept an invitation to join the BYU faculty in 1972. This created many professional difficulties for me, but it opened the way to pursuing spiritual issues in a more concerted way. Despite opposition among various scholars, including some at BYU, there was enough support to provide me and like-minded individuals, such as Victor Brown, Jr., the freedom and opportunity to explore the spiritual side of emotional distress and treatment. This was truly a breath of fresh air provided, paradoxically, by a university thought by some to be too parochial. My experience had been the opposite. It was the major research universities that were, from my perspective, parochial and entrenched in conceptual tradition.

There were several years of transition at BYU during the 1970s, characterized by starts and stops, trial and error; but for the past fifteen years (1980–95), the spiritual force in psychology and related disciplines has grown abundantly and has gained a place of respect. My own work[5] has earned national awards from three organizations, including the American Psychological Association (APA); those of us who desire to put spirituality back into understanding and healing the psyche have made tremendous progress in gaining recognition for our viewpoint. One of my papers[6] elicited more than a thousand responses, including letters from many prominent professionals, some of which are excerpted below. They imply a strong but hidden interest in these issues that has since become public.

> I congratulate you for saying what I believe has needed to be said for a long time. . . . I very much hope that this paper will, in retrospect, be considered one of the most important to have been published in the area in the new decade.
>
> —ELLEN BERSCHIED, PROFESSOR, DEPARTMENT OF
> PSYCHOLOGY, UNIVERSITY OF MINNESOTA

> I think this is a landmark article that says several things that many people must have been thinking for years. You have done us all a great service.
>
> —TED LOREI, VETERANS ADMINISTRATION,
> WASHINGTON, D.C.

> [I] am extremely sympathetic with the hypotheses you describe.
>
> —LISA WALLACH, LECTURER, DEPARTMENT OF
> PSYCHOLOGY, DUKE UNIVERSITY

> I commend you on your excellent article.
>
> —KARL MENNINGER, THE MENNINGER
> FOUNDATION, TOPEKA, KANSAS, PAST-PRESIDENT OF
> THE AMERICAN PSYCHIATRIC ASSOCIATION

> On the whole, I am very much in agreement although we may differ on some aspects. . . . Major values in human relations are woven into various religious systems, and they seem to be universally true regardless of what a therapist's attitude toward a Supreme Being might be.
>
> —HANS STRUPP, DISTINGUISHED PROFESSOR,
> DEPARTMENT OF PSYCHOLOGY, VANDERBILT
> UNIVERSITY, PAST-PRESIDENT, APA DIVISION OF
> CLINICAL PSYCHOLOGY

Whether it be the role of religious values in the science and practice of psychology, humanism, radical behaviorism, or social learning theory, such ideas touch the lives of people in the field because certain proponents were willing to state them, whatever the reactions of others might be. It is through writings such as yours that religious values will receive greater consideration in psychotherapy.

—ALBERT BANDURA, PROFESSOR, DEPARTMENT OF PSYCHOLOGY, STANFORD UNIVERSITY, AND PAST-PRESIDENT, APA

I don't disagree as much as you might think. . . . I do believe there is some kind of a transcendent organizing influence in the universe which operates in man as well. . . . My present, very tentative, view is that perhaps there is an essential person which persists through time, or even through eternity.

—CARL ROGERS, CENTER FOR STUDIES OF THE PERSON, LA JOLLA, CALIFORNIA, AND PAST-PRESIDENT, APA

These new trends did not occur in a vacuum. People gradually became more supportive throughout the discipline. BYU and other religiously sponsored institutions provided a safe haven for the incubation of a new trend in psychological thought. A broad cultural shift also occurred in western culture during the 1970s and 1980s that was evident in resurgent public interest in spiritual matters, along with steady growth of organizations, publications, and conferences devoted to such matters. Religious social scientists and mental health professionals have led the way. I share common spiritual feelings with many of these people. They come from diverse persuasions, but we have high regard for each other's perspectives, and we share the conviction that there are God-given, universal moral standards.

Symbolic of this new trend is a book on religion and the clinical practice of psychology to be published by the APA; the book includes a chapter I coauthored with BYU faculty members Reed Payne and Scott Richards.[7] Success in this effort is already challenging us to demonstrate that these new views will make a positive difference unattainable in other ways. The chance to rigorously bring this to pass is a great opportunity and responsibility.

I am proud of my colleagues around the world who are engaged in this movement,[8] including many at BYU who are making names for themselves as competent, original, and provocative thinkers. There are too many to name individually, but of the centers for new thought about human behavior, BYU has to be considered a leader.

This is all refreshing and rewarding to me. I am excited about the future as cadres of younger faculty and students have their own visions of what can be done. They have an open field, relatively unfettered by traditional obstacles. Beachheads have been won and a new day is on the horizon—one that I believe will be marked by open faith in religious truth as it guides us to new ways of thinking and living anchored by spiritual subspecialties in the behavioral and mental health fields. As this happens, younger spiritually oriented social scientists might consider the following points of advice:

• Become competent and establish professional credibility in at least one area of nonspiritual specialization or expertise. This will provide your passport into the academic or professional world.

• Build all spiritual inquiries on a solid base of scholarship and be willing to absorb negative evidence about your views. Don't make a career out of attacking other people's positions; positively pursue your own. Be caring toward others, including academic authorities who disagree with you. Militancy may win battles in the short run, but in the long run we all have to live together—peacefully, we hope.

• Seek divine inspiration in your work and your life; if you receive specific direction, keep it private. Let your scholarly products speak for themselves as a witness of your insight and creativity.

• Be courageous in holding to your beliefs and moral values despite derision or opposition.

• Be gracious in giving credit to others for helping you advance your goals for the field, including those whose views differ from yours but from whom you have learned much.

Let me return, in closing, to the quest for faith with which I began this essay. I have never found my hard-won new faith to be wanting. I only find myself wanting in my ability to keep up with its momentum as it courses forward into a new millennium under the leadership of the Lord and his servants. Naturally, like others, I see some defects in the culture of church and university that cause me a measure of consternation. I believe that, despite its imperfections, this religious culture is the embryo of the kingdom of God on earth. The deficiencies are part of the human condition and not fundamental. The cure is not to make a career out of criticism. The cure is to do our own duty well—creatively, with compassion and inspiration.

The key for me, as I look back to my conversion forty years ago, in 1955, has been to give the revealing will and Spirit of God top priority in the ways of knowing. Research and reason are essential allies in the search for truth, but if either of them becomes dominant, God's natural order is upset. We become, to paraphrase Emerson,[9] professional monsters—a good analyst or thinker, a great methodologist, or a penetrating writer, but never a whole human being.

At the same time, I glory in the academic. Universities, research centers, writing, study, and publication are my world. But I have discovered that Bob Thomas was right. It is possible to contain spiritual conviction and academic excellence in the same mind. I am thankful that my church generously supports Brigham Young University, an institution dedicated to a knowledge of Jesus Christ and his ways, and to truth in general. I hope the future brings even more support and more freedom with which we can explore the whole truth of every subject in innovative and inspired ways. To the extent that our inquiries are absolutely penetrating, they can become absolutely revealing.

I know, however, that if every academic trapping were stripped away, I would still thrive, because of more important things—my family of nine children and twelve grandchildren, my eternal marriage with Marian, and my faith in God. I know that God, our Eternal Father, lives. His influence is a daily spiritual experience for me. Nothing is more precious. It affects everything else. There is no trial or doubt that can displace or subsume this conviction of the holy.

His Son, Jesus Christ, is not an abstraction to me. He is real. He has commissioned his church and sanctioned its leadership. He is my Redeemer. I have faith in him whom I know through unseen experiences. He has guided me during forty eventful years. I feel his love and aspire to be his disciple. My feelings for him are beyond words, and my knowledge of him is priceless.

Given such a foundation in spiritual knowledge, additional truth flows abundantly. Albert Einstein said, "I want to know how God created this world. I am not interested in this or that phenomenon. . . . I want to know His thoughts, the rest are details."[10] Becoming attuned to the mysteries of God opens the way for discoveries that transcend ordinary inquiry. I hope for such at BYU and among the community of faithful scholars everywhere. May we conduct our inquiries with an eternal vision that embraces whatever is honest, true, chaste, benevolent, and virtuous. Then, we shall know by personal experience that "to be learned is good if [we] hearken unto the counsels of God" (2 Nephi 9:29).

NOTES

1. An earlier version of this article was delivered as the Kenneth and Mary Hardy Annual Lecture, a Brigham Young University Psychology Forum address, March 28, 1995.

2. Allen E. Bergin, "Nephi, a Universal Man," *Ensign*, September 1976, 65–70.

3. Allen E. Bergin, "Psychotherapy and Religious Values," *Journal of Consulting and Clinical Psychology* 48 (1980): 95–105.

4. Allen E. Bergin and Sol L. Garfield, eds., *Handbook of Psychotherapy and Behavior Change* (New York: Wiley, 1971).

5. Allen E. Bergin, "Values and Religious Issues in Psychotherapy and Mental Health," *American Psychologist* 46 (1991): 394–403.

6. Bergin, "Psychotherapy and Religious Values."

7. E. Shafranske, ed., *Religion and the Clinical Practice of Psychology* (Washington, D.C.: American Psychological Association, 1996).

8. D. B. Larson and S. S. Larson, "The Forgotten Factor in Physical and Mental Health: What Does the Research Show?" (Arlington, Virginia: National Institute for Healthcare Research, 1992).

9. Ralph Waldo Emerson, "The American Scholar," delivered at Harvard University in 1837. In *The Complete Essays and Other Writings of Ralph Waldo Emerson,* ed. B. Atkinson (New York: Modern Library, 1950), 45–64.

10. Albert Einstein, quoted in Ronald W. Clark, *Einstein, the Life and Times* (New York: World Publishing Company, 1971), 19.

Chapter 2

A Legacy of Faith

Susan Easton Black
*Associate Dean of General Education and Honors, Professor of
   Church History and Doctrine, Brigham Young University*

T ELL ME A STORY," I would plead of Grandma as a child. Though I wanted to hear of Cinderella, Snow White, or Sleeping Beauty, she would say, "Susan, I can only tell you stories that are true. If you want to hear truth I have something to say." Not wanting to sleep, I enthusiastically listened to stories of Jesus, the Prophet Joseph Smith, the Book of Mormon, and those whose sacrifices created our legacy of faith.

Though I believed in the truthfulness of Grandma's stories, there was one that caused me discomfort. It was of a young pioneer girl named Sarah Ann who was in danger of being trampled by stampeding buffaloes. In this perilous situation she knelt and prayed for protection. "In answer to her prayer," said my grandmother, "she remained unharmed, even though hundreds of buffalo stampeded around her." Instead of marveling with wonder at the miracle, I emphatically pronounced, "That's impossible!" Grandma countered, "It is not impossible to those who have faith. Susan, it was because Sarah Ann had faith and you don't."

Such forthrightness caused me to ponder, then and now. I attended Church, paid tithing, and said my prayers, but the essence of faith, the substance of "things which are hoped for and not seen" had eluded me (Ether 12:6). As the years passed my outward demeanor mirrored faith, but my inner faith was lacking. I rationalized faithful events as good fortune, favorable circumstances, and just being "plain lucky." Would I ever have a faith like Sarah Ann's?

The answer was slow in coming, but in retrospect paralleled my desire for faith. That desire was ignited my freshman year at Brigham Young University. On a whim, a girlfriend and I decided to spend the weekend in Salt Lake City. While sitting with suitcase in hand at Temple Square, my friend casually remarked, "The President of the Church, David O. McKay, lives just across the street in the Hotel Utah." Her continual nods of assurance and our curiosity led us to the hotel. Speaking with the bellboy and hotel manager about where the famous resident lived was frustrating. Their refusal to disclose his whereabouts, punctuated with security implications, fell on deaf ears. We left them, determined to answer the question, "If I were a prophet of God, behind which door in this hotel would I choose to live?"

After hours of knocking on doors and greeting blank stares from grumpy hotel guests, we staked out three floors. An innocent chambermaid on one of the floors revealed the answer. Excitedly, we hugged each other as only BYU freshmen can. Our enthusiasm was boundless, until we decided to see if the prophet was home. Being the smaller of the two, I was designated to knock on the door. If the knock was answered, I was programmed to say, "We are selling early orders for Girl Scout cookies; would you care to place an order?"

As I walked toward the door I felt reticent; yet, as my feet faltered and heart pounded, my friend pushed me forward. It wasn't until I reached the door and was knocking that she ran like a flash of light to the far end of the hall. I was just turning to run when the door opened and before me stood the prophet. He looked surprised but didn't say anything. Neither did I; I couldn't. I felt like I had a key to the celestial kingdom but did not belong—I was not worthy to be in his presence. I started to cry and then to sob. He took me by the hand and said, "Won't you come in?" I waved to my friend down the hall, whose open mouth betrayed her surprise, and entered the prophet's home. Our discussion remains personal, but the resulting impact of that meeting was to change my inner direction dramatically. I resolved, as never before, not just to mirror faith, but to know of faith, to be faithful like Sarah Ann each day of my life so I would be worthy to see again a prophet, my Savior, and my Father in Heaven.

O that I could say I had always lived up to that resolve. I can echo Nephi in saying, "My heart sorroweth because of my flesh; my soul grieveth because of mine iniquities. I am encompassed about, because of the temptations and the sins which do so easily beset me. And when I desire to rejoice, my heart groaneth because of my sins" (2 Nephi 4:17–19).

To strengthen my resolve, I consciously determined that I would study in depth the scriptures, doctrinal discourses, early Church records and histories, and biographies of the righteous. I can say with Parley P. Pratt, "I [have] always loved a book. If I worked hard, a book was in my hand in the morning. . . . A book at evening; . . . a book at every leisure moment of my life."[1] After decades of reading and reading and reading more I learned: "If ye will awake and arouse your faculties, even to an experiment upon my words, and exercise a particle of faith, . . . let this desire work in you" (Alma 32:27). That inner working has now resulted in a knowledge of the great truths about faith. From the scriptures I have learned that "the Lord is able to do all things according to his will, for the children of men, if it so be that they exercise faith in him" (1 Nephi 7:12). We must "ask in faith, nothing wavering" (James 1:6) because "it is by faith that miracles are wrought" (Moroni 7:37). "Jesus [is] the author and finisher of our faith" (Hebrews 12:2); "your hearts are changed through faith on his name; therefore, ye are born of him and have become his sons and his daughters" (Mosiah 5:7). We all yearn to hear, "Thy faith hath made thee whole" (Enos 1:8).

These truths are not new but eternal. The followers of Christ in the meridian of time and the Saints of the latter days made the discovery of these truths years before and lived lives of enduring faith. But I needed to discover those truths anew to reach an understanding of who I am in the eyes of Deity and why Jesus loved me so much he would atone for my sins that I might return to my Father in Heaven.

Helping me in the process of discovering faith have been the journals and histories of early Saints who knew and loved the Prophet Joseph Smith. I stand amazed at their resolve to cling tenaciously to their faith amid the Extermination Order, the Haun's Mill Massacre, and the prospects of war. It seems to me that they echoed the words of Joshua, that no matter what trial beset them, they resolved, "As for me and my house, we will serve the Lord" (Joshua 24:15). For, like Job, "Though he slay me, yet will I trust in him" (Job 13:15). And like Joseph Smith, "What power shall stay the heavens? As well might man stretch forth his puny arm to stop the Missouri river in its decreed course, or to turn it up stream, as to hinder the Almighty," and yes, his faithful Saints from worshiping him (D&C 121:33).

The names and stories of those who remained faithful and endured in righteousness are not lost. They are told and retold by their thankful posterity from generation to generation. As we remember with gratefulness our legacy, let us recall the faithful declarations of the past. Near Liberty, Clay County, Missouri, Samuel Bent was the object of religious persecution. He was tied to a tree and whipped by a mob, and saw his wife die from the effects of these privations.[2] Yet he nobly declared, "[My] faith is as ever and [I feel] to praise God in prisons and in dungeons and in all circumstances whatever [I] may be found."[3]

Titus Billings's escape from mobocracy in Missouri was plagued with starvation and frostbite: "For three days and nights he had only slippery elm bark for food." His feet were "frozen so badly the flesh came off in pieces."[4] Yet, like Samuel Bent, he praised God for his faith.

When Joseph Smith, Sr., was imprisoned for a $14 note of indebtedness against him, he was promised he could go free if he renounced the Book of Mormon. His thoughts turned to the Apostle Paul: "I was not the first man who had been imprisoned for the truth's sake; and when I should meet Paul in the Paradise of God, I could tell him that I, too, had been in bonds for the Gospel he had preached."[5]

Another of those who epitomized the faith I wanted to obtain, a faith like Sarah Ann's, was John Murdock. At age seventeen John "came near bleeding to death; yea death stared me in the face, but I covenanted with my Heavenly Father that if he would preserve my life, I would serve him." True to his resolve, John turned to prayer and meditation and began his search for the gospel of Jesus Christ that professed and practiced the ancient ordinances.[6] He first united with the Lutheran Dutch Church, but "soon found they did not walk according to the Scriptures." He next joined the Presbyterian Cedar Church, but he said, "I soon became dissatisfied with their walk, for I saw it was not according to the scriptures." He then united with the Baptists, but withdrew himself from them when he recognized "their walk not to agree with their profession."[7]

Continuing his search for truth, John turned to the Methodist faith, but discovered "when I did not please them I would have to be silent among them awhile." By 1827 he had joined the Campbellites. "It caused me to rejoice believing that I had at last found a people that believed the Scriptures," wrote John. For three years he faithfully attended their meetings, but as the ministers denied the "gift and power of the Holy Ghost," John lost interest and concluded that "all the [religious] Sects were out of the way."[8]

Then in the winter of 1830 his prayers were answered. Four missionaries sent to the Lamanites arrived in Kirtland from the state of New York. They preached, baptized, and built up the Lord's church after the ancient order. Curious, John journeyed twenty miles to see the new preachers for himself and rebuffed a Campbellite who tried to dissuade him. "I told him I was of age, and the case was an important one, of life, and death, existing between me and my God, and I must act for myself, for no one can act for me."[9]

He arrived at Isaac Morley's home in Kirtland about dusk and was introduced to the four men and presented with a copy of the Book of Mormon. He said that as he read the new scripture, "the spirit of the Lord rested on me, witnessing to me of the truth of the work. . . . About ten oclock [the next] morning being Nov 5th, 1830, I told the servants of the Lord that I was ready to walk with them into the water of baptism."[10]

John wrote, "This was the third time that I had been immersed, but I never before felt the authority of the ordinance, but I felt it this time and felt as though my sins were forgiven." After being ordained an elder, he returned home rejoicing and endeavored to bear testimony. To his joy, "my family gladly received me and my words, Thank the Lord."[11]

It was John Murdock who, after the death of his wife, gave his surviving twins, Joseph and Julia, to Joseph and Emma Smith to rear. It was John that served a mission with Hyrum Smith to Missouri (D&C 52:8–9). On the trek his feet became wet: "I took a violent cold by which I suffered near unto death. . . . [But] I could not die because my work was not yet done."[12]

Truly, it was not complete. The calls of the Lord from his prophets would take him from house to house, from village to village, and from city to city, proclaiming the everlasting gospel to all who would listen, from the eastern United States to Australia. On October 14, 1852, a letter from Brigham Young released John from his final mission: "Return in peace. Your Mission is accomplished and others are on the way to follow up and build upon the foundation which you have laid."[13]

Who were those sent to build upon the foundation he laid? Could they include me, if I am faithful "at all times and in all things, and in all places" to the truths I have learned? (Mosiah 18:9). The Saints of yesteryear, when the winds of adversity, the trials of faith, or the Abrahamic test raged and beat upon their houses, stood firm because their foundation was in Christ (see Matthew 7:25). These Saints accepted the name of Christ by baptism and did not allow their faith to be tossed to and fro like the waves of the sea (James 1:6); nor did they stray from the strait and narrow path to the filthy waters or spacious building of Lehi's dream (1 Nephi 8).

They were not like their contemporary, Jared Carter, who recognized that "the spirit of God in a measure has left me," but failed to rectify the problem.[14] Nor were they like William McLellin, who maintained his testimony of the Book of Mormon but denied the Lord's chosen leaders, saying:

> When a man goes at the Book of M. he touches the apple of my eye. He fights against truth—against purity—against light—against the purist, or one of the truest, purist books on earth. . . . Fight the wrongs of L.D.S.ism as much as you please, but let that unique, that inimitable book alone.[15]

The faithful Saints learned and willingly embraced truth. They did not approach the gospel feast as a smorgasbord, offering a nibble here, a bite there, a taste, a smell, or even a desire to change the recipe. They accepted the gospel harvest as a feast of thanksgiving and embraced the truth as they came unto Christ and partook.

Through faith they had found the passageway to eternal life and clung to the rod of iron amidst the refiner's fire, the fuller's soap, and the trials that tested their integrity and tenacity. For them and for thousands and now millions of Latter-day Saints, faith increased to knowledge until they knew in whom they trusted: they knew their Redeemer lived (see Job 19:25).

I need to repeat that remembered legacy of faith. Their external trials of life are obviously different from mine, but my internal resolve must be comparable to theirs. May I forever be grateful to my Father in Heaven for the gospel in its fulness and for the opportunity to read preserved records and to ponder and choose the path of faith. May I endure in righteousness as I nurture my faith and strengthen my resolve to commit myself to a Christlike life. May I choose the path trodden by our faithful forefathers, who knew that yesterday's faith needed to be nurtured today.

As I partake of the Lord's supper, his feast, his delicious fruit, my hope of eternal brightness grows as I contemplate an infinite joy with the Saints of the Most High God—Abraham, Joseph Smith, John Murdock, and, yes, I could say with my grandmother, even Sarah Ann.

....
NOTES

1. Parley P. Pratt, *Autobiography of Parley Parker Pratt*, 6th ed. (Salt Lake City: Deseret Book, 1966), 2.

2. Andrew Jenson, *Latter-day Saint Biographical Encyclopedia: A Compilation of Biographical Sketches of Prominent Men and Women in the Church of Jesus Christ of Latter-day Saints*, 4 vols. (Salt Lake City: Andrew Jenson History Company, 1901–36), 1:368.

3. Donald Q. Cannon and Lyndon W. Cook, eds. *Far West Record: Minutes of The Church of Jesus Christ of Latter-day Saints, 1830–1844* (Salt Lake City: Deseret Book, 1983), 222.

4. Melvin Billings, comp., "Titus Billings, Early Mormon Pioneer" (n.p., n.d.), 21, in author's possession.

5. Lucy Mack Smith, *History of Joseph Smith by His Mother*, ed. Preston Nibley (Salt Lake City: Bookcraft, 1958), 185.

6. Journal of John Murdock, typescript, BYU Archives, 3.

7. Ibid., 5, 7.

8. Ibid., 4–5.

9. Ibid., 6.

10. Ibid., 7.

11. Ibid., 7–8.

12. Ibid., 10.

13. Reva Baker Holt, "A Brief Synopsis of the Life of John Murdock" (n.p., 1965), 12, in author's possession.

14. Autobiography of Jared Carter, typescript, LDS Church Archives, 28. Grammar has been standardized.

15. Larry C. Porter, "William E. McLellin's Testimony of the Book of Mormon," *BYU Studies* 10, no. 4 (Summer 1970): 486.

CHAPTER 3

OF CONVICTIONS AND COMMITMENTS

ROGER B. PORTER
IBM Professor of Business and Government, Harvard University

I FIRST VISITED England the summer I turned seventeen. I would spend half of the next ten years living and traveling through Great Britain as a missionary, student, and teacher.

The English at that time were buoyant and at peace, but many of my conversations, prompted by an abiding interest in twentieth-century history, harked back to the Second World War. Those with whom I spoke responded eagerly and candidly to my questions about their experiences during those dark and difficult days. Repeatedly they expressed their conviction that the cause in which they had been engaged was right. They talked about the commitment they had to see the struggle through to the end, whatever the personal cost or sacrifice.

Those conversations impressed upon me the power associated with firm convictions and how genuine commitment gives one's life focus and direction, inspiring great courage and selflessness. As I prepared for my chosen profession as a teacher and scholar, I determined to develop a set of convictions that would provide a similar focus for my efforts.

I returned from my first trip to England to enroll at Brigham Young University. As an undergraduate I spent many happy, productive hours studying in what was then the J. Reuben Clark, Jr., Library. I selected a quiet place where I would go regularly, a place at once familiar and dedicated to study. While I was there, my mind was concentrated and my energies focused.

To arrive at this location on the fourth floor, I climbed the stairs past a verse etched in the wall, quoting from the eighty-eighth section of the Doctrine and Covenants:

> And as all have not faith, seek ye diligently and teach one another words of wisdom; yea, seek ye out of the best books words of wisdom; seek learning, even by study and also by faith. (D&C 88:118)

Seeing those words each day inspired me as I considered my convictions and commitments.

On December 27, 1832, Joseph Smith received the most detailed revelation on education of this dispensation. It was from this revelation that the words etched in the library wall were taken. Also in the eighty-eighth section of the Doctrine and Covenants, the Lord instructed his Saints to build a temple: "Organize yourselves; prepare every needful thing; and establish a house, even a house of prayer, a house of fasting, a house of faith, a house of learning, a house of glory, a house of order, a house of God" (D&C 88:119). The Saints were further directed to begin a School of the Prophets, which Joseph Smith promptly established during the winter of 1833. Five principles guided that early undertaking and form the core of my convictions regarding learning and testimony.

First, the gospel embraces all truth. Rather than restricting us to a narrow, limited vision, the gospel offers a breadth of things to learn and subjects to master. The Lord commanded his people to gain an understanding

> of things both in heaven and in the earth, and under the earth; things which have been, things which are, things which must shortly come to pass; things which are at home, things which are abroad; the wars and the perplexities of the nations, and the judgments which are on the land; and a knowledge also of countries and of kingdoms. (D&C 88:79)

Accordingly, the curriculum of the School of the Prophets was ambitious. In March 1833 the Prophet was instructed that those attending the school should "study and learn, and become acquainted with all good books, and with languages, tongues, and people" (D&C 90:15). They studied English grammar, arithmetic, geography, history, penmanship, science, Hebrew, Latin, and Greek, as well as theology.[1] The school's curriculum reflected the view articulated by Brigham Young that "every art and science known and studied by the children of men is comprised within the Gospel."[2]

This injunction to seek all truth runs counter to two powerful tendencies in modern society—the tendency to specialize and the tendency to compartmentalize. Many see the path to success as one of greater and greater specialization, of becoming preeminent in a narrow, particular specialty. Others compartmentalize their lives, seeking to separate the secular and the spiritual, often neglecting one or the other. Some view the secular and the spiritual as in conflict; others consider one relevant and the other irrelevant.

The path the Lord outlined widens horizons and challenges us on every front. Those who retreat into the comfort of the cozy confines of a narrow specialty unwisely limit themselves, as do those who compartmentalize their lives between secular pursuits and spiritual matters.

Second, truth is revealed incrementally. The Lord has outlined the process by which he reveals truth and by which we learn wisdom:

> For behold, thus saith the Lord God: I will give unto the children of men line upon line, precept upon precept, here a little and there a little; and blessed are those who hearken unto my precepts, and lend an ear unto my counsel, for they shall learn wisdom; for unto him that receiveth I will give more; and from them that shall say, We have enough, from them shall be taken away even that which they have. (2 Nephi 28:30; see also Isaiah 28:10 and D&C 98:12)

It is a process that rewards patience and persistence. We learn wisdom by moving through levels of understanding. Advancing to a new level requires desire and effort, openness and receptivity. Learning is an experience more like climbing a mountain than jumping a ditch. It occurs step by step.

Third, learning truth involves teaching one another. The School of the Prophets was designed not merely to teach the Saints in order that they could magnify their callings, but it was also intended to produce a community of believers. The Lord instructed them: "And I give unto you a commandment that you shall teach one another the doctrine of the kingdom . . . and teach one another words of wisdom" (D&C 88:77, 118). In certain respects, our study of the gospel is a collective effort and a collegial enterprise. Each is able to help others and to receive help.

Fourth, learning truth comes by study and by faith—the particular method by which we are commanded to learn. The combination of study and faith has many dimensions. Dedicated study can contribute to strengthening our faith and deepening our convictions. The more knowledge we acquire, the greater our understanding of a principle or a practice, the stronger our faith and convictions.

Likewise, faith can contribute to our scholarly efforts. It is easy, indeed commonplace, for people to become prisoners of conventional ways of thinking. Among the most powerful vested interests are those of the mind. These interests often cause intellectual arthritis, leading people to a sense of unwarranted certitude. Faith in the Lord and in his promise to continue to reveal truth to us line upon line makes us less dependent on conventional wisdom and more open and receptive to new ideas and new approaches. The combination of study and faith can both deepen commitments and help keep one intellectually limber.

Fifth, learning a fullness of truth requires dependence on the Lord. Life is filled with a variety of temptations. One of the most seductive is that of intellectual arrogance. Jacob follows his compelling explanation of the power of the Atonement by noting the common temptation of a pride that rejects the need for divine direction. He warns:

> O that cunning plan of the evil one! O the vainness, and the frailties, and the foolishness of men! When they are learned they think they are wise, and they hearken not unto the counsel of God, for they set it aside, supposing they know of themselves, wherefore, their wisdom is foolishness and it profiteth them not. And they shall perish.
>
> But to be learned is good if they hearken unto the counsels of God. (2 Nephi 9:28–29)

The gospel teaches us to depend on the Lord, to "look to God" (Alma 37:47) rather than to lean on our own learning and understanding. Joseph and Oliver were counseled early in their ministries: "Look unto me in every thought; doubt not, fear not" (D&C 6:36). I had been taught these principles intellectually in my youth. I was to learn them experientially in England.

As a student at Oxford I felt like Joseph in Egypt, apart and alone. When I arrived to begin my graduate studies, I was the only Latter-day Saint, faculty or student, at the university. Although alone in some ways, I was far from lonely. The opportunities were immense and the challenges exhilarating. The days provided much time for reflection, reading, solitude, spirited conversations, and long walks down quiet lanes.

Best of all from my standpoint, the method of instruction at Oxford placed a premium on individual motivation and imposed few formal requirements. Students, working with a faculty tutor, prepared for exams they would take at the end of two or three years of study. Three eight-week terms consisted of lectures and tutorials. The lectures were optional. The tutorials focused on large questions designed to help the student master a subject. The remaining twenty-eight weeks of the year were spent in what was commonly referred to as reading vacations.

Shortly before arriving at Oxford, I reread the eighty-eighth section of the Doctrine and Covenants and was impressed again by the Lord's counsel:

> Teach ye diligently and my grace shall attend you, that you may be instructed more perfectly in theory, in principle, in doctrine, in the law of the gospel, in all things that pertain unto the kingdom of God, that are expedient for you to understand;
>
> Of things both in heaven and in the earth, and under the earth; things which have been, things which are, things which must shortly come to pass; things which are at home, things which are abroad; the wars and the perplexities of the nations, and the judgments which are on the land; and a knowledge also of countries and of kingdoms—
>
> That ye may be prepared in all things when I shall send you again to magnify the calling whereunto I have called you, and the mission with which I have commissioned you. (D&C 88:78–80)

This injunction expanded my view of what I should study, prompting me to attend lectures in a dozen subjects along with my tutorials in economics and politics. At the same time, I determined to reread the standard works from cover to cover.

By consistently devoting a set time each day to studying the scriptures, I was amazed at how much I learned and how quickly the time and the pages passed. The scriptures were opening to my understanding line upon line, precept upon precept. On many occasions, I concluded those sessions drenched with joy.

I also reflected frequently on the injunction to "teach one another the doctrine of the kingdom." On Sundays, I taught the Gospel Doctrine course and my share of priesthood class lessons, but something seemed missing. That void was filled by organizing a family home evening group that grew and led to several baptisms. Ultimately, we added a small seminary program, which I taught, for some of the newly baptized adults in the area. Most importantly, I had several spiritual experiences that confirmed for me the intensity of God's love, the reality of personal revelation, and the power of his priesthood.

Throughout this experience I discovered anew the need and the place for both reason and revelation. The two are inextricably bound together. We are to seek learning by study and by faith. It is hard to identify where one begins and the other ends. This pattern of learning applies to the doctrines of the gospel, and "all things that pertain unto the kingdom of God, that are expedient for [us] to understand" (D&C 88:78).

At Oxford, I had both the freedom and the motivation to learn about everything. I discovered that learning comes incrementally, that it involves teaching others, and that the combination of study and faith strengthens rather than weakens scholarship. My greatest insights, the times of greatest scholarly accomplishment, have come at times of faith. It is at such times that we are most open and receptive because we have a deeper sense of dependence on the Lord. Those convictions, learned intellectually, experientially, and spiritually, have deepened my commitment to the gospel and to the restored church.

One afternoon, I was reading the concluding pages of Arnold

Toynbee's *A Study of History* when the following passage washed over me with great force:

> When we set out on this quest we found ourselves moving in the midst of a mighty host, but, as we have pressed forward, the marchers, company by company, have fallen out of the race. The first to fail were the swordsmen, the next the archaists and futurists, the next the philosophers, until only gods were left in the running. At the final ordeal of death, few, even of these would-be saviour gods, have dared to put their title to the test by plunging into the icy river. And now, as we stand and gaze with our eyes fixed upon the farther shore, a single figure rises from the flood and straightway fills the whole horizon. There is the Saviour; "and the pleasure of the Lord shall prosper in his hand; he shall see of the travail of his soul and shall be satisfied" (Isaiah 53:10–11).[3]

That Savior is the Lord Jesus Christ. The knowledge of his reality greatly strengthened me while far from home and continues to sustain and deepen for me the sacred convictions and commitments that are part of his gospel. To play a part, however small, in bringing to pass his eternal purposes is a privilege that lifts us and inspires us and will fill us with great joy.

NOTES

1. See James B. Allen and Glen M. Leonard, *The Story of the Latter-day Saints* (Salt Lake City: Deseret Book, 1976), 96; John A. Widtsoe, *The Message of the Doctrine and Covenants* (Salt Lake City: Bookcraft, 1969), 138; William E. Berrett, *Teachings of the Doctrine and Covenants* (Salt Lake City: Deseret Book, 1961), 223–24.

2. In *Journal of Discourses*, 26 vols. (Liverpool: Latter-day Saints' Book Depot, 1869), 12:257. Brigham Young also declared that it was the duty of the Elders of the Church "to gather up all the truths in the world pertaining to life and salvation, to the Gospel we preach, to mechanisms of every kind, to the sciences, and to philosophy, wherever it may be found in every nation, kindred, tongue, and people, and bring it to Zion" (in *Journal of Discourses* 7:283–84).

3. Arnold J. Toynbee, *A Study of History*, abridgement of vols. 1–6, by D. C. Somervell (New York: Oxford University Press, 1947), 547.

Chapter 4

MAN AGAINST DARKNESS

Truman G. Madsen
Emeritus Professor of Philosophy, Brigham Young University
Past Director of BYU Center for Near Eastern Studies, Jerusalem

M AN AGAINST DARKNESS." This was the title of an article I read decades ago by British-American philosopher W. T. Stace. Of Western civilization he wrote, "We are told the truth shall make us free. In fact, we have only been able to live by lies, and the truth may very well destroy us." The truth, Stace argued, was that religion in all its forms was an impediment and a burden. Whatever the costs, it should be jettisoned.

Years later, after a more than academic encounter with Eastern religions, Stace wrote a book, *Time and Eternity.*[1] In it he argued that scientific methods lead to truth in one realm, that the religious, mainly mystical, approach, leads to truth in another, and that these are utterly different realms. No interplay, no compatibility, no reconciliation.

Stace, as many I have read since, illustrates two axioms that intersect my own life. First, the "absolute presuppositions" of a given era change. Second, much of the history of thought, and especially religious thought, can be rewritten as an attempt, often ingenious, to separate what cannot be separated and unite what cannot be united. One might make a case for this in a lengthy tome. Here what is called for is a brief treatment.

Today, not for the first time, the cry in academia is increasingly that there is no truth or, more modestly, that every discipline is in the same arbitrary boat.[2] Strangely, this points to a fact of life. Neutrality in matters of value and religion is rare. But while it is the business of philosophers to sleuth assumptions and prior assumptions, I am not with those who want to argue that all assumptions are created equal. The major disputed assertions (a pre-programmed slip of my computer from "assumptions") of my religion have startlingly old and startlingly new credentials. Thereby hangs a tale.

An Ultimate Religious Question

As a child I had a recurrent nightmare: It was as if everything "out there" was surrounding me and closing in. It left nothing behind, and then condensed, with me, into nothingness. When my father awoke to my outcries he came anxiously to my bedside. "What is the matter?" he asked. I usually answered, "Nothing." Maturity has brought me to see what I sensed as a child, what I take to be the beginning and end of the religious quest: Is there any meaning in all this? Is there, as most religions affirm, a Grand Design?

For me, intimacy is ultimate. Is there anyone in this vast universe who cares about and for us? Who cares with power enough to reach us, reassure us, and enable us to become what we have it in us to become? Is there anything deep enough in me to care and to give in return? I have a need, even a desperate need, to overcome my debilitating ignorance, strident sins, perennial flaws and follies. Hence, the promise from any quarter of enlightenment, forgiveness, healing, or redemption resonates with me. Just as anguishing are the broken harmonies of relationships with those close to me. In my own body and mind I face irreversible losses. And death.

A colleague once said to me, "You can't choose your parents or your religion." Clever—but mistaken. One cannot avoid the choosing and the rechoosing. The refusal to choose is a choice with infinite consequences.

I had four sets of ancestors who burned all bridges to make the Mormon *aliya*, that is, to come at appalling sacrifice from their European roots to America for freedom, then up to the "mountain of the Lord's house" because, as they believed, everything in the New

Testament was happening all over again. The original vitality of the community of Jesus Christ and his disciples was being rediscovered in a modern Zion. A new book of Acts was underway.

My mother died when I was two, leaving three little boys, and I have no memory of her. A close-knit family closed ranks after her death. My father did not remarry until after my own marriage. In a neighborhood high overlooking the promised valley, my grandparents and we thirty grandchildren lived in each other's homes and absorbed the verve of all-consuming kinship and dedication. So it may be said that I was cradled in the full-bodied vision of family love as the supreme blessing of life. I have been asked by friendly and hostile associates: "Were you born a Mormon, were you a convert, or were you reconverted?" The answer is yes. "But didn't you ever doubt?" Yes, sometimes I doubted everything. But like Descartes I could not doubt my own existence.

It would follow, and did follow, that my propensities for the history of ideas and the voluminous study of my own heritage were natural. Since my teens I have been thrust into the teaching mode, sometimes on the side, then as vocation, but always as predisposition. Over the years I have offered many reasons for my professional focus. They may be good reasons, but they are mostly after the fact. The real reason is twofold: my mentors encouraged me in the direction of comparative literature, psychology, and philosophy on grounds of aptitudes and interests; and a scholarship opened up after I won a philosophical essay contest. Still, that is not the whole truth. I felt nudged by something inner—something more than inner. But that is ahead of the story.

Assurance and Cynicism

Religious assurances aside, all of my life in this world has been attended by a pessimism without bottom. One may learn from the recent past that we seem to learn nothing from the past. No solid line, for example, protects me, my children, or anyone else from a fury-fueled holocaust. Five years in Jerusalem brought me nose to nose with people who would much rather shed anybody's blood, even their own, than make peace. But worse deaths are also around and in us. In this shrinking world, the stings of ethnic hate are on the next block and imaged night and day in our living rooms. No invisible shield separates a normal, functional person from one in the dark corner of an asylum. Further, who or what can counter the headlong self-absorption that permeates our time? It is my considered judgment that multiple bromides seduce us to adjust to our sicknesses rather than to overcome them. I will be asked, "Who is to say what is sickness?" The cemeteries say, as the result of alternative death-styles. But who is to say what it means to be healed and to overcome? It is a fair question if one is really interested in an answer.

As Dostoevsky's character Dmitri Karamazov tells his friend Rakitin, "If God does not exist then everything is permitted."[3] That widely quoted notion may help explain why many want to hold the funeral. For me, God dead or absent or utterly mysterious or silent all comes to the same thing: namely to nothing. I have devoted much study to the intellectual frameworks that argue for the existence of God. Even if the classical arguments were valid, and as formal structures they are not, conviction of existence, without a clue to God's nature, is not yet a relationship that motivates and masters. Unless from somewhere there is moving appeal, unless there is power to galvanize the will and burn out or reverse human impulses toward the violence and vapidity and narcissism of our time, what hope is there?

I prop myself up, as many do: give us more self-correcting science, more technology, better communication, a new generation, more education, and civilization will flourish. But will it? I have not lost my nerve, but I have lost my faith in the sufficiency of most backups for breakdowns, just as I lost some of my secular faith while attending three graduate schools—Utah, the University of Southern California, and Harvard.

When I arrived at Harvard, I had an M.S. degree in the history of philosophy. I was for a time preoccupied mainly with ethics: I could see in that discipline direct connections to life, to choice, to solutions. Slowly it became clear that every question leads to other questions and that how one views reality has implications for everything else.

At the time, logical positivism was the dominant trend. Aside from symbolic logic and mathematics, anything not sensate was nonsense. This criterion, it was assumed, undercut all traditional ethical, aesthetic, and religious "pseudo-statements." The history of philosophy, except philosophy of science, was seen as a history of mistakes. Meaning was reduced to verifiability and verifiability to sense-testing in the laboratory. Physics was archetypal. W. V. Quine, Morton White, Carl Hempel, and Philipp Frank made language analysis the focus, and Gilbert Ryle and Ludwig Wittgenstein were models. So we did linguistic exercises on topics such as these: Can the analytic and synthetic be reconciled? Is there empirical certainty? How are the theories of truth related? Is freedom compatible with determinism? Is reason the slave of the passions? Can altruism be reduced to egoism? Are good and obligation separate categories? Is the verifiability criterion itself verifiable? What possible justification can there be for induction? Are there new models for moral discourse?

In the other department, which might as well have been on the far side of the planet, I studied history of theology—Jewish philosophy, Augustine, Aquinas, Luther, Calvin, Karl Barth, Emil Brunner, and Rudolf Bultmann. I had tutoring in Buddhism—hinayana and mahayana—and Continental philosophy, especially Heidegger. This was before hermeneutics became the slogan for the philosopher's vocation. Between analytic philosophy and existentialism there was an ocean. I troubled my professors, for opposite reasons, by taking both quite seriously.

Studying the Bible

During this same period I pursued biblical and literary studies with Robert Pfeiffer, Amos Wilder, Krister Stendahl, and later Helmut Koester. More recently, I have become indebted to text experts who have also become friends—Frank Cross, James Charlesworth, W. D. Davies, David Noel Freedman, Raymond E. Brown, and in Israel, David Flusser, R. J. Zwi Werblowsky, and members of a new Jewish and Christian Dead Sea Scrolls team. I labored at form criticism, redaction criticism, textual and contextual analysis, linguistic comparisons, conflation, gloss, variant readings, and historiography of texts.

I wrote something close to a master's thesis on Maurice Goguel's *Life of Jesus.* Was there a "Q" (an original source used by the synoptic writers)? And which redaction was first? Change one assumption and you have to start over.

The apparatus I learned was dismantled within two decades. In fact, I was asked to write an addendum to my doctorals because I showed a mastery of the "Welhausen era," the multiple-document hypothesis of the Pentateuch, but less of the newly influential H. H. Rowley and others who ascribed more historicity and prophetic content to the sources than had earlier Higher Critics.

Today, prolonged probing of the fifty-plus volumes of the Anchor Bible, and new Bible dictionaries, will show revised and reversed methodologies at work. Many of the premises and conclusions we worked with are passé. Keeping up with the literature is a prodigious task. One net effect is a change in dating: Both Old Testament and New Testament sources have been pushed back from very late to much earlier. Otherwise, there is almost no consensus.

Except one. Like the speed of light for Einstein, there has been one constant in biblical studies since Albert Schweitzer wrote his *Quest of the Historical Jesus:* the Jesus of history is beyond recovery. What he was, what he taught (especially about himself), what he did, are blurred beyond recognition. Jesus as Christ, these scholars say, is a construct built out of centuries of Church polemic and institutional distortion. Just now the Jesus Seminar is using a five-color code for expunging the presumably invented or imposed sayings in the Gospels by degrees of probability. My own background had put me on the alert: texts can indeed be marred, mutilated, and manipulated—by moderns as well as by ancients.

In distinguished company I have raised questions: Are there things out of the Bible that should be in it, and things in it that should be out? From many outside and inside the circles of faith (Jewish, Christian, and Muslim), the standard responses are "Don't touch"; "No need for more"; "One canon is enough"; "I am a minimalist." Yet almost every biblical scholar I know would give a great deal for documents close to or contemporary with Jesus. Else how could the Dead Sea Scrolls, dated 150 B.C., have taken center stage in recent discussion?

Which brings me to the Book of Mormon. Krister Stendahl, formerly dean of the Harvard Divinity School, who did his homework comparing the Sermon on the Mount in Matthew and the teachings of Christ in 3 Nephi, writes with self-critical candor:

It struck me how cavalier we biblical scholars have been in our attitude toward the biblical "after-history." Every scrap of evidence for elucidating the origins of Christianity and its first formative periods receives minute attention and is treated with great seriousness, however marginal. But, as this essay makes clear, the laws of creative interpretation by which we analyze material from the first and second Christian centuries operate and are significantly elucidated by works like the Book of Mormon or by other writings of revelatory character.[4]

For myself, I consider the Book of Mormon to be just what it purports to be. It is evidence. And it is evidenced. It is not a historical novel. It is a novel history. I have pulled this collection of writings through every critical wringer that has come to hand. I have applied measuring sticks ranging from Christology to wisdom literature, from the use of divine names to contextual tests of narrative, from Semitic allusions to aesthetics. It is an understatement to say I am filled with increasing wonder and appreciation. I probe and respond to the book, especially to the portrait of Christ in 3 Nephi, with an intensity comparable to the Hasid and his Talmud, the Jesuit and his Thomistic sources, or the cabalist and his Zohar. All these works, I should note in passing, are treated as if they were scripture by their adherents.

But religiously speaking, appreciation is only a start. When a whole way of life is at stake, one cannot wait on the morning's mail for the latest best guess on whether there were two or three Isaiahs (recent scholarship has come full circle and it is trendy now to speak of the "unity of Isaiah"). The clock is ticking. Life is to be lived.

So strategies for skirting these probabilistic queries have arisen. One may impose a general theory of meaning upon the whole received text of the Bible, including the four Gospels. Such a theory was the subject of my dissertation, which brought to bear in one project my analytic training, my studies in existentialism, and my biblical studies. The result was a critical analysis of Paul Tillich's theory of symbols, an analysis that he himself and two of his Harvard exponents encouraged.

Tillich makes a radical distinction between sign and symbol. The Bible is for him a constellation of symbols—not of signs. Symbols have functions that signs do not: they reach into the "depth self";

they point beyond themselves; they express depths otherwise inexpressible; and unlike signs they cannot be consciously coined or invented. They are organic; they grow, live, and die. Tillich warns against saying "only a symbol" because in religion symbols are all we have. He insists that everything we say about God must be symbolic. Likewise, everything in the language of scripture is symbolic.

For example, the words "eternal life" permeate the New Testament. A priori, Tillich says, religious language must never be taken literally. So one can circumvent hard historical questions of the intent of the writer, the root words in Greek, the background in the milieu, and so forth. As a symbol, "eternal life" is to be tested by its reverberations in one's ultimate concern, which is Tillich's definition of religion. If we ask what does the symbol point to, Tillich answers: to being-itself, that is, God. But aside from this function, does the symbol "eternal life" have any meaning? After laborious processing in his systematic theology he transforms "eternal life" into "life beyond ambiguity."

In his theory and its applications I found a tissue of fallacies that cannot be labored here. But one core issue was and is, What do Tillich's existential translations such as "life beyond ambiguity" mean? Unless we are to have an infinite regress of symbolic pointing, we have in each phrase what Tillich was systematically concerned to avoid: literal meanings. These meanings are intended to undercut other meanings, also literal, that Tillich is attempting to replace—for example, everlasting life beyond the grave. If his "life beyond ambiguity" has no literal meaning, how can it negate, which he concedes it has, the often-ascribed meaning of everlasting life?

My committee was searching and searing in their review of my thesis. They followed me through Tillich's contradictions. Their response was: "Maybe in this realm contradiction is unavoidable." But Tillich had written in his *Systematic Theology* that he must submit his conclusions to formal logic. My argument—too long to present here—is that the whole enterprise Tillich himself symbolizes is based upon a fundamental and pervasive confusion. It is an untenable dualism. It can be said correctly that all language, even the mathematical posits of science, is metaphorical. But metaphors either float in midair without designation, or they sooner or later come down to designation and description. One may study an allegory as allegory. But the question then is what does the allegory mean? The attempt, beginning as early as Philo and Rabbi Akiba (both of whom lived in the first century A.D.), to "save" the scriptures by saying that they are primarily allegory is deceptive. Other genres are there: narrative, propositions, laws, instructions, ordinances. All of them, however attenuated, are cognitive. So are the sayings and parables of Jesus and the sayings about Jesus. The radical dualism of symbolic and literal needs demythologizing.

So is there an alternative? One of the acknowledged authorities on comparative religion, with whom I have had long correspondence, has written to me,

> Do you understand how unique the record of your origin-events is? Do you realize what it means to have objective shared visions, to have witnesses of Divine conferrals? For you, God, Christ, angels, spirits are seeable and hearable. You do not advocate a transcendent escape from the space-time continuum. As in Judaism you advocate their enhancement. There is close continuity and similarity between this world and the next. You have taken the confluence of Judaism and Christianity and emancipated it from unverifiable metaphysical hangovers. You have a kind of theological empiricism. Do you realize how distinctive, refreshing, and yet Biblical this is?

Yes. I think I do.

The Lost Manuscript

Early on in graduate school I wrote a master's thesis on William James and have continued to read everything he wrote, and have tried to keep up with the critical literature. Just now he is being given new recognition as a forerunner of phenomenology. But that is another story. In his *Varieties of Religious Experience,* both the raw material and his generalizations, I found impetus for comparative work in this field.[5]

One day at Harkness Commons in Cambridge, I heard myself tell a colleague I would someday write a *Varieties of Mormon Religious Experience.* It would present the richness, the diversity, but also the unity of Mormon experiences. The book would place this summation in its nurturing setting, the prophetic heritage of Jewish-

Christian antiquity. It would show the contrast to extreme mysticism: retreat into ineffability, the denial of the subject-object distinction, aspiration to the cosmic loss of the individual, and the disparagement of the senses. Instead it would derive from men and women who left a straightforward record of what they saw, heard, and felt—and whose outlooks had, and have, a way of making a tangible difference in the real world.

Over the decade that followed, amid other consuming tasks, I built just such a collection of materials combing journals, autobiographies, letters, and memorabilia, beginning with Joseph Smith. My only copy of this rough draft manuscript was in a brand-new suitcase, which I took to Berkeley before a lecture. The case was stolen out of a car trunk. And the manuscript? Probably tossed in the bay. I did not have the heart to begin over. And anyway I was having second thoughts: How enlightening is the extended display of others' experience? Does second- and thirdhand knowing about knowing yield significant knowledge by acquaintance? One can conceivably master all there is to know about eyes and still be unable, or unwilling, to see. The point of my religious background is to duplicate, relive, bring what is vital into the present tense. Here again I find myself uncompromisingly with the prophets and specifically with Joseph Smith:

> Reading the experience of others, or the revelation given to *them*, can never give *us* a comprehensive view of our condition and true relation to God. Knowledge of these things can only be obtained by experience through the ordinances of God set forth for that purpose. Could you gaze into heaven five minutes, you would know more than you would by reading all that ever was written on the subject.[6]

Of course you would, if you could. But who can? The answer of the Latter-day Saints is, finally, everyone can.

In the academy and in other more or less secular settings, a curious etiquette forbids such experimental attempts. Moreover, the gifts and fruits of authentic convictions and conversions belong to a category our generation has almost entirely lost: the holy. They are not treated kindly, or objectively, in most circles. The operative rule is when in Rome, especially in the Forum, speak in the secular vernacular.

Friendship, however, may allay this rule. For two decades my role was to represent the Richard L. Evans Chair, an endowed chair at BYU, underwritten by persons of many backgrounds, designed for serious religious and interdisciplinary exchange. So it happened that I was often in academic settings with students and faculties of diverse outlooks and philosophies. I have visited more than a hundred universities here and abroad and invited double that number of scholars to symposia and intercultural meetings. Linguists, scientists, philosophers, and advocates of all the world religions participated. In the spirit of fellowship they have welcomed cross-examination of their own views.

Whatever their stance on the way or ways of knowing, I take their religion to be what they live by. It is more apparent than they realize. Some do not live down to their disbeliefs. Many perform and decide and even risk everything by "yeas" and "nays" that use data they officially tone down or repudiate in the academy. Some will never give a straight answer on religious matters, but are striving sentimentalists. All live, as bookish people do, lives of quiet perspiration.

I have learned that as hopes and fears may get in the way of truth, they may also lead to it. I have no illusions about how in the very moment of calculated discounting of religious impulses some may be haunted with doubts about their doubts and become seekers. Then their inquiries may be both more objective (will this rope break?) and subjective (it is a long fall from this cliff!) than they have ever been about their professional studies or the conduct of their lives. Moreover, from renowned figures in the world, including some notoriously secular, and in many languages, I have heard whispers of genuine envy. This from people who know enough to know that the Latter-day Saints are onto something, but who just can't stand the cost of embracing that something.

About the cost. If religion does not demand our all, if it does not order our most lasting concerns, it does not qualify as religion. But what if it yields everything worth having and giving, and worth becoming and being? There is a certain logical neatness in giving all for all. Is that too much to be expected of Christ? Not of the Christ I know.

Reconciliation

My testimony, with that of others, is a witness arrived at through and attended by the Spirit of God. That Spirit is to me and those close to me recognizable, even tangible. Like a fine-edged sword it goes to the marrow of the bone. God is present in the real world as person, and immanent through his Spirit. Christ is the full revelation of God and of the possible destiny of man. He has empowered authentic prophets throughout human history and in our own time. Moses saw God; so did Joseph Smith. Living prophets are in the world today. All testify of Christ.

Again, how can one know? Only if he finds the revelation in himself. "Here," says the unreconstructed naturalist, "you leave us. Here you abandon science and reason. Here you lapse into irrationalism." One reply is that so does everyone else, whatever his positive or negative faith. But I believe that understates the case. The case is that whatever I, and you, consider evidence has been provided or is available.

The cumulative testimony of this modern Mormon movement is, much of it, public, shareable, and repeatable. That makes it not the least empirical religion in the world, but the most. At the same time, it is without the traditional piling of paradox on paradox. Contradictions, even when enshrined in creeds, do not bring one closer to God. Reason can show that this accumulated body of Latter-day Saint convictions is both consistent and coherent, though incomplete. The movement is also pragmatic. It works. Measurable effects follow when one learns what can be learned only by doing. Just as surely, the Mormon movement is revelatory in the most comprehensive sense. And it is open to further disclosure. I know of no other religion so responsive to the entire range of human awareness.

Humanity, however darkened, still stands against darkness. And the darkness cannot totally extinguish the light. It is not the truth that will destroy us. Truth as embodied in Christ can alone save us.

NOTES

1. W. T. Stace, *Time and Eternity: An Essay in the Philosophy of Religion* (Princeton: Princeton University Press, 1952).

2. See Richard Bushman's article, "The Social Dimensions of Rationality," in this volume.

3. Fyodor Dostoevsky, *The Brothers Karamazov*, part IV, book 11, chapter iv.

4. Krister Stendahl, "The Sermon on the Mount and Third Nephi in the Book of Mormon," *Meanings: The Bible as Document and as Guide* (Philadelphia: Fortress Press, 1984), 99.

5. William James, *The Varieties of Religious Experience: A Study in Human Nature;*

Being the Gifford Lectures on Natural Religion Delivered at Edinburgh in 1901–1902 (New York: New American Library, 1958).

6. *Teachings of the Prophet Joseph Smith,* comp. Joseph Fielding Smith (Salt Lake City: Deseret Book, 1961), 324; emphasis in original.

CHAPTER 5

"HUMAN LIFE DIVIDED BY REASON LEAVES A REMAINDER"

STEVEN D. BENNION
President, Ricks College

THERE IS A beautiful symmetry between the spiritual and the intellectual in the mosaic of the restored gospel of Jesus Christ. My testimony that God lives, that Jesus is the Christ, that Joseph Smith is the mighty prophet of the Restoration, that each of his successors through President Gordon B. Hinckley have held the same keys and authority, and that the Book of Mormon is a marvelous witness of Jesus Christ is based on treasured spiritual experiences. My testimony is also based on understanding that has come through serious study and reflection. Simultaneous quests for spiritual understanding and secular learning have been a part of my life since I was quite young. The first and great commandment urges us to love God with all of our hearts, minds, and souls (Matthew 22:37). I believe that we demonstrate our love for the Lord by serious study and intellectual growth as well as by serving him with all our hearts and souls.

I can never remember feeling that spiritual growth and intellectual pursuits needed to be pitted against each other. The scriptures clearly indicate that wisdom and learning come "by study and also by faith" (D&C 88:118). Even the mortal growth of our supreme exemplar, Jesus Christ, came in all dimensions of his life—mental, physical, spiritual, and social (see Luke 2:52). Jacob, the brother of

Nephi, reminds us that "to be learned is good if [we] hearken unto the counsels of God" (2 Nephi 9:29). I am grateful for these scriptural perspectives. I can remember as a college student hearing the eminent LDS chemist Henry Eyring share the general idea that there are not really any major conflicts between science and religion. As we come to know more about God and about science, we see many gaps closed, and ultimately we will understand that there are no major conflicts, that all truth fits together in a perfect framework. The perceived conflicts are the result of man's limits in learning.

In the meantime, we can adopt the attitude Alma did regarding unresolved conflicts that exist in our own minds between religious truths and intellectual pursuits: "These mysteries are not yet fully made known unto me; therefore I shall forbear" (Alma 37:11).

I have reflected upon the odyssey of my own spiritual and intellectual growth during the prolonged process of my formal education and a working career spanning nearly three decades (principally in higher education). I thank God beyond expression for my priceless testimony of the restored gospel. Though I have always had warm feelings for the Church and the restored gospel, my testimony has grown through study, service, and prayer—as well as through my work. And while I have had a handful of exceptional spiritual experiences, I feel that the growth of my testimony and my faith in God and his Beloved Son has come "line upon line, precept upon precept" (D&C 98:12)—more through this sacrament meeting and that Sunday School lesson, or through opportunities to serve and home teach, than through dramatic experiences. I would like to share four foundational experiences that have been important in the development of faith and testimony throughout my life.

My parents, Lowell and Merle Bennion, set an important template for me in serving, learning, and studying. The world of ideas was exciting to both Mother and Dad. In their later years, although their physical health seriously declined, they fortunately retained clear minds and eyesight. They relished reading about a variety of subjects. This quest and hunger for learning have been powerful examples to me and my siblings. The differing intellectual and spiritual interests of both parents have enriched our perspectives. In fact, just over a year ago, when I dropped in one day to visit my homebound parents, I asked Dad what he had been reading. He said, "The Book of Mormon." When I asked him where he was in this reading, he said, "I read the whole book on Monday and Tuesday of this week!" While frail physically, his mind and spirit seem to soar. (Mother passed away in September 1994.)

My father devoted much of his life to teaching religion. He was the founding director of the LDS Institute of Religion at the University of Utah and served in that capacity for nearly thirty years. He taught by faith and also by reason. I believe he blends them in a uniquely wonderful and powerful way. I thank him for that, and I have heard literally hundreds of his former students offer similar expressions of gratitude. Institute classes from Dad and his associates, such as Elder Marion D. Hanks and Brother T. Edgar Lyon, were highlights of my college years. Perhaps a picture of Dad's approach can best be painted by quoting from a talk he gave on education at the Church general priesthood meeting in April 1968:

> Buddha said, "In eating, fearing, and sleeping, men and beasts are alike. Man excelleth the beast by engaging in religious practices; so why should a man, if he be without religion, not be equal to the beast?"
>
> When I first read this, it struck home. In eating, fearing, and sleeping, men and beasts are alike. Man excelleth the beast by being human, by engaging in things of the spirit, of the mind, of the heart.
>
> . . . how often do you contemplate the wonderful qualities and aspects of your mind? Imagination is one of the qualities of a human mind that I cherish deeply; it is the ability to take single images and to put them into a new image that has never existed before. Only a human being can reorganize life around him after his own image. . . . Only human beings keep the entire past with them. You and I can live with Jesus, Beethoven, Socrates, and our grandfathers. Animals . . . [tend to] live in the present. . . . Only human beings have language, the power to symbolize feelings and ideas and to communicate. Imagination, memory, language—these are wonderful gifts of the human spirit.
>
> Until a year or two ago I kept a pig. My pig never got his eyes above the trough, except when I came to feed him; and . . . when I went out to feed my pig, I thrilled at the color on Mt. Olympus, and I pondered its geology, and I worshiped at the foot of the mountain. I sang "O Ye Mountains High" to myself alone, and "For the

Strength of the Hills." I like animals, but believe me, I am grateful for those qualities which are distinctly human and which are divine.

You and I were not only created in the physical image of our Father in heaven; we were also created in his spiritual image. And if the glory of God is intelligence, then the glory of man is also intelligence. If God is Creator, man must be creative to satisfy his soul. If God is love, man must be loving. If God is a person of integrity, then we must also be honest, to be true to our own nature, which we have inherited . . . from him.[1]

"Develop Spiritually Apace with Your Mental Development"

Another foundational experience that left an indelible imprint on me was receiving my patriarchal blessing about the time I turned eighteen. I was preparing to leave for military service, and thus I may have been more humble and spiritually receptive. The counsel I received from that inspired patriarch, who knew me only by name, included the following:

> I bless your mind that it will be alert and retentive, and urge that as you are acquiring your education, you continue in the service of our Father in Heaven. Magnify your calling in the priesthood, attend to church meetings and give your attention, time and energy to whatever assignment is given you, that you may develop spiritually apace with your mental development.

At that time I did not know what my educational plans would be. But from the time I began college as a freshman in the spring of 1960 until I completed a Ph.D. seventeen years later, in 1977, I was engaged in school full time or part time for all but four years. While time was precious to meet family, church, work, and study responsibilities, I am grateful for that counsel not to ignore spiritual pursuits during those busy years.

After completing both bachelor's and master's degrees, I accepted an employment offer in Wisconsin. By this time we had two young sons. Two years later I decided to enroll in a doctoral program at the University of Wisconsin-Madison. With encouragement from my wife, Marge, I began work on this program. During the next year and a half, I was able to take two classes each semester and do quite well. Just as I began my fourth semester, we were surprised by my call to serve as bishop of the Madison First Ward. No doubt the ward was even more startled, for I was still in my twenties. We accepted the call and I placed my Ph.D. program on a slower back burner. With a young family, a job that required about fifty hours a week, and a call to serve as bishop, I knew that I did not have the time and energy to work aggressively on a Ph.D. program. I worked on a class here and there, and with encouraging support from my employer and faithful counselors in the bishopric, I took a three-month leave to prepare for comprehensive exams and write the first chapter of my dissertation. I was able to successfully complete this phase of my program.

After just less than five years, I was released as bishop and I launched back more intensively into the doctoral program. I completed several more classes. We had added two more sons to our family while I served as bishop. A fifth child, our only daughter, was born about five months before I completed my doctorate. I was still employed full time in order to provide for our growing family. When it was time to finally complete my dissertation, I had saved up five weeks of vacation and requested an additional week of unpaid leave. Our two oldest sons went to Utah for a few weeks with grandparents, leaving Marge to wrestle with the three youngest while I dissertated. It was early June and hot and humid in Madison. With only two chapters of the dissertation written, I knew it would be a mammoth undertaking to complete the balance in six weeks; then I would have to successfully defend it before my faculty committee.

From Monday through Saturday I would arise at 4:30 A.M. and read and write until 9:00 or 9:30 P.M. I would take a break once or twice in the day, but for the most part, I was glued to our study and old typewriter. I had completed only 90 pages and two chapters before the six-week writing marathon. I had four chapters to go, projected at more than 300 additional pages. I needed to write about 50 or 60 pages a week. I had done my research, but the writing had to flow fast. My dear Marge shouldered the challenge of caring single-handedly for the children's needs day and night and also helping me with meals and editorial recommendations. The adrenaline was moving quickly as the clock went into fast forward. I finished the next three chapters and about 260 pages in five weeks and four days. I had only two days left before I had to have the last chapter ready for typing by two special friends and sisters in the ward.

The first day was an exercise in frustration. I struggled at length through that day and produced only 4 pages. By 9 o'clock that evening, I was discouraged and desperate: I had only two nights and a day left to compose a compelling concluding chapter. I decided to get a good night's rest the first night, leaving myself only a day and a night to complete the chapter. I remember offering special prayers both that evening and the next morning. I pleaded my need to the Lord, reminding him of my good wife and family and their faithful support while I worked on the dissertation and served as bishop. I acknowledged gratitude for opportunities and then asked for special spiritual help to quicken my mind and spirit for the monumental challenge of completing the final chapter in a single day.

I arose the next morning at 4:30 and began to write. The words flowed as I had never before experienced. The next 42 pages came far more easily than the first 4 had the day before. Heaven smiled on me and my family in a way I can describe only as miraculous. I wrote those 42 pages during that day and night and finished at 5 o'clock the next morning. I crashed for two short hours of rest, completely exhausted but greatly relieved.

When I awoke, I asked Marge if she would review the final chapter before we ran it to the typists. Marge chopped the first 4 pages up brutally; then to our mutual amazement, she did not suggest one change in the final 42 pages. I readily acknowledged then, as I do now, that there was a remarkable blessing in that undertaking. My heart was filled with gratitude and also tremendous relief. Those splendid typists efficiently completed their work, and I successfully defended the dissertation about a week later.

Now, more than seventeen years later, my heart is yet filled with gratitude for the wonderful blessing that came from the Lord after my herculean effort to write most of the dissertation in a short six weeks. I realized then, as now, that, more important than completing my dissertation and doctorate, I could be grateful for a growing testimony of the Lord and his restored gospel. I also knew I could rejoice in my feelings of faith and in the gospel's special influence in my life and my family's lives through the long years of formal education.

The Pivotal Role of Faith in Jesus Christ
and Our Church Leaders

My faith and understanding were further strengthened by two foundational experiences that helped me to better understand the pivotal role of faith in Jesus Christ and faith in our Church leaders. I have learned that these two are inseparable (see D&C 1:38).

As a young priest in our East Mill Creek Ward, I heard an inspired lesson by Bishop Stephen C. Richards. Bishop Richards indicated that he and his wife were married in the temple by a Church leader who had subsequently lost his Church membership. He went on to say that their temple marriage was just as valid as if the current prophet, President David O. McKay, had performed it. Our good bishop then went on to note that the first principle of the gospel is not just faith, but faith in Jesus Christ. Jesus is our exemplar, Savior, and ultimate role model. He said that in our lives we might encounter people we admired, possibly even a trusted Church leader, who on occasion would disappoint us. Then he pleaded with us to remember the importance of anchoring our faith in the Lord Jesus Christ, who would not disappoint us. Bishop Richards assured us that the First Presidency would not lead us astray and that we need not let our faith and testimonies of the Savior and his restored gospel be weakened by the failings or misdeeds of others.

When I was in my twenties, I had a second experience related more directly to the Lord's direction and calling of his prophets. When I was serving in the administration of the University of Wisconsin, some of us younger employees would sometimes have brown-bag lunches and discussions together. In January 1970, President McKay passed away. There was much speculation in the press that with the likely successor to President McKay being the ninety-three-year-old Joseph Fielding Smith, the Church would consider deviating from its pattern of installing the senior apostle as president of the Church in favor of a younger leader. At one of those lunch sessions I was posed that same question, with a dozen colleagues listening intently. I told them I did not think that would happen. When they asked why, I told them that I believed the Lord controls through life and death who will be his prophet and that President Joseph Fielding Smith had been preserved for that season of prophetic service. I also indicated that a prophet had many associates to help him in his leadership of the Church. Several shook their heads in wonder, and the subject shifted.

A year and some months later, as a relatively new bishop, I had the privilege of attending a general conference in Salt Lake City. I was seated near the back of the Tabernacle. The audience suddenly arose as President Smith walked across the stand. As I looked at this white-haired prophet, I had a powerful feeling run from the crown of my head to the tips of my toes. Tears came to my eyes, and I knew without a doubt that we were in the presence of God's prophet. I know that President Gordon B. Hinckley has been similarly preserved for his service today. Through this experience and others, I have been impressed by the truth of a statement by a member of the Council of the Twelve, as quoted by President Harold B. Lee: "That person is not truly converted until he sees the power of God resting upon the leaders of this church, and it goes down into his heart like fire."[2]

I do not wish to imply that I have arrived spiritually. Far from it! I firmly believe that spiritual growth must be a daily quest throughout our lives. This is the pattern to follow. I have learned that while we may be blessed to learn from wonderful minds while pursuing our formal or informal education, it is important that we keep our eyes focused on our prophets. They see farther than any of us—no matter how brilliant we may be as teachers or students. They are the Savior's chosen mouthpieces. How can we ignore them if we hope to follow the Savior, who speaks through them?

Missionary Work Is Matchless

Missionary experiences loom large in the development of my testimony and outlook on life. During my mission to Scotland in 1961 through 1963, I had the privilege of serving with an inspired mission president, Bernard P. Brockbank, in an era when the Church expanded the number of missions in Great Britain from one (which had been the case for 123 years) to about eight within two or three years. In this period, many missionaries had the opportunity to serve as branch presidents as we expanded from four or five branches in Scotland to thirty-two in a matter of months.

President Brockbank was a pioneer. He inspired us to serve with faith, to set goals, and to work hard. Every missionary meeting was positive and focused on the basic fundamentals of faith, repentance, love, service, and work. I do not remember attending a meeting with President Brockbank without being inspired or finding an answer to some question that had been on my mind. In particular, I remember a meeting about a week after I was first assigned as a senior companion. The mission was young, and I was young in the mission. I badly wanted my new junior companion to have a positive experience. The only week of my mission in which we did not receive an invitation into a home during our tracting was that first week I served as a senior companion. I was blaming myself for the numerous rejections we had received.

At the next missionary meeting, President Brockbank spoke at length about free agency. As missionaries we are called to present the message, but it is the choice of others to accept or reject what we present. A great burden was lifted from my shoulders that day. I realized we had been working hard but that people still must choose whether or not to listen to us and accept our message. Many similar messages came through this wise, practical, loving, and inspired leader. More than thirty years later, I find myself referring to marvelous memories and lessons of those days in Scotland.

These, then, are but a few of the fundamental experiences of my life, learning, and faith. How grateful I am for them! I am excited about the opportunity to learn and to grow both in mind and spirit. For more than a dozen years I have had the opportunity to serve at the rural, residential colleges of Ricks and Snow and to work with freshmen and sophomores. I have witnessed the synergy that comes into the lives of these young students who are at crossroads in their lives. I have watched countless students grow spiritually apace with their mental and academic growth. There is a confidence and joy that radiates from those who pursue this balanced growth. It is clear and evident, but perhaps not measurable in the same way educators measure intellectual progress.

The German poet Goethe said, "Human life divided by reason leaves a remainder."[3] Faith deals with the large remainder. I believe that reason, common sense, and the development of the mind are vital to our success and happiness. We enjoy so many blessings from the worlds of medicine, science, technology, agriculture, and business because of such developments. But there is much more to life. The world hungers for it and even looks for it in its leaders—people whose character and spiritual and moral depth warrant our trust. Theodore Roosevelt reflected this need for balanced growth when he said, "To educate a man in mind and not in morals is to educate a menace to society."[4] Reason alone does not provide all the answers, even though we need a solid foundation of reason and common sense.

Faith in God and in his Son, Jesus Christ, and in his gospel adds a beautiful framework for learning. I will be eternally grateful not only for the opportunity to learn, but also for the opportunity to learn through the framework and perspective of a testimony of the restored gospel of Jesus Christ. It makes a vital difference. And because of it, I can echo the words of an unknown author, which perhaps best express my feelings: "I believe in Christ as I believe in the rising sun. Not only because I can see it, but because of it, I can see everything else more clearly."

NOTES

1. Lowell L. Bennion, in Conference Report, April 1968, 97; or "Seek Ye Wisdom," *Improvement Era*, June 1968, 92–93.
2. Harold B. Lee, *Stand Ye in Holy Places* (Salt Lake City: Deseret Book, 1975), 63.
3. Bennion, *Religion and the Pursuit of Truth* (Salt Lake City: Deseret Book, 1959), 123.
4. Richard L. Evans, *Richard Evans' Quote Book* (Salt Lake City: Publishers Press, 1971), 69.

Chapter 6

Revelation and Reason
A Productive Harmony

Gerald N. Lund
Zone Administrator, Church Educational System

There are times in one's life that may seem trivial or only marginally important at the moment they happen, but as the years roll on, they prove to have been like the switch points on a railway line. In a fast-moving train, one is hardly aware of passing over those points where two lines are joined, separated by no more than an inch or two of space. Yet, depending on how the switch is thrown, one can end in destinations as divergent as New York and Los Angeles.

As I have reflected on the factors that have shaped my testimony of the gospel, several such switch points stand out as having been of particularly profound importance to me. Describing three of those influences may well be the best way to express my personal testimony of the gospel of Jesus Christ.

A House of Learning, a House of Faith
I grew up in a home that was fairly typical of mid-twentieth century America. My father was a pipe fitter at the Garfield Smelter at the southern tip of the Great Salt Lake. We lived in a small house on three and a half acres in the western part of Murray, Utah, which at that time was a mostly rural part of Salt Lake County. We lived simply but

comfortably, though I suppose by today's standards we would have been below the poverty level and would have qualified for all sorts of benevolent help from the government. Despite our poverty, my mother believed strongly that her occupation was the care and nurturing of her children, and throughout my growing-up years she never worked outside the home.

My father always said he was an "uneducated" man. He did well in high school, but unfortunately, three weeks after he was accepted into the engineering program at the University of Utah, Black Thursday—October 24, 1929—struck and the nation was plunged into the Great Depression. That dashed any hopes for "higher education," and my father became a laborer for the rest of his life. Only much later did I come to realize that his self-imposed title of "uneducated" could not have been more undeserved.

Just a year ago, while visiting with an ailing uncle—the brother that was closest to my father in both age and temperament—I learned something about my father I had not known before. My uncle told me that while my father was in high school, the math teacher in an adjoining town found a trigonometry problem in the textbook that he was unable to solve. Perplexed, he asked other math teachers in the area for help. They were stumped as well. He asked the math teacher at my father's school for help, but he could not solve it either. "Let me give it to Jewell Lund," he said. "He's the best math student I've got." Within a day or two, Dad had solved the problem on his own. It was such an event in that rural community that it made the front page of the weekly newspaper.

It was that analytical tenacity, coupled with an abiding curiosity and inquisitiveness, that characterized my father's whole life of "informal" education. And he bequeathed that gift to us. Books were always a part of our lives. He loved to learn and to know and encouraged us to feel the same way. He constantly pushed us to think critically and logically. He demanded not negativism, but an examination of the rationale behind what was being postulated. What were the assumptions? Were those assumptions logical? Was the thinking consistent? Did it square with known truth?

In most homes, the dinner hour is a time for quiet talk and relaxed visiting. In our home the "amen" of the blessing signaled the opening of the debate. One of us would raise this topic or that, and away we went. It was always vigorous, frequently intense, and occasionally downright heated. (I only realized that this was not normal for all families when I brought my wife-to-be to our home for dinner for the first time, and she threatened my life if I left her alone in that forensic fray for one moment.) We never had to agree with Dad in these discussions, but we quickly learned that we had better be prepared to defend our positions properly or else abandon them.

The thing that kept this demanding scrutiny from becoming mere intellectual gymnastics was my father's deep love for the gospel and the scriptures. He often stressed the fact that the scriptures were called "the standard works" because they are "the measure by which you judge all things." And we learned to do so. Everything we read and learned about was couched in terms of and laid up against the gospel plan. He would note simple things in nature that bore silent witness to the hand of God. We would compare the principles and doctrines of men to the principles and doctrines of God.

I mention my upbringing because occasionally I have had people say to me, "Well, you were raised a Mormon. It's only natural that you would accept your theology without question." I just smile. That may be true in some homes, but it was not in mine. The gospel was put to the same intense scrutiny and debate as any other topic. But here again, this scrutiny came from a foundation of faith, not skepticism. "Whatever God says is right," Dad would often say. "If something God says or does doesn't make sense to you, it's because of your limitations, not God's."

My mother's contribution in shaping this wonderful gift of inquiry was as enormous as my father's, though in a much less dramatic way. My mother has always been a gentle, patient woman. Her temperament is such that she raised her voice in anger only when her children, particularly three teenaged sons, drove her to it, and that was rarely. Not that we did not try, but her capacity for patience was prodigious.

Mom has always been a peacemaker in the fullest sense of the word. Her nature was not to plunge into those verbal duels that were so much a part of our life. She would mostly sit and listen. Occasionally, when we would begin to defend our intellectual turf too vigorously, she would quietly note that we had stopped listening. That always pulled us up short. Or she might make us all feel a little sheepish by noting some core principle we had totally overlooked, or by making a simple declaration of faith that brought the discussion back to its proper moorings.

Only now do I fully understand how important her gentle balance was for us in that climate of inquiry, which could easily have become only strident. She was always there to remind us that one could disagree without being disagreeable. My father taught us to combine reason with revelation, and that was a superlative gift. But my mother did something equally important. She showed us how to keep our balance so that rationalism did not become radicalism.

Teaching, a Lifelong Love

A second influence began with a simple question at the end of a religion class at BYU. "Jerry," the professor asked, "have you ever considered teaching seminary?" I had not, but the idea had instant appeal to me. I enrolled in the training classes and within the year was teaching seminary for the Church Educational System. To that point I had been working toward a career in social work, with an eye toward working with juvenile delinquents. Talk about a switch point!

I have now completed my thirtieth year with CES, serving as a teacher in both the seminaries and the institutes of religion, as a curriculum writer, and as an administrator. For the last three decades I have been privileged to devote my full occupational time to studying, teaching, and writing about the gospel of Jesus Christ. Day in and day out, it has been a requirement of my employment to immerse myself in the scriptures. For thirty years I have pored over them, studied them, drawn lessons from them, answered questions about them and from them. I have examined them with telescope, microscope, calipers, and slide rule. Whether taking the macro or the micro view of the scriptures, I have found in them an incredible, wonderful, miraculous depth and consistency that cannot be fully plumbed. Over and over I have been asked to teach or to write about a particularly dismaying block of scripture—blocks like Leviticus, Chronicles, or Philemon. "There is nothing much of importance in that particular block," I would say to myself. But, given little choice,

I would dive in. And there is where my father's training would begin to pay off. "The problem is not with God," I would remember. "It is your own limitations that make his word difficult." Again and again I would be stunned at the richness of the ore to be mined from that ground I had assumed was barren.

A "Non-Christian" among Christians, a Gentile among Jews

As I neared the completion of a master's degree in sociology at BYU, I began looking in earnest at various graduate programs around the country. I had enjoyed my studies in sociology and was committed to a doctorate in that same field. My wife and I took an opportunity to visit several major Midwestern universities with strong doctoral programs in sociology. When we returned home some ten days and three thousand miles later, we were sure of two things. First, we discovered we were quite naive about the world out there, and particularly about the world of higher education. Second, we knew a doctorate in sociology was not for us.

Still desirous of pursuing a doctoral degree, I began to look at programs in either biblical studies or Near Eastern studies. After considerable examination, I applied for and was accepted at the Claremont Graduate School in southern California. At that time, Claremont was considered one of the preeminent schools in this field in America. Though my wife and I had always facetiously stated that there were two places we did not want to go—hell and Los Angeles, and we weren't sure in which order to list them—life has a way of working its will on you. We volunteered to go to California for CES to teach in the institutes of religion. One year later, in September 1969, I was standing in the registration line at Claremont with my tuition check in hand.

The program at Claremont was impressive. For the doctorate, in addition to the base languages for a Ph.D., it was required that a person have a working knowledge of Hebrew, Greek, Aramaic, Akkadian, and Ugaritic. Unfortunately, I had also learned that while they had an impeccable academic reputation, the program in biblical studies was in the mainstream of liberal theological thought. For example, some of the faculty there had been prominent in the development of the "death-of-god" movement that had swept theological circles during the sixties. I felt some misgivings about this kind of program, but I had my acceptance in hand and I wanted an advanced degree.

As I stood there in the California sunshine, waiting for my turn at the cashier's window, the misgivings went from a disquieting whisper to a deafening roar. Three places away from the cashier's window I suddenly asked myself, "What are you doing here? This is not what you want." I gulped a little, turned on my heel and left, tearing up my tuition check as I walked away. And with that, in what very much seemed at the time like a frivolous, if not a downright foolish, decision, the switch was thrown and I started down a different track entirely.

Still wanting to do something in biblical studies, I began to look around southern California to see what else was available. I investigated everything that had anything close to my interests. I still smile when I think of the bewildered look on the face of the dean of admissions at a Baptist theological seminary when I tried to explain why a Mormon was interested in studying the Bible with the Baptists. Finally, I learned of a small private school in Los Angeles called Pepperdine College. It offered a master's degree in the New Testament. The Church of Christ, which owned and operated Pepperdine and several other schools of higher education, had a fine reputation for conservative biblical scholarship. I applied, was accepted, and, one year after walking away from Claremont, began my studies at Pepperdine.

The Church of Christ and Mormonism go back a long way together. Thomas Campbell and his son, Alexander, began the movement that eventually founded the Churches of Christ throughout America. One of their centers of influence was in the Kirtland, Ohio, area. When Parley Pratt and other missionaries came through Kirtland, they met with Sidney Rigdon, who was a Campbellite minister. The message of the Restoration struck a responsive chord among the Campbellites, and hundreds joined the Church. Not surprisingly, a strong feeling of antipathy on the part of the Campbellites resulted, which has continued to this day. The Church of Christ still believes that the LDS Church is a source of serious error and deception. It was common during my stay at Pepperdine to see notices on the bulletin boards announcing anti-Mormon seminars or classes for the religion faculty and students. Along with other denominations, they label us "non-Christian." With almost all the religion faculty at Pepperdine drawn from the ranks of Church of Christ ministers and with virtually every student in the graduate religion program preparing for the Church of Christ ministry, I was the only "non-Christian" in a devoutly Christian graduate program.

After a couple of semesters of studying the New Testament, I wanted to do some studies in the Hebrew language as well. There were a few community education classes close to home, but these were conversational Hebrew and moved at a very slow pace. Finally, I found a little college in Hollywood called the University of Judaism, which was run by the conservative branch of Judaism. Like Pepperdine's graduate program, the University of Judaism catered primarily to students who wanted to prepare themselves for the religious life. But I applied, was accepted, and, along with my studies at Pepperdine, attended Hebrew classes in Hollywood. Once again I found myself a minority of one. Not only was I a "non-Christian" in a Christian school, but now I was also a Gentile among the Jews.

But I am happy to say that while my enrollment in both schools caused numerous raised eyebrows, I was accepted graciously and treated with courtesy and respect in every case. By the time I had finished the equivalent of a master's degree in New Testament studies and three semesters of Hebrew, I knew that my choice to walk away from Claremont was a wise one. As the years have gone on and life has unfolded, I can see so clearly that my decision that day was another one of those profoundly important "switching" moments in my life. What a grand thing my experience at both of those universities proved to be. I could write a whole treatise on how those years at Pepperdine and the University of Judaism affected my testimony, but I will briefly note only a few examples.

First, I learned very quickly that Latter-day Saints do not have a corner on sincere devotion and service to God. I think of a black student at Pepperdine with whom I came to be friends. He ran a neighborhood ministry in the heart of Watts and was hated by some of his own people for being a "black honkey." I stood in awe of his love for the Savior and his courage in serving him. I think of my biblical

Hebrew teacher who invited us to attend a conservative synagogue service one Saturday. One of the students offered him a ride. The young instructor quietly indicated that he honored the restriction of his faith that forbade lighting fires on the Sabbath. Since an automobile engine ignites the gasoline in order to run, he could not ride in an automobile without violating that commandment. Instead, he and his wife and two little boys walked the four miles back and forth. It was not done in a boastful or self-righteous manner. It was just a quiet willingness to sacrifice comfort to principle.

Second, I learned how to study the Bible. I learned the full meaning of taking an exegetical approach to scripture study. (*Exegesis* comes from the same root as *exodus* and means "to draw out," suggesting that through exegesis one draws out the meaning of a scriptural passage.) The Churches of Christ accept the Old Testament but believe that it was fulfilled when Christ came. The New Testament is the basis for their belief, and they study it with an intense passion. In my studies at Pepperdine, I learned how to study the linguistic, historical, cultural, and contextual settings of scripture. We analyzed and criticized and dissected and debated. I wrote fifteen- and twenty-page papers on two or three verses of scripture. Over and over I was filled with wonder at the power of the scriptures, at their incredible consistency, and at the marvelous inspiration of Peter and Paul and John and the other early writers.

Third, with all of that academic emphasis, I also came to more fully appreciate two statements I had heard repeatedly in our church. I learned just how strongly the world feels that one cannot preach the gospel unless one has been trained for the ministry. That was the primary qualification for service in the minds of these sincere and wonderful young ministerial students and their teachers. Academic expertise was the prime qualifier, not priesthood authority or revelatory experience. I also saw just how successful the adversary has been over the centuries in teaching the philosophies of men mingled with scripture. It always intrigued me that it was stated that way, and not the other way around—that is, scripture mingled with the philosophies of men. By the time I was through with my studies there, I understood that the first was the better description of what had happened: The philosophies of men took first priority.

Fourth, and most important, I came to learn just how much we owe to Joseph Smith and the Restoration. I learned what a rich treasure-house of doctrine we have in the Book of Mormon and other latter-day scriptures. Over and over I saw examples of the simplicity of the doctrine restored under the hand of the Prophet. I came to know firsthand how the Book of Mormon restored many of the "plain and precious truths" that had been stripped out of the Bible by careless transcribers and designing priests.

One day in a class on the book of Revelation, we ended up in a major discussion about the "natural paradox," as the professor called it, found in Revelation 2:26–27. As part of the promise to the faithful who endure to the end, the Lord said they would receive "power over the nations," "rule them with a rod of iron," and break the nations to "shivers." "Do you see the paradox?" the professor asked. "The image is that of a tyrant, smashing nations to pieces like clay pots, but the promise is given to the faithful. How do you reconcile faith and tyranny in the same breath?" I wanted to tell him that the Book of Mormon makes it clear that the rod of iron is a symbol for the word of God, and that the faithful were leading with God's word, not some tyrannical weapon. But since references to the Book of Mormon and Joseph Smith were not warmly received at Pepperdine, I bit my tongue.

On another occasion, I wrote a long exegetical treatise on Peter's references to Christ's visit to the spirit world (1 Peter 3:18–20; 4:6). I dug into the writings of the early patristic fathers (those who wrote within a few years of Christ's death) and found that they clearly taught the idea of doing work for the dead. I cited Paul's writings. I explained the theological logic behind the position. When my professor (a fine man and a wonderful teacher who was the Church of Christ minister over a large congregation in Glendale, California) handed me back the paper, he said something like this: "Jerry, I know what you Mormons believe about vicarious work for the dead. I know about your work in the temples. And frankly, I will have to admit that it makes sense. The scriptures are with you. The patristic fathers are with you. Logic is with you." Then he shook his head. "But I can't accept it. I just can't accept it." To say such experiences came every day would be a bit of an exaggeration, but they came nearly every week. It was a wonderful academic experience that constantly reaffirmed testimony rather than calling it into question. Time after time during the three years that I studied at Pepperdine and the University of Judaism I saw evidence of the truthfulness of the Church and of God's work.

A Witness of the Truth

There they are—three influences that have had a profound effect on me and on my feelings about the gospel of Jesus Christ. I was raised in a home of faith, but one in which inquiry and reason were championed. I have spent thirty years studying and teaching the scriptures and the gospel. And I was privileged to examine the Bible under the tutelage of some very fine scholars and teachers. There were, of course, other important influences, but those three have proven to be the most important. Together they have combined, in what one person called a great "confluence of influence," to build my testimony. Because of those three factors, I now can boldly declare my witness:

I know that God the Father lives and that Jesus Christ is our Redeemer and Savior. I know that God is a loving, caring Father. He not only hears and answers prayers and shows an almost incomprehensible degree of long-suffering for my stumblings, but he also nurtures us and guides our steps, helping to pull those "switches" that send us down tracks we did not even know were out there. I know that he so loved the world that he sent his Only Begotten Son, a being of such perfection that even a lifetime of study only begins to lift the curtain enough that we catch the slightest glimpse of his majesty and power. The foundations for this testimony of the Father and the Son were laid during my early childhood years by wonderful parents. But a lifetime of searching, studying, questioning, teaching, trusting, and learning have only shown me all the more how truly God and Christ live and how profoundly they are involved in my life.

The scriptures are a repository of miraculous truth and power. The words of God have withstood every scrutiny, shone brightly through every challenge, brought power and wisdom and peace through every examination I have given them. The hand of God is evident throughout the standard works. They are like a great, interwoven tapestry of truth. The principles and practical guidelines weave through the whole fabric with an absolutely incredible complexity, consistency, and genius of design. The scriptures are simply a miracle. There is no other adequate word to describe them. No human hand could have produced their power and their wisdom.

Joseph Smith was called of God, labored under his direction, and surely stands high among the list of noble and great ones God chose to do his work. The work of the Restoration in this dispensation is of such magnitude, such majesty, and such scope that it can be described only as "a marvelous work and wonder." I have studied the writings of some of the world's most learned men and women, people with enough letters behind their names to provide a serious game of Scrabble. They are brilliant, erudite, scholarly, and articulate—but compared to Joseph Smith, they are like children beginning a study of the alphabet. I have learned that God's prophets are not only his servants, but truly become his spokesmen. What a statement of confidence that God should say of them, "whether by mine own voice or by the voice of my servants, it is the same" (D&C 1:38).

The Church of Jesus Christ of Latter-day Saints is the only "true and living" church on the face of the earth. I have come to admire and respect other faiths and the people who sincerely hold to those faiths, but oh how keenly has it been made manifest to me that this is His church! It is filled with struggling, quick-to-falter Saints, but the organization reflects the divine hand of God and it is led by his Son. It moves forward in the face of swirling change and intense opposition. Again and again I have had carried into my heart the witness that the Brethren who lead it are doing God's work and are his servants. The Church is indeed the stone cut out of the mountains without hands, and I know that it will continue to roll forth until it fills the whole earth. I am humbly grateful that my Father saw fit to send me to a home where the Church would become part of my daily life.

Finally, and perhaps most important because it is the validation of all of the above, I bear witness of the reality of the Spirit's whispered guidance. In my earlier years as a teacher I used to say that I believed the Holy Ghost spoke to us daily. I am sure now that hourly would be a much more likely description. I know that he comforts, testifies, enlightens, guides, verifies, prompts, warns, directs, compels, restrains, leads, and witnesses to me. I know that it was his voice during all those years with my parents, and during all those years of teaching, and during all those months of study and learning in California, that over and over whispered to me, "This is true! This is true!"

What an unthinkable gift, to be given the presence of a member of the Godhead as a personal guide and companion. And I thank my God for it and the testimony that is the result of that influence.

PART 2

STUDY AND FAITH

Chapter 7

The Social Dimensions of Rationality

Richard Lyman Bushman
Gouverneur Morris Professor of History, Columbia University

I RECENTLY ATTENDED a conference on religious advocacy sponsored by a group of Christian scholars who feel that religious belief is unduly restricted in academic discourse. The starting point for the conference was the evident fact that political convictions are freely advocated in classrooms and scholarly writing. These political positions are ideological and value laden, so why not introduce religious views too? If history can be taught from a Marxist perspective, why not from a Christian viewpoint?

At the conference, scholars with a wide range of personal outlooks, some religious, some not, addressed the question of how their personal beliefs affected their teaching and writing. The paper of one of the less-believing participants reminded me of how academics commonly think of Mormon belief. He was looking for an outer limit to what rational people would dare bring into serious academic conversation, and the example he chose was Joseph Smith. Forgetting that I was a Latter-day Saint, he proposed the idea of an angel delivering gold plates as an example of a religious phantasm so far beyond the boundaries of plausibility as to preclude any consideration in college classrooms or scholarly writing.

When we got to the discussion segment of that session, I

reminded him that I had written a book on Joseph Smith founded on the very assumption that an angel delivered golden plates on a New York hillside.[1] The writer did not press his point and generously acknowledged in private conversation that he should read my study of Joseph's early life. Neither of us suffered embarrassment, but his candor brought out an attitude that I know many of my colleagues share. Belief in angels is beyond the pale of academic conversation. After all, what can be said about events so far beyond the bounds of ordinary experience?

Belief in angels and golden plates apparently does not disqualify a person for other kinds of scholarly activity. I am asked to give papers and review books and have never felt that my religion prevents me from engaging in all the usual routines of modern academic life. Apparently, the crazy Mormon side of my mind is envisioned as sequestered in some watertight compartment where it cannot infect my rational processes. Beliefs inhabit a realm of feeling and traditional loyalties where we are not called to rational account and where eccentricities and bizarre ideas can be tolerated. Probably my colleagues have peculiar notions of their own that they would not want to defend before a panel of academic critics.

When a graduate student or a colleague does ask about my beliefs, I am often asked if I was reared a Mormon. The question is, of course, a hypothesis. They are explaining my belief not as a rational choice made in the face of other choices but as one component of an elaborate cultural system intertwined with my family, the culture of my home, loyalty to old friends, the fundamentals of my personal identity. They think I am Mormon the way many people are Jewish or Polish; they think that's simply me. My belief in the angel and the plates cannot be extricated from my personal culture. I am a Mormon, they implicitly presume, not because I *believe* in Mormonism. I believe in Mormonism because I *am* a Mormon—by upbringing, affection, and cultural construction.

I accept this explanation and go one step further. I believe in the doctrine and the miraculous events because they sustain life. I need them to carry on from day to day. The God whom I worship and who dwells in the midst of Mormon scriptures is the God who heals me when I am wounded, who corrects me when I err, who restores me to good when I fall into evil. My religion is a crutch, an absolutely necessary crutch that I need to hobble on through life. Far from rationally judging every historical event in the fabulous life of Joseph Smith or weighing the worth of each doctrine, I believe in the God of the Mormon scriptures because I need that God. My beliefs grow in the dark, warm realm of feelings, the place of fears and agonizing human needs, of desires beyond naming, the place where my soul has its roots.

All this is a simple fact of my religious life, perhaps of all religious life. Does this mean, therefore, that all religious doctrine is irrational, that all the events of Mormon history are beyond discourse, that one cannot make an argument for Mormon beliefs? Obviously not. Those arguments are made constantly. I have myself made a historical case for the authenticity of the Book of Mormon. Hugh Nibley has devoted his life to assembling evidence in rational support of Mormon scriptures. The Foundation for Ancient Research and Mormon Studies (FARMS) has mobilized an army of people who publish hundreds of pages a year in support of our beliefs. This scholarship is not generally acknowledged outside of Mormon circles, but that does not mean it is trivial. The people at FARMS are trained in accredited graduate schools, learned in languages, informed about current scholarship, and careful in argumentation. They abide by all the canons of rational discourse. Nor can it be claimed that they are emotionally unbalanced or congenitally stupid. They bear every evidence of psychological stability and intellectual acuity. These people, and many others not directly associated with FARMS, have brought their considerable powers to bear in support of Mormon beliefs about history and God. If my colleagues consider my beliefs outside the realm of rational discourse, these Mormon apologists do not. They maintain, and I concur, that a more persuasive argument can be made for belief in God and Christ through the Book of Mormon than through any of the arguments of conventional Christianity.

The cultural position of Mormon belief, then, is strangely anomalous. For me it grows out of family culture, a thousand personal associations, and deep human needs. At the same time, it is girded up with forceful (though never unassailable) rational arguments based on conventional scholarly methods and the rules of rational discourse. My colleagues are correct in placing my beliefs in the realm of feeling and deep loyalties, where it is tactful not to call for rational explanation; on the other hand, if they wished to take the trouble, I could provide them with shelves of scholarship in support of the Book of Mormon and Joseph Smith's story. Belief is irrational and rational at the same time.

My academic colleagues would explain away the apologist scholarship in the way they account for my belief. All the other Mormon scholars argue on behalf of their faith for the same reasons I do: because they are personally grounded in Mormon society, where they live and move and have their being. Social environment has made Mormons of these people, and they devote their lives to a defense of the faith in order to sustain their own social and personal identities.

This explanation has served to put believing Mormon scholars in their place largely in contrast to another kind of scholarship that is thought to be beyond social loyalties or deep personal needs: the scholarship of science and objective reason, best exemplified by the physical sciences. Over the past four centuries, scientific scholarship has developed rigorous methods for screening out personal preferences and arriving at conclusions based on objective, measurable reality and cool, disinterested reasoning. This kind of scholarship is responsible for breathtaking advances in physics, chemistry, and biology, and it inspires a hope that the study of history and sociology, the sciences of the human spirit, can make comparable progress.

By the standards of this rigorous scientific inquiry, Mormon scholars with their obvious personal commitments do not measure up. To practitioners of objective science, the findings of Mormon scholars are necessarily polluted by their personal interest in the outcome. Mormon scholars have a form of scholarship but deny the power thereof, and hence can be dismissed as special pleaders rather than as serious claimants to objective truth.

That is where Mormon scholarship was located, anyway, until about twenty years ago. Now, that perspective on belief is undergoing a fundamental shift, not because of changes in Mormon scholarship but because of the way modern thinkers are conceiving scholarship as a whole. We live at a moment in history when the Enlightenment dream of scientific scholarship has been eaten away by doubts about the possibility of scholarly objectivity. A host of thinkers, many of them French, have called into question the very possibility of dispassionate inquiry. They are arguing not merely that objectivity is an impossible achievement for human beings, who can never detach their minds from the rest of their being, but that the pretense of objectivity is an exercise in self-aggrandizement. Objectivity disguises a play for power by those who pretend to the authority of objective scholarship when they are every bit as self-interested in the outcome as any religious apologist. The scientific authorities of an era, according to current theory, claim to speak only for truth against error, when in actuality they stand to benefit by promoting their particular truth and vanquishing all others. No truth, not even the most rigorously scientific, is objective. All truth is colored by personal interest of some sort.

That is harsh criticism of the scientists whom we have all learned to admire, and I, for one, am loath to go all the way with postmodernist thinkers. It is very hard to relinquish faith in some measure of objective scholarship. We all can think of utterly biased and self-serving scholarship that we are sure would not hold up under scrutiny, or history writing that is filled with factual errors. We want to reserve the right to correct this corrupted work in the name of some kind of objective truth.

But if we cannot go all the way with the critics of the Enlightenment, we must at least acknowledge that no scholarship, no truth, exists in a social vacuum. Though it is rarely mentioned in the work itself, all scholarship is tied to a community of some kind and bears the marks of that community's influence. Scholarship is the product of people who are located in institutions—universities, research institutes, or circles of like-minded thinkers. They publish their work and want to have it read by others. Their reputations, promotions, pay raises, and appointments depend on how that work is received. When they write, they use the language, the mannerisms, the forms of their scholarly community. In taking an intellectual position, they silently, but inevitably, associate themselves with people of a similar outlook. Scholars take pleasure in hearing references to their work at scholarly meetings or seeing it mentioned in publications. They can imagine being part of a distinguished community of learned people whose intelligence and character are admired. In the scholarly work itself, a conclusion is presented as the outcome of careful scrutiny of the facts and rigorous analysis; but the assumptions, the perspective of the work, the fundamental attitude come from some community, from a society with which the scholar is implicitly and probably quite hopefully associating.

Every form of scholarship is rooted in a society, an imagined community of scholars in which the teachers or writers live and move and have their being. We cannot take a position on a scholarly issue without implicitly forming or breaking a social relationship. Everything we write and say links us to other people, with all the tangled consequences for our self-esteem, our personal identities, our hopes and aspirations. There is a social and personal dimension to every form of rational discourse, which means that all beliefs, not merely religious beliefs, are both rational and irrational. We may indeed become persuaded rationally that the Book of Mormon is a nineteenth-century production. There may be hundreds of facts we can invoke to sustain this position. But in making that assertion we are forming and breaking human relationships that unavoidably influence our thinking, just as the memories of a religious upbringing (or of a transforming conversion) coil around the work of the Mormon apologists.

The explanation for faith that I imagine in the minds of my academic colleagues has never intimidated me. I acknowledge my subjectivity and the influence of a million personal associations. But this recognition of my own limitations has made me deeply skeptical of all who claim to escape their subjectivity, who think they have rid themselves of the prejudices of their tribe. We all have our tribes. The desire to form tribes, to join tribes, to triumph within our tribes drives and shapes our scholarship. Every form of discourse, every rationality is rooted in a society and serves social purposes. However much we enjoy the pursuit of truth for its own sake, these social purposes are preeminent. Without a society behind the scholarship, we would never do the research or write the books. Every truth is socially conditioned and socially motivated. When we take an intellectual position, we are announcing the society to which we wish to belong and the kind of people we want to be. The very explanation that my academic colleagues offer for my belief is what I use to understand theirs. All truth, Mormon and scientific, is of necessity social truth and profoundly conditioned by human associations. The pretenses of Enlightenment scholarship have been torn away in recent decades, and the inescapable contingencies of this profoundly human endeavor have been laid bare.

In what, then, can we put our trust? If truth always grows from a particular society, how do we choose among the perplexing confusions of multiple and conflicting truths? If the Enlightenment quest has faltered and the pursuit of knowledge seems mired in subjectivity, if scholarship is entwined in the corrupting pursuit of power, what can we cling to? What can replace objective scientific truth as a foundation for culture and personal identity? Where do we go when we are post-Enlightenment, postmodern, post-everything?

I begin with an insistent question that shoulders aside even truth in demanding our attention: How should we live a life? It may take a long time to discover the truth, especially if we follow the tortuous path of scientific rigor. But we must answer the question of how to live a life every second of every day. We may have only tentative answers, to be replaced from day to day, but some answer we must find for the inescapable query, What is good? What is worth pursuing? What should we give our time to? How should we treat other people? How should we think of them? How should we feel and act? These questions thrust themselves insistently upon us and demand immediate answers in our actions and thoughts. We cannot wait to hear from science or the universities about these matters. We are in the middle of the fray the minute we open our eyes each morning.

We sometimes think that if we knew the true, then we would know the good. The right way to live should grow out of the right way to understand. A goodness based on falsehood would be faith built on the sand. The true and the good should come together, we want to think, and indeed may be close to equivalent. In the pragmatic tradition that has influenced my thinking, I carry that hope one step further to say that what we find to be truly good is the truth. The only truth we can know is the truth that works.

One of the perplexities of academic scholarship is how it shies away from goodness. Classroom teachers make a point of saying that they have no intention of telling students how to live their lives. It is true that a certain set of moral precepts grows out of scholarship—accuracy of expression, an honest reading of evidence, clarity of reasoning, diligence, empathy. But objective scholarship will not reveal what it means to be a good husband or wife, how to learn to be generous, how to bless people. Those who are academics have values, of course, but they bring these political and ethical principles into their teaching from other sources—from their religious backgrounds, their families, their communities. Except in the narrow realm of scholarly methods, the Enlightenment pursuit of truth does not provide answers to the question of how to live a life. In fact, it explicitly denies responsibility for finding the good. Scholarship has no doctrine of repentance because it has no doctrine of good. I consider that a damning lack.

Scientific scholarship is the official truth of our culture. The government will grant you money to investigate questions by scientific methods; you will never get money to answer inquiries by spiritual means. And yet, that official culture holds no promise of ultimately discovering what is good or of helping people to attain it. We are left on our own to discover the truth that teaches us what is worth doing in life and how to be a good person.

As I said at the outset, I find goodness in the God of the Mormon scriptures. There I find truth to live by, which to my way of thinking is the most significant, the most useful, the most compelling kind of truth. But is this Mormon truth real? We cannot help asking, Is it anything more than a hopeful fabrication? That question comes from the ghost of the Enlightenment, the ghost that tells us we can escape our subjectivity and find a truth above human frailty, a truth that all reasonable people will be forced to accept. But it is a ghost that speaks to us; the hope of objective truth has been slain. No one is capable of finding that dreamed-of reality by scholarly methods. Objectivity is the claim of people who think they are gods now, not of persons worshiping God and striving to be like him, nor of persons who understand the reality of finite human life without God. It is a magnificent phantasm, a blind and futile aspiration—futile not just because we can never escape ourselves, but because in the end the Enlightenment project fails us. Even when science has done its work to perfection, it fails to tell us how to live a life.

The Mormon truth, above all, tells us how to be good and helps us to get there. Faith and repentance are wrapped up together. The goodness that I see in the Mormon lives about me, and day after day in my own life when I construct myself as the scriptures direct, is every bit as real as the abstractions of scientific scholarship. I can, if I wish, cast an aura of rationality over this belief in an effort to explain and justify myself to my academic colleagues. Our valiant apologists will go on defending the faith with scholarly evidence, to keep up our connection with the academic establishment. But I hold to my beliefs not because of the evidence or the arguments but because I find our Mormon truth good and yearn to install it at the center of my life. After losing many followers when he taught an especially hard doctrine, Jesus asked his disciples, "Will ye also go away? Then Simon Peter answered him, Lord, to whom shall we go? thou hast the words of eternal life" (John 6:67–68). The truth we have is truth to live by.

....

NOTE

1. Richard L. Bushman, *Joseph Smith and the Beginnings of Mormonism* (Urbana: University of Illinois Press, 1984).

CHAPTER 8

DILIGENCE AND GRACE

BRUCE C. HAFEN
Provost, Brigham Young University

SHORTLY BEFORE he died, Johannes Brahms granted an intimate interview about his life, in which he described the powerful place of heavenly inspiration in his composing. He ascribed much of his gift to direct impressions from "the great Nazarene," even though he had little use for the established churches of his day. He also predicted that no atheist would ever compose great and lasting music, because without belief in God, a composer has no access to the source of divine inspiration. But then Brahms added that even inspired melodies would never amount to great music unless they were crafted and developed through the intellectual "structure" of rigorous musical forms.[1]

I see this same connection between inspiration and structure in the Lord's revelation to Joseph Smith: "Teach ye diligently and my grace shall attend you" (D&C 88:78). I wish to testify about the interaction between professional diligence and heavenly grace by describing the relationship I see between those two forces at Brigham Young University. The BYU community is engaged in a large, diverse, and incredibly successful educational enterprise. At its best, this enterprise combines both the grace of inspiration and the diligence of structure. The university's dual heritage gives us membership in and allegiance to two different worlds—the world of higher education and the world of the Church. As a description of that heritage, I offer a simple visual model.

Imagine two circles representing the two worlds of higher education and the Church. Color the higher education circle red, and color the Church circle blue. Bring the two circles toward each other until they overlap somewhat. The overlapping area will, of course, be purple, the color resulting from mixing blue and red. Given its deliberately dual nature, BYU belongs in the purple area of overlap—it is genuinely part of the Church, yet genuinely also part of American higher education; it is inevitably affected by what happens in either world. In this unique domain we have found a more perfect way to teach and learn.

Yet some people in the red world of education look at a purple BYU and say, "But you're not red like us, so you must not be a real university." And some people in the blue world of the Church say, "You're not blue like us, so there must be something wrong with you." Such comments from both directions can give BYU people, and many other LDS scholars, feelings of tension, if not an identity crisis—despite their being part of the great purple tradition of religious higher education. But that tension and our unique identity are the sources of our greatest contributions to both the red and blue worlds—and our ability to contribute is improved every time someone in either of those worlds understands how our purple nature can bless them in ways that a simple blue or red entity never could.

Despite a tradition of higher education that has made American colleges and universities the world's finest, not everything about U.S. higher education today is healthy. Hence, BYU's membership in the community of universities does not mean we uncritically accept every new academic trend or value. But in the simplest, most general sense, BYU is clearly a player on the field of higher education. It thus differs in certain respects from other agencies sponsored by the Church, which explains its direct reporting line to a distinct board of trustees. BYU's sponsorship and its educational mission do make it accountable first of all to the Church, and if it ever has a truly irreconcilable conflict between higher education and the Church, it will always choose the Church.

But the BYU community is also accountable in very serious ways to accrediting bodies, government agencies, the academic disciplines, the professions, and even the general public. The day the Church created BYU as a serious university, it made a substantial contribution to the public interest. BYU is obliged to prepare its students to function successfully in that public world as well as in their private worlds of family and Church. BYU will never be *of* the public world, but it is unavoidably and wholeheartedly *in* that world.

In this spirit, I salute the growing numbers of Latter-day Saint scholars at BYU and elsewhere who are major contributors to their academic and professional fields. The Church's scholars, artists, and researchers are making a difference in a society that sorely needs their inspired and creative genius—precisely because their religious commitments give them access to authentic inspiration. Then their professional rigor lets them add structure to that inspiration, thereby giving their inspired ideas lasting value in the real world. As Oliver Wendell Holmes said, "It is required of [us] that [we] should share the passion and action of [our] time at peril of being judged not to have lived."[2] LDS scholars whose work reflects both inspiration and structure are already being judged as having lived.

Our commitments to the blue world that gives us inspiration and the red world that gives us intellectual structure teach us how to integrate the academic and professional disciplines with the gospel. As Alma taught Korihor (see Alma 30), the divinely given sacred map of the universe is large enough to encompass the secular map, but the secular map is too small to include the sacred map. This perspective teaches me to have a sacred, as opposed to a profane, perspective on the whole of life. But this does not mean I *exclude* secular maps—I just see them in perspective. This understanding can also inform me when some value-laden premise from the red world is simply wrong. But that red world still offers much that is "lovely, or of good report or praiseworthy" (Articles of Faith 1:13).

Because of their active participation in the red world of higher education, LDS scholars are inevitably affected by—and must therefore come to terms with—developments in the academic disciplines. I note especially the newly radicalized disciplines with which all major universities are now concerned. In my own field of law, for example, the critical legal studies movement, which partakes of several post-modernist elements, has challenged not only the very foundations of legal education and law practice, but the very idea of a system of law. This movement asserts that law has no objective legitimacy and is simply a euphemism for power. Similar claims in the humanities and elsewhere challenge every discipline they touch.

Many of these arguments have value, forcing us to rethink prevailing paradigms and helping to unmask remaining pockets of discrimination and unfairness. But while some radical advocates have staked claims to new theoretical constructs, they also convey anti-intellectual overtones when they rely on simplistic conspiracy theories urged by "true believers" who refuse to deal rationally with the arguments against their positions. Some of these radicals are waging war against American universities, uprooting established disciplines and turning departments on many campuses into what one writer described as islands of repression in a sea of freedom.

Some proponents of change put power-oriented "activism" ahead of rational discourse in their teaching and scholarship, a step that raises troubling questions for those of us who thought universities were designed to liberate us from making decisions in the streets. And, as New York University's Joseph Salemi writes, "Academic freedom . . . [to some] means [their own] freedom . . . to be hired and tenured without the inconvenience of competition or the necessity of producing real scholarly work."[3]

The new movements are asking large and searching questions, and we must not dismiss them out of hand. We must maintain open minds and a willingness to debate the issues honestly. BYU must be among the universities that thoughtfully distinguish the legitimate from the illegitimate arguments in this area. And as we encounter these contemporary currents, we must help our friends in both the blue and red worlds understand that not everything about these trends is bad. Moreover, the noisy debates the movements foster can, if conducted civilly, be a sign of educational health, not a sign that BYU is falling apart. At the same time, BYU also belongs to the Church world; thus, its faculty who accept activist premises must not take lightly their need for the understanding and support of main-stream Church members.

Consider now a few implications of BYU's belonging to the blue world of the Church. First, we do not dilute everything blue with a dose of red. The doctrines of the Restoration inform and shape BYU and LDS scholars in utterly undiluted ways. In that sense and in other ways, my three-colored metaphor, like most metaphors, is obviously subject to important qualifications. Let us also note that BYU's Church sponsorship is, and has always been, the source of its greatest strength. For one thing, the Church and its members are deeply committed to BYU, providing a very stable and secure source of financial as well as moral support. In addition, BYU's blue background gives its educational mission a unique hue, enabling a truly distinctive contribution to society and to all the academic and professional disciplines. As other institutions become increasingly alike, the need for this contribution has never been greater.

BYU's belonging to the Church world liberates rather than confines it in all of its campus activities. In nearly all matters of hiring, curriculum, academic programs, research projects and methods, organizational matters, and social activities, authorized faculty or staff have enormous personal discretion. These people must always strive for mature professionalism, but because of the religious world view held by virtually all BYU people, Church values obviously shape their discretionary judgments in appropriate ways—not because they *have* to follow Church values, but because they *get* to follow them. Sometimes the blue world defines BYU in ways that people in the red world cannot understand, but those limits do what the Lord's discipline always does: enable greater, not less, educational perfection than the red world knows.

So LDS scholars and BYU as an institution live in two worlds—the red world of higher education and the blue world of the Church. I realize that some people see red when they think BYU looks blue, and other people turn blue when they think BYU looks red. Still, I hope that those who see mostly one or the other of these worlds will experience the other world more fully. We all work within a complex sphere, even though some disciplines naturally deal more with one color than another. It hurts us and drives the Lord's Spirit from our midst when some, who think mostly in either red or blue terms, sit in harsh judgment on those who think mostly in terms of the other color.

With the Church growing so rapidly all across the globe, we must continually rethink why BYU exists and draw on the best of these two worlds in ways that, above all, serve the long-term interests of the Restoration.

The eighty-eighth section of the Doctrine and Covenants, first given to guide the Saints in Kirtland in 1832, is still the best perspective on building Zion with a more perfect form. This revelation speaks of the light of Christ, which enlightens every person and fills every space. That light, said Parley P. Pratt, is the source of "instinct in animal life, reason in man, [and] vision in the Prophets."[4] It is the light of human conscience and of natural laws in the universe.

Those who leave the light will become without feeling or conscience, for they seek "to become a law unto [themselves], and [will] to abide in sin" (D&C 88:35). But for those who live in the light, section eighty-eight unfolds an amazing pattern of personal progression. As we grow in understanding and obedience, we receive more light. This includes the prompting of the Holy Ghost, then the gift of the Holy Ghost, then ratification by the Holy Spirit of Promise. As the light increases according to our faithfulness, the day will come when our calling and election is made sure (see D&C 88:4). Then we are prepared, taught Joseph Smith, to receive in this life the Second Comforter—the presence of Christ. And finally comes glorious sanctification in the Father's holy presence. So it is that "he that receiveth light, and continueth in God, receiveth more light; and that light groweth brighter and brighter until the perfect day" (D&C 50:24).

Students and scholars love to learn. They seek to comprehend the mysteries of life. Thus, no more stirring promise could fill their ears than that of D&C 88:67–68, which describes the culmination of the fulness of light:

> And if your eye be single to my glory, your whole bodies shall be filled with light, and there shall be no darkness in you; and that body which is filled with light comprehendeth all things.
>
> Therefore, sanctify yourselves that your minds become single to God, and the days will come that you shall see him; for he will unveil his face unto you, and it shall be in his own time, and in his own way, and according to his own will.

After giving this promise, the Lord speaks of a solemn assembly where the laborers for Zion may purify themselves, so that he by his atoning power may make them clean. He testifies of that cleansing power and asks the laborers to fast and pray. Then from this stirring train of thought flow these powerful words:

> And I give unto you a commandment that you shall teach one another the doctrine of the kingdom. Teach ye diligently and my grace shall attend you, that you may be instructed more perfectly in theory, . . . in doctrine, . . . Of things both in heaven and in the earth, . . . things which have been, things which are. . . . Seek ye out of the best books words of wisdom; seek learning, even by study and also by faith. (D&C 88:77–79, 118)

These phrases and those that surround them are the most celebrated lines in all scripture on the subject of teaching and learning. What are these verses doing in section eighty-eight, mixed with the promises of sanctification and being filled with light?

Could it possibly be that if we learn and teach with enough diligence, and if our eyes really are single to God's glory, the grace of the holy Atonement would attend us in every dimension of our lives? What is the connection between "comprehending" and learning and receiving more light? What is "an eye single to the glory of God"? What must we do to invite this understanding into our lives? Seeking the answers to these questions is the quest of a lifetime. It is the quest for light, and more light, until the perfect day.

As BYU's new Joseph Smith Memorial Building was nearing completion a few years ago, it needed some kind of artistic capstone that captured and conveyed the crucial place of religious education on the university's campus. Franz Johansen of the BYU art faculty was invited to propose possible designs for a large relief sculpture near the building's entrance. He brought in several beautiful sketches of Joseph the Prophet, but something was missing: the connection between Joseph Smith and the very idea of BYU—a magnificent school of learning that is filled with the Spirit of the Lord.

After a prayerful search, we found the answer in the eighty-eighth section: "And I give unto you a commandment that you shall teach one another the doctrine of the kingdom. Teach ye diligently and my grace shall attend you" (D&C 88:77–78). The Lord actually commands us to teach and to learn—even to the point of promising that once we exhaust our own efforts to understand "the best books" and "things both in heaven and in the earth" with utmost diligence, his divine grace will attend us. And when we sanctify ourselves to make room for the light of that grace, it will fill our very souls to the point that we comprehend all things.

Brother Johansen captured this idea with a sculpture showing Joseph the Prophet with outstretched hands, intently teaching a young BYU couple who will one day teach other people, including their own children, just as Joseph is teaching them. From above the Prophet's head streams the grace and light of heaven, not only into his soul, but also into the souls of his students. Next to the figure of the Prophet are inscribed the Lord's words of commandment to learn, followed by his words of promise: "Teach ye diligently and my grace shall attend you." This is the best way to teach and learn.

When all the primary colors—red, blue, and yellow—are displayed in colored lights so that the colors overlap one another, the color at the very center of the overlap is not purple, but pure white. Perhaps as students and scholars join the blue world of the Church and the red world of education with a yellow world symbolizing a personal quest to sanctify themselves before the Lord, their bodies will be filled with the pure light of infinite comprehension—not a light reflecting the absence of color, but a light that reflects the combination of every color. By diligence and grace, the Lord's process of learning expands rather than limits us, until, with minds single to God, we know every color and comprehend all things.

....
NOTES

1. Arthur M. Abell, *Talks with Great Composers* (New York: Philosophical Library of New York, 1954), 5–6.

2. *The Occasional Speeches of Justice Oliver Wendell Holmes,* comp. Mark DeWolfe Howe (Cambridge: Belknap Press of Harvard University Press, 1962), 6–7.

3. Joseph S. Salemi, "Enduring the MLA Convention," *Measure,* no. 116 (May 1993): 4.

4. Parley P. Pratt, *Key to the Science of Theology* (Salt Lake City: George Q. Cannon & Sons, 1891), 41.

5. *Teachings of the Prophet Joseph Smith,* comp. Joseph Fielding Smith (Salt Lake City: Deseret Book, 1961), 150.

Chapter 9

Study and the Prayer of Faith

James W. Cannon
Orson Pratt Professor of Mathematics, Brigham Young University

Y OU SHOULD PRAY about your research," my wife, Ardyth, would tell me. "You've been working hard trying to serve other people and you could use some help with the things you like best."

"But I don't want help," I argued. "Half or three-quarters of the fun is figuring things out for yourself. I'm not just interested in the answer; I want to understand. I'm not concerned with being the first to discover these things; without doubt other people elsewhere in space or time already know all the things I'm thinking about if those things are worth anything at all. After all, space is big and time is long, and there are a lot of smart, curious beings in the universe."

"Still," Ardyth insisted, "you should pray about your research."

And so I decided, why not? It would be an interesting experiment. I started early in a summer that was to be devoted to research. The problem I was considering was a hard one that I had been working on, off and on, for five years. I felt that I was really near the end. I felt that just one little insight was all I needed—the ideal occasion for praying and receiving an answer. And so I would hide in the library at the beginning of each day, think about what direction might be the right one to pry loose that additional bit of needed insight (the one that would explain everything), pray for direction and enlightenment, and set out to work. And, amazingly to me, each day I would feel instructed and directed. I would feel at day's end that I had traveled a great distance, and that only a *little* bit of insight was still needed to finish the problem. And so the next day would begin, just a little way from the end of the problem, and I would travel another great distance until I understood a great deal more and only a little distance remained to travel.

So went the months until at the end of the summer I was, actually, at the end of the problem. I understood it, and the little bit of needed insight was spread over the summer and was full of miraculous mathematical wonders, much deeper than I had dreamed—and I marveled. I marveled not so much at the mathematics, because I had seen beautiful mathematics before, had occasionally had a hand in its discovery, and had even come to expect things to be richer and more beautiful than I could dream or than I could have made them had I been the creator of the universe; rather, I marveled at the naïveté that led me to expect my hard problem to have an easy answer, to assume that one little inspiration was all I needed, that I needed just one little word in the ear. I marveled at the distance I had traveled and at the length of my instruction. The specific theorem is of little consequence to the reader, but to me it is a miracle theorem that taught me a lot about prayer, about instruction, and about patient beings who care about our concerns.

My answers to prayer have been mostly nonspecific, with a few exceptions. There was the one that told me when I was first counselor in a bishopric about to be dissolved, "No, you won't be called as the new bishop, but the new bishop will call you as Scoutmaster." When we were considering coming to BYU after seventeen wonderful research years at the University of Wisconsin in lovely, cold, hot, humid, green Madison, an answer to another prayer told me, "No, you will not have great success in your research at BYU." This last answer is one I try to forget and bury in hard work.

Lauren was our fourth child, of six. She was born with Down's syndrome and a multitude of attendant problems: mental retardation, no rectal opening, heart valve problems, a floppy neck, small limbs, tongue thrust. She spun her crib toys with her feet since her legs reached farther than her short arms. We thought of her as our

Raggedy Ann baby. If she were living now, she would be twenty-three years old (she was born in 1973) and would exactly fill the gap between Michael and Jonathan.

Circulatory problems made Lauren susceptible to respiratory difficulties, and during her first year she was often sick. Pneumonia took her in and out of the hospital. We came to know most of the nurses. One morning at 2:00 we awoke to her sudden cry—and found that she had stopped breathing. Before help arrived, Ardyth managed to get Lauren breathing again with a thump to the sternum. Lauren was sick during most of the month of December and wanted only Ardyth to care for her. By Christmas morning, Ardyth was exhausted. We decided that Lauren surely needed a priesthood blessing. As always, I was very anxious since I felt responsible to be worthy and to say the right things—as though it were I who gave the blessing rather than God.

Shortly after I had pronounced the blessing, Ardyth said, "She wants you."

"Right!" I thought doubtfully, "She never wants me; she always wants her mother."

But Ardyth was right: Lauren would not be at peace that Christmas day unless I was holding her. She would not sleep unless I held her. She would not nurse at her mother's breast unless I was plainly in sight over her mother's shoulder. For one day, Lauren's only Christmas day, Lauren was her father's girl rather than her mother's. For precisely one day of her one and a half years, Lauren was not her mother's girl but mine. At the time we thought that it was a wonderful priesthood gift to Ardyth to save her from total exhaustion. We have come to view that day as a gift to me. For one day of her life, Lauren was my girl.

When doctors tried to repair Lauren's faulty heart valves the following September, we fasted and gave her a blessing. For the last time I felt terrible anxiety as I gave a priesthood blessing. We so wanted her to live and to be healthy, and I blessed her to do so. And I was wrong, and she died. We could hardly bear to break our fast. It gave us such comfort. For the first time we understood the scripture wherein the Lord says, "that thy fasting may be perfect, or, in other words, that thy joy may be full. Verily, this is fasting and prayer, or in other words, rejoicing and prayer" (D&C 59:13–14). I resolved never again to be anxious about a priesthood blessing, but to listen as carefully as I could to the Spirit, for it is the Lord who blesses.

After our move to BYU we found friends who wanted to read the Book of Mormon with us. President Benson had just asked us all to read it individually every day. With these friends, I enjoyed feeling the exuberance of the angel who, as he instructed Nephi, could not restrain his own comment:

> Knowest thou the meaning of the tree which thy father saw?
>
> And I answered him, saying: Yea, it is the love of God . . . ; wherefore, it is the most desirable above all things.
>
> And he spake unto me, saying: Yea, and the most joyous to the soul. (1 Nephi 11:21–23)

I love an angel who bursts out with such exclamations. I also love the unity of truth taught by the temple ceremony and by the scriptures:

> Wherefore, I beseech of you, brethren, that ye should search diligently in the light of Christ that ye may know good from evil; and if ye will lay hold upon every good thing, and condemn it not, ye certainly will be a child of Christ. (Moroni 7:19)

I love the same unity of truth taught by one of the world's great mathematicians, Henri Poincaré:

> Truth should not be feared, for it alone is beautiful.
>
> When I speak here of truth, assuredly I refer first to scientific truth, but I also mean moral truth. . . . I cannot separate them, and whosoever loves the one cannot help loving the other. . . . These two sorts of truth when discovered give the same joy; each when perceived beams with the same splendor, so that we must see it or close our eyes. . . .
>
> In a word, I liken the two truths, because the same reasons make us love them and because the same reasons make us fear them.[1]

I love the example of people around me who live my every dream of holiness. Some of them hold high positions in the Church or the community; some of them hold none. For me, goodness is more important than knowledge and knowledge is more important than power. It is a miracle to me that the most powerful being in the universe is also good. Power and goodness are not highly correlated in our world. I would rather do what is good and right than have a testimony that the Church is true, and I consider it a miracle that the evidence I trust indicates that it is true. I am delighted when I see heroes and heroines around me living its precepts. I am saddened at the occasional person who values its authority more than its goodness. I find most compelling the sentiments of George Cannon, the immigrant who, upon reading the Book of Mormon, uttered the following evaluation: "An evil-minded man could not have written it, and a good man would not have tried to write it with intent to deceive."[2] I feel the goodness of the Book of Mormon as I study and pray, and I rejoice, and "Yea," says my personal angel, "it is most joyous to the soul."

NOTES

1. Henri Poincaré, *The Value of Science* (New York: Dover, 1958), 11–12.
2. Beatrice Cannon Evans and Janath Russell Cannon, eds., *Cannon Family Historical Treasury* (Salt Lake City: George Cannon Family Association, 1967), 35.

Chapter 10

Knowledge by Faith

Robert L. Millet
Dean of Religious Education, Brigham Young University

I HAD AN EXPERIENCE as a young missionary in the eastern states that taught me something about the heart and the mind. My companion and I had moved into a small town in New Jersey only to find that the local Protestant ministers had prepared their parishioners for our coming. At almost every door we approached, we were met by a smiling face and the words, "Oh, you must be the Mormons. This is for you." The people would then hand us an anti-Mormon tract. We saved the pamphlets, stacked them in the corner of the living room of the apartment, and soon had a rather substantial pile of material. Out of sheer curiosity we began to read the pamphlets during lunchtime. I can still recall the dark and empty feelings that filled my soul as I encountered question after question about selected doctrines and specific moments in the history of the Church. My senior companion was no different; he was as unsettled as I was.

For weeks we did our work, but our hearts weren't in it. We went through the motions but, without saying much to each other, we sensed that we could not carry on indefinitely. I broke the ice one afternoon with the rather brutal query: "Elder Dyreng, what if the Church isn't true?" He responded, "I don't know." I followed up: "What if the Baptists are right?" (There was a strong contingent of

Baptists in the area.) He said, "I just don't know." Third question: "What if the Catholics are right? What if they have had the authority all along?" He responded, "I've been wondering the same thing." Then, presumably in an effort to cheer me up, he asked, "Elder Millet, do you think we are doing anything wrong? I mean, even if we are not a part of the true church, are we hurting anyone?" I sheepishly replied that we were probably not doing anything destructive. "Then," he added, "maybe we should keep working." I asked, with much pain in my voice, "Is that supposed to make me feel better? If so, it doesn't." He indicated that under the present circumstances it was the best he could do.

I am ashamed to admit that before that time I had never prayed intently about my testimony. I was raised in the Church. Mom and Dad had a testimony, and I knew that they knew. That had always seemed adequate. But now I was up against the wall of faith, and suddenly what they knew did not seem sufficient to settle my troubled heart. I prayed and pleaded. I begged the Lord for light, for help, for anything! These vexations of the soul went on for about a month. I had actually concluded (though I had not confided it to my companion) that if relief were not forthcoming shortly, I would pack my bags and go home. It did not seem proper to be engaged seriously in a cause about which I could not bear my testimony.

We came home for lunch a few days later and my companion set about the task of making the soup and preparing the peanut butter sandwiches. I collapsed in a large chair in the living room, removed my shoes, and loosened my tie. As I began to reflect once more on my testimony problem, my heart ached. My feelings were close to the surface at this point, and I yearned for deliverance from my pain. For some reason I reached to a nearby table and picked up a copy of the pamphlet *Joseph Smith Tells His Own Story*. I began reading the opening lines. I came to the Prophet's statement that he was born on December 23, 1805, in Sharon, Windsor County, Vermont, and I was suddenly and without warning immersed in the most comforting and soothing influence I had ever known. It seemed at the time as if I were being wrapped in a large blanket as I began to be filled with the warmth of the Holy Spirit from head to toe. I wept as the spirit of conversion encompassed me, and as I came to know assuredly that what we were doing was right and true and good. I did not hear specific words, but the feelings on that occasion seemed to whisper: "Of course it's true. You know that now, and you've known it for a long time." The other feeling, terribly pertinent to what I want to express in this article, was to the effect that the answers to what was troubling me were for the time being beyond my present capacity to comprehend. In time the answers would come, answers that would be as satisfying to the mind as they were soothing to the heart. The answers came, in fact, within a matter of months, and I marveled at the time how it was that something so simple could have been so problematic before.

The Spirit touched my heart, told me things my mind did not yet understand, and I was then in a position to proceed confidently with my work until my head caught up with my heart. That experience has served me well over the last thirty years or so. It continues to reinforce in my life important principles pertaining to study and faith. I believe in study. I find great joy in reading broadly and expanding my mind on a myriad of subjects. I think we are expected to do that as much as our time and circumstances allow. I believe it is good for men and women to specialize, to focus their attention and efforts on certain disciplines or fields of study, to master the disciplines, to become expert on what the great minds have discovered or uncovered. In short, I believe it is good to be learned. I am sincerely grateful for noble teachers, Mormon and non-Mormon alike, who have motivated me—set me on fire—in regard to the social and behavioral sciences as well as the ancient world of the Bible. At the same time, I thank God for those great minds whose faith in the true, eternal but unseen verities, has inspired me to prioritize. I have come to know that although ours is a thoughtful faith, one that requires reason as well as revelation, it is often necessary to place our unanswered questions on a shelf, to suspend intellectual judgment while findings from study manage to catch up with the feelings and impressions obtained from the Spirit of God.

All truths are not of equal worth, nor are they acquired in the same way. Elder Dallin H. Oaks observed:

> Seeking learning by study, we use the method of reason. Seeking learning by faith, we must rely on revelation. . . . Reason is a thinking

process using facts and logic that can be communicated to another person and tested by objective (that is, measurable) criteria. Revelation is communication from God to man. It cannot be defined and tested like reason. Reason involves thinking and demonstrating. Revelation involves hearing or seeing or understanding or feeling. Reason is potentially public. Revelation is invariably personal.[1]

Surely we are put here on the earth to learn as much as we can in science, in art, in language, in history and foreign culture, and so on. And, to the degree that we can master some of these fields, we are better able to present the truth understandably and appropriately to more and more people. (See D&C 88:78–80.)

But I have a conviction that some truths matter more than others. It is valuable to know of gravity or the laws of motion, but it is vital to know of the reality of a Redeemer. It is helpful to know the laws of thermodynamics, but it is essential to know how to repent and call upon God, in the name of his Son, for forgiveness. The idea that spiritual truths are of greater worth to our eternal welfare than the fields to which we have dedicated our professional lives should not be threatening to anyone, nor should it cause us to be defensive about our own disciplines. The perpetuation of eternal truth and the conversion of individual souls must be more important to us than the discovery or dissemination of this or that idea. We are children of God, followers of Christ, and devotees to disciplines in that order. When we get out of order we open ourselves to trouble; we begin the gradual dilution of our discipleship.

I am convinced that Mormonism is robust enough to open itself to rigorous study and analysis. It is commendable when a member of the Church, when confronted by a challenging issue, responds with the simple statement of testimony. Every one of us will be in that position at one time or another. And yet there is a particular power associated with the bearing of testimony informed by adequate study, testimony that represents, in the words of the apostle Peter, a reason for the hope within us (1 Peter 3:15). I refuse to allow my commitment to the faith to be held hostage to the latest fads and trends in the academic world. I cannot, for example, afford to postpone believing in Christ until New Testament scholars come to a consensus on what Jesus really did and what he really said. I cannot allow my witness of the Book of Mormon to rest on archaeological evidences in North, Central, or South America any more than I can prop my faith in the Book of Abraham on what a handful of Egyptologists make of the Joseph Smith papyri. Forty years ago Hugh Nibley reminded us that

> the words of the prophets cannot be held to the tentative and defective tests that men have devised for them. Science, philosophy, and common sense all have a right to their day in court. But the last word does not lie with them. Every time men in their wisdom have come forth with the last word, other words have promptly followed. The last word is a testimony of the gospel that comes only by direct revelation. Our Father in heaven speaks it, and if it were in perfect agreement with the science of today, it would surely be out of line with the science of tomorrow. Let us not, therefore, seek to hold God to the learned opinions of the moment when he speaks the language of eternity.[2]

There are few things more desperately needed in our day than faith—faith in the unseen, or as one astute observer of Christianity has noted, "Faith that bridges the chasm between what our minds can know and what our souls aspire after."[3] I have come to believe that there is nothing weak about faith, even (or especially) in one dedicated to the life of the mind; faith is not whimpering acquiescence, not timid and spineless hope for happiness, for pie in the sky in the great by-and-by. Faith is active. Faith is dynamic. Faith is based on evidence, internal evidence, the kind of evidence that men and women acquire when they search and pray and open themselves to the infinite, refusing to yield to cynicism or arrogance.

One need not surrender cherished values to live in a modern world. One need not suspend his or her intellectual faculties to be a faithful Latter-day Saint. A member of the Church need not fall prey to the increasingly vocal voices of those who choose to preach from the forums of dissent; one can have implicit trust in the Church and its leaders without sacrificing or compromising anything, not the least of which is intellectual integrity. Having said all that, I hasten to add that one must be willing to put first things first, to establish a hierarchy of loyalties. If my attitude is "The kingdom of God or nothing!" then whatever I may encounter in my intellectual pursuits that is seemingly at variance with the scriptures or the counsel of living prophets will be placed in its proper perspective. One who is grounded in the witness of the Spirit deals with ambiguity and intellectual dissonance with patience and faith.

Though one need not be simpleminded to have faith, one may need to be simple in his or her approach to life and its challenges in order to enjoy the fruits of faith. There are times when faith requires us to act in the face of what the world would consider to be the absurd. Abraham was asked to put to death his beloved and long-awaited son, Isaac, the one hope Abraham had for the fulfillment of the promise that his posterity would be as numberless as the sands upon the seashore or the stars in the heavens. Jehovah had spoken. Abraham had entered the realm of divine experience, knew the voice of the Lord, and knew what he had encountered was real. Therefore, when the awful assignment came to offer up Isaac in sacrifice, he obeyed, even though, rationally speaking, there was no way the promises could thereafter be realized. But the father of the faithful had implicit trust in his God, "accounting that God was able to raise [Isaac] up, even from the dead" (Hebrews 11:19). Abraham knew God and he knew that his purposes were just; the finite mind yielded to the infinite, knowing fully that "whatever God requires is right, no matter what it is, although we may not see the reason thereof till long after the events transpire."[4] His leap of faith was prerequisite to his ascent to glory.

This kind of faith may be particularly difficult for one who is devoted to research and study and dependent solely on external evidence; it requires that we put first things first, that we not judge the restored gospel—its history or doctrines—by the canons of our own discipline, but that we judge our own disciplines by the standards of the gospel. That is, faithful scholarship does not, as some have naively supposed, entail hiding from the truth or hiding the truth, but rather viewing all things through the lenses of the Restoration. It is only then that we are able to see things as they really are and as they really will be. One of the challenges a person faces is to learn the strengths—and thus the limitations—of his or her own field of study, what it can teach and what it cannot teach. It just may be that faithful scholarship requires more, not less, mental discipline. Faithful scholarship requires that we not live a divided or disjointed life, that we not be psychologists or historians or chemists during the week and Latter-day Saints on Sunday, but that we take the restored gospel seriously and incorporate it into all areas of worthwhile investigation. The apostasy was long and broad and deep; it made its influence felt in the pure sciences, the social sciences, the arts, and, of course, theology. The Restoration is destined to have an impact not only in the explication of doctrine and the delivery of divine authority (as vital as those things are), but also in all areas of study. When disciplined minds and creative artists open themselves to the enlightening powers of the Holy Ghost and are imbued with the spirit and power of the restored gospel, learning and discovery and creativity reach beyond the paltry bounds of what has been done heretofore and open us to new vistas of understanding and expression.

Indeed, faith has its own type of discipline. Some things that are obvious to the faithful sound like the gibberish of alien tongues to the faithless. The discipline of faith, the concentrated and consecrated effort to become dedicated to God, has its own reward, a reward that includes the expansion of the mind. Those who enter that discipline come to be filled with light and are able in time to comprehend all things (D&C 88:67). It is worth considering the words of a revelation given in Kirtland, Ohio. Having encouraged the Saints to call a solemn assembly, the Lord continued: "And as all have not faith, seek ye diligently and teach one another words of wisdom; . . . seek learning, even by study and also by faith" (D&C 88:118). We note that the counsel to seek learning out of the best books is prefaced by the negative clause, "And as all *have not* faith." One wonders whether the Master did not intend something like the following: Since all do not have sufficient faith—that is, according to Elder B. H. Roberts, since they have not "matured in their religious convictions" to learn by any other means[5]—then they must seek learning by study, the use of the rational processes alone. In other words, if all *did* have the requisite faith, then what? Perhaps learning by studying from the best books would then be greatly enhanced by revelation. Honest truth seekers would learn things in this way that they could not know otherwise.

Could this be what Joseph Smith meant when he taught that "the best way to obtain truth and wisdom is not to ask it from books, but to go to God in prayer, and obtain divine teaching"?[6] It is surely in this same context that another of the Prophet's famous, yet little-understood statements yields meaning: "Could you gaze into heaven five minutes," he declared, "you would know more than you would by reading all that ever was written on the subject" of life after death.[7]

"I believe in study," President Marion G. Romney stated. "I believe that men learn much through study. As a matter of fact, it has been my observation that they learn little concerning things as they are, as they were, or as they are to come without study. *I also believe, however, and know, that learning by study is greatly accelerated by faith.*"[8]

President Harold B. Lee spoke to BYU students, just weeks before his death, of the rigors of learning by faith:

> The acquiring of knowledge by faith is no easy road to learning. It will demand strenuous effort and continual striving by faith. In short, learning by faith is no task for a lazy man. Someone has said, in effect, that "such a process requires the bending of the whole soul, the calling up from the depths of the human mind and linking the person with God. The right connection must be formed; then only comes knowledge by faith, a kind of knowledge that goes beyond secular learning, that reaches into the realms of the unknown and makes those who follow that course great in the sight of the Lord."[9]

On another occasion, President Lee taught that this idea of "bending . . . the whole soul" is accomplished "through worthy living to become attuned to the Holy Spirit of the Lord, the calling up from the depths of one's own mental searching, and the linking of our own efforts to receive the true witness of the Spirit."[10]

Learning by faith requires that we be as rigorous in our pursuit of sacred things through the established channels—scriptures, living prophets, personal revelation—as we are in our research and study of secular things. Sometimes members of the Church dismiss outright or at least underestimate the power of the gospel message because they have not paid a sufficient price to plumb the depths of those things God has made known. Elder John A. Widtsoe stated:

> It is a paradox that men will gladly devote time every day for many years to learn a science or an art; yet will expect to win a knowledge of the gospel, which comprehends all sciences and arts, through perfunctory glances at books or occasional listening to sermons. The

gospel should be studied more intensively than any school or college subject. They who pass opinion on the gospel without having given it intimate and careful study are not lovers of truth, and their opinions are worthless.[11]

Learning by faith seems to entail something else as well. An episode in the Book of Mormon highlights another very important principle. "Now it came to pass," Mormon writes, "that there were many of the rising generation that could not understand the words of king Benjamin, being little children at the time he spake unto his people; and they did not believe the tradition of their fathers. They did not believe what had been said concerning the resurrection of the dead, neither did they believe concerning the coming of Christ." And now note this powerful statement: "And now *because of their unbelief they could not understand the word of God;* and their hearts were hardened" (Mosiah 26:1–3; emphasis added). Because of their unbelief—their refusal to believe, to accept the true but unseen, to surrender and yield to God—they denied themselves the right to understanding. To give a modern-day example, one who approaches the reading of the Book of Mormon with a cynical eye is not likely to mine its doctrinal gold or gain a witness of its truthfulness; there must be a willful suspension of disbelief, an inclination to accept the truth when confronted with it, an openness to the possibility that something just might be true.

I think this is what the Lord has in mind when he counsels us to "search diligently, pray always, and *be believing*," with the promise that all things shall thereafter work together for our good (D&C 90:24; emphasis added; see also D&C 100:15 and Romans 8:28). God does not ask us to be gullible or to obey blindly. "Of those who speak in his name," President Joseph F. Smith declared, "the Lord requires humility, not ignorance."[12] Neither ignorance nor blind obedience adds strength to the kingdom. Instead, the Omniscient One simply asks of his Saints that they believe, that they be willing to trust in him, in his plan, and in those who direct the destiny of his Church. Some knowledge may come by study, but intelligence or the glory of God requires diligence and obedience (D&C 130:19). In a revelation to President Brigham Young, the Savior explained: "Let him that is ignorant learn wisdom by humbling himself and calling upon the

Lord his God, that his eyes may be opened that he may see, and his ears opened that he may hear" (D&C 136:32).

I have learned a few things as I have studied over the years. I thank God for the formal education I have received, for the privilege it is (and I count it such) to have received university training and to have earned bachelor's, master's, and doctoral degrees. Education has expanded my mind and opened conversations and doors for me. It has taught me what books to read, how to research a topic, and how to make my case or present my point of view more effectively. But the more I learn, the more I value the truths of salvation, those simple but profound verities that soothe and settle and sanctify human hearts. I appreciate knowing that the order of the cosmos points toward a Providential Hand; I am deeply grateful to know by the power of the Holy Ghost that there is a God and that he is our Father in Heaven. I appreciate knowing something about the social, political, and religious world into which Jesus of Nazareth was born; I am deeply grateful for the witness of the Spirit that he is indeed God's Almighty Son. I appreciate knowing something about the social and intellectual climate of nineteenth-century America; I am deeply grateful to have burning within my soul a testimony that the Father and the Son appeared to Joseph Smith in the spring of 1820, and that the work set in motion is truly the kingdom of God on earth. In short, the more I encounter men's approximations of what is, the more I treasure those absolute truths that make known "things as they really are, and . . . things as they really will be" (Jacob 4:13; see also D&C 93:24). In fact, the more we learn, the more we begin to realize what we do not know, the more we feel the need to consider ourselves "fools before God" (2 Nephi 9:42).

Those who choose to follow the Brethren, choose to believe in and teach the scriptures, and choose to be loyal to the Church—no matter the extent of their academic training or intellectual capacity—open themselves to ridicule from the cynic and the critic. Ultimately, doctrinal truth comes not through the explorations of scholars, but through the revelations of God to apostles and prophets. And if such a position be labeled by some as narrow, parochial, or anti-intellectual, then so be it. I cast my lot with the prophets. I sincerely believe that education need not be antithetical to conversion and spiritual commitment and that study can contribute to faith in the ways I have described in these pages. It all depends on where one places his or her trust. Elder Bruce R. McConkie testified:

> True religion deals with spiritual things. We do not come to a knowledge of God and his laws through intellectuality, or by research, or by reason. . . . In their sphere, education and intellectuality are devoutly to be desired. But when contrasted with spiritual endowments, they are of but slight and passing worth. From an eternal perspective what each of us needs is a Ph.D. in faith and righteousness. The things that will profit us everlastingly are not the power to reason, but the ability to receive revelation; not the truths learned by study, but the knowledge gained by faith; not what we know about the things of the world, but our knowledge of God and his laws.[13]

NOTES

1. Dallin H. Oaks, *The Lord's Way* (Salt Lake City: Deseret Book, 1991), 16–17.
2. Hugh Nibley, *The World and the Prophets* (Salt Lake City: Deseret Book and FARMS, 1987), 134.
3. Malcolm Muggeridge, *Jesus: The Man Who Lives* (New York: Harper & Row, 1975), 20.
4. *Teachings of the Prophet Joseph Smith*, comp. Joseph Fielding Smith (Salt Lake City: Deseret Book, 1961), 256.
5. Harold B. Lee, in Conference Report, April 1968, 129; or "Seek Learning, . . . Faith," *Improvement Era*, June 1968, 102.
6. *Teachings of the Prophet Joseph Smith*, 191.
7. Ibid., 324.
8. Marion G. Romney, *Learning for the Eternities* (Salt Lake City: Deseret Book, 1977), 72; emphasis added.
9. Harold B. Lee, "Be Loyal to the Royal within You," in *Speeches of the Year: BYU Devotional and Ten-Stake Fireside Addresses, 1973* (Provo, Utah: Brigham Young University Press, 1974), 91.
10. Harold B. Lee, in Conference Report, April 1971, 94; or "The Iron Rod," *Ensign*, June 1971, 10.
11. John A. Widtsoe, *Evidences and Reconciliations* (Salt Lake City: Bookcraft, 1987), 16–17.
12. Joseph F. Smith, *Gospel Doctrine* (Salt Lake City: Deseret Book, 1970), 206.
13. Bruce R. McConkie, in Conference Report, April 1971, 99; or "The Lord's People Receive Revelation," *Ensign*, June 1971, 77–78.

CHAPTER 11

FROM THE CRADLE OF CREATION
The Beliefs of a Young Botanist

PAUL ALAN COX
Dean of General Education and Honors, Brigham Young University

Consider the lilies how they grow: they toil not, they spin not; and yet I say unto you, that Solomon in all his glory was not arrayed like one of these.

—LUKE 12:27

FOR AS LONG as I can remember, I have loved plants. Some of my first memories are of rough juniper seeds, the damp smell of lilac in the morning, and the glory of purple irises along a ditch bank. Theodore Roethke wrote that "morning's a motion in a happy mind," and just as surely plants were a joyous presence in my earliest thoughts. As I grew older my enthusiasm for plants continued unabated. While other boys joined Little League, I planted dahlias and built greenhouses. There is an ineffable aesthetic about plants that I have always found astonishingly beautiful. Some of my happiest hours have been spent studying plants.

My father was a park ranger and my mother was a fisheries biologist. They were very supportive of my interests in plants. When I was ten, I received permission from Gasquet forest to collect several rare cobra lilies (*Darlingtonia californica*), so my parents drove me one weekend from Provo to Crescent City, California, to collect the plants. I spent the first several nights home in my greenhouse with the cobra lilies, trying my best to recreate with extension cords and humidifiers the early morning and afternoon coastal fogs that characterize their native habitat.

As a tropical rain forest biologist, I have spent the last two decades of my life studying plants in South and Central America, Africa, the Far East, Australia, and the Pacific and Caribbean islands. I usually work alone in the forest and spend my nights in small villages. Many people ask me if my work is frightening. They do not understand that the rain forest is not at all like the "jungle" portrayed in the movies: the rain forest is serene and gentle, very much like the Sacred Grove. When I walk through the rain forest, I feel as though I am walking through a living masterpiece painted by the Creator. When I see the sun streaming through the rain forest canopy like light pouring through the stained glass windows of a cathedral, I feel very close to Heavenly Father. I always feel his Spirit in the rain forest. It is abundantly clear to me that plants and animals are spiritual entities worthy of our care and respect. We demonstrate respect for the Creator when we show respect for his handiwork. I have devoted my life to conservation because I believe the rain forests, oceans, mountains, and deserts are the very handiwork of God.

My Life as a Scientist

I have both a deep testimony of the gospel and a deep appreciation of science. I see no contradictions between the truths of the gospel and the truths of science. I do not wish to belittle the struggles of those who wrestle with contradictions they perceive, but merely to indicate that I detect no essential contradictions.

There are a few teachers on both sides of the question who promulgate the belief that science is irreconcilable with religion. I fear that this stance can be damaging to the spirituality of our youth. When I hear of such controversies, I think on the words of the Savior to the Nephites:

> And there shall be no disputations among you, as there have hitherto been; neither shall there be disputations among you concerning the points of my doctrine, as there have hitherto been.
>
> For verily, verily I say unto you, he that hath the spirit of

contention is not of me, but is of the devil, who is the father of contention, and he stirreth up the hearts of men to contend with anger, one with another. (3 Nephi 11:28–29)

For this reason I have been reluctant to discuss my views about science and conservation within Church settings, and indeed I was hesitant to accept the invitation to write this chapter. I realize that my own views on these matters might be objectionable to some, and I do not wish to inadvertently offend any fellow member of the Church.

I think Paul had a similar issue in mind when he wrote:

For one believeth that he may eat all things: another, who is weak, eateth herbs.

Let not him that eateth despise him that eateth not; and let not him which eateth not judge him that eateth: for God hath received him. . . .

Let us not therefore judge one another any more: but judge this rather, that no man put a stumblingblock or an occasion to fall in his brother's way. . . .

But if thy brother be grieved with thy meat, now walkest thou not charitably. Destroy not him with thy meat, for whom Christ died. (Romans 14:2–3, 13, 15)

Because I believe so deeply in the Church, I do not wish my views on science or conservation to become a "stumblingblock" that might anger or destroy a fellow member "for whom Christ died." The price paid for each of us was so great that we cannot afford to endanger the salvation of another. Besides, it behooves all of us to speak meekly about these issues. As scientists we must be humble about our conclusions, because new information can radically change our understanding of the world. And as Latter-day Saints we should be modest about our personal interpretations of the scriptures because new revelation can profoundly change our understanding of the gospel.

My personal views about the compatibility of the gospel and science were deeply influenced by interactions I had, as a student, with two remarkable individuals. The famous Latter-day Saint chemist Henry Eyring taught that "the Church only requires you to believe what is true," an expansive vision of the compatibility of all truth that defuses many potential contradictions between science and religion.

President Harold B. Lee told a group of us "never to accept any single-scripture theology. If the Lord wants this people to know something, he will not bury it in some obscure verse, but will make it abundantly apparent throughout the scriptures."

Both of these sentiments, one by a prominent Latter-day Saint scientist and the other by a prophet of God, led me to focus on the weightier matters of the gospel, such as faith in Christ, repentance, and baptism, rather than on tangential areas of possible conflict. It is now clear to me that religion and science speak to very different questions. Science has very little to offer on important "why" questions: Why was the world created? Why are we here? Why does God love us? However, the scriptures offer little information on mechanisms that are sought in "how" questions: How old is the earth? How were plants and animals created? What are the laws governing the origin and expansion of the visible universe?

Not only do science and religion address different realms of truth, but they also have very different consequences. The truths of science can be known to any diligent investigator regardless of personal worthiness. These truths can be useful for building aircraft or devising new medicines. But the treasures of eternity are available only to those who humbly seek the Lord through faith, repentance, and obedience to the commandments. The truths of the gospel, if followed, can lead one to Christ and salvation. One can be saved without a knowledge of population genetics or quantum mechanics, but little eternal progress is possible without a knowledge of the principles of repentance or the power of prayer. There is also a certainty about gospel truths that is unparalleled in science. The divinity of Jesus and the power of his atonement will never change, while it is possible that many of our scientific understandings will change as further information becomes available.

My Life as a Scholar

Perhaps because I am a botanist, spending my life in peaceful forests, working with organisms that are silent and gentle, I tend to shun debate and controversy, particularly concerning religious issues. The weightier matters of the gospel, the doctrines that unite rather than divide us as brothers and sisters in Christ, are the parts of the gospel that I find most compelling. In short, I seek "the peaceable things of the kingdom" (D&C 39:6) rather than the areas of controversy.

I do not feel that I fit comfortably into either camp of scholars who have led much of the recent discussion on "Mormon scholarship," camps that have been termed by some "the Mormon liberals" and "the Neo-orthodoxy." As a scholar, I do not see my employment as any better or worse than that of a park ranger, a plumber, a farmer, a fisherman, or any other honorable occupation that Latter-day Saints pursue. Whatever our endeavors, we should strive for excellence, serving our employers and our communities with our best efforts. The true Saints have never been artificially divided by status, wealth, or opportunities for education. We are told that when such divisions did occur, the Church suffered:

> And the people began to be distinguished by ranks, according to their riches and their chances for learning; yea, some were ignorant because of their poverty, and others did receive great learning because of their riches.
>
> Some were lifted up in pride, and others were exceedingly humble; some did return railing for railing, while others would receive railing and persecution and all manner of afflictions, and would not turn and revile again, but were humble and penitent before God.
>
> And thus there became a great inequality in all the land, insomuch that the church began to be broken up; yea, insomuch that in the thirtieth year the church was broken up in all the land save it were among a few of the Lamanites who were converted unto the true faith; and they would not depart from it, for they were firm, and steadfast, and immovable, willing with all diligence to keep the commandments of the Lord.
>
> Now the cause of this iniquity of the people was this—Satan had great power, unto the stirring up of the people to do all manner of iniquity, and to the puffing them up with pride, tempting them to seek for power, and authority, and riches, and the vain things of the world. (3 Nephi 6:12–15)

I am uncomfortable with recent discussions about the role and import of "Mormon intellectuals," and I really do not have much to contribute to that dialogue. One extreme seems to argue that the Lord's servants, particularly those who are not "scholars," should somehow be limited in their ministry and utterances, or even distrusted. The other extreme suggests that those who pursue scholarly careers may damage themselves and the Church—unless they disengage themselves from traditional scholarship and pursue a unique form of "Mormon scholarship."

Imagine if Mormon plumbers had a similar controversy, one side arguing that the Lord's servants should not be followed if they lacked a detailed knowledge of plumbing, and the other side arguing that we must abandon plumbing altogether and invent a unique "Mormon" method of sending water coursing through pipes.

I am grateful that I can spend my days in enjoyable professional pursuits, but I do not believe that my scholarly endeavors give me any special advantage in discerning the mysteries of godliness, an undertaking that will depend solely on my willingness to humbly follow the Savior. Yet as a scholar, I do not believe that my Church affiliation excuses me in doing poor-quality work or allows me to invent some unique "Mormon" formulation of my discipline. My work as a rain forest biologist should be accessible to my academic peers regardless of their religious affiliation.

My Life as a Latter-day Saint

The most precious thing to me in the world is my membership in The Church of Jesus Christ of Latter-day Saints. I will be eternally grateful that I was able to be baptized at the age of eight into the Church and receive the wonderful blessings of the atonement.

When I was a twelve-year-old, I read the Gospels, which record the earthly ministry of Jesus. I found his teachings to be both vivid and compelling. He taught us to love our enemies, to do good to those who treat us badly, to pray in secret, and to do our alms in a quiet and unobtrusive way. As I read, I knew inside that his doctrine was true. If, of all the scriptural texts, only the Sermon on the Mount survived, I would find it to be compelling evidence that Jesus is who he said he was, the Son of God. A mere man could not invent such beautiful but deeply radical doctrines. If the entire world lived the teachings of the Sermon on the Mount, nearly all our problems would disappear. Reading that sermon, I believed with my entire being that Jesus is the Christ and that because of his sacrifice, each of us will be resurrected and can receive a remission of our sins if we repent and are baptized.

Later I read the Book of Mormon, cover to cover, many times. I have a deep testimony of the truthfulness of the Book of Mormon. I cannot read a single page without feeling power and righteousness flowing from the book. I have the same feeling of peace when I read the Book of Mormon as when I read the New Testament. I know that both are true.

I believe with my whole heart that our church is led by inspired servants of God. They are good men and women, but more compelling to me than their own personal merits is the fact that they were called by the Lord. It hurts me when people speak unkindly or sarcastically of our leaders, because I know that when I listen carefully, I can hear the voice of the Lord speaking to me through them. I am so grateful that the Lord left us with a solid tripod on which to ground our faith: the scriptures, the living prophets, and most important, the Spirit. All are united in testifying of the divinity of the Savior and the reality of his love for us.

Jesus offers us such a bargain. He allows us to repent of our sins. Through him, we can approach the Father in prayer. He makes possible a remission of sins, so that the Father can send his Spirit to be with us. And he offers us the saving ordinances of the priesthood that are precious beyond price. I am so grateful that I have been sealed for time and all eternity to my wife, children, parents, and other family members. No matter what happens to us, if we are faithful, we will again be together. Those seals are real. I testify of the reality of the "good tidings" of the gospel of Jesus Christ.

As a botanist, I find it poignant that the prophet Isaiah referred to the Savior as a plant: "For he shall grow up before him as a tender plant, and as a root out of a dry ground: he hath no form nor comeliness; and when we shall see him, there is no beauty that we should desire him" (Isaiah 53:2).

Isaiah's metaphor is apt. Rather than being defined like so many animals (and many of us!) by what he consumed, Jesus, like a plant, is characterized by what he produced. Like many plants, he healed wounds. Like many seeds that fall and grow in untoward places, Jesus was born and reared in a humble place. As his mortal life unfolded, he always grew toward the light. Like a small forest herb, he was meek and gentle, silent in the face of oppression. Like plants that use dirt, earth, and other common things to produce beautiful flowers, Jesus took simple things, common experiences, and lowly people, and produced great teachings, beautiful proverbs, and magnificent servants. Jesus Christ is the master botanist, the creator not only of the rain forest flowers and architect of Eden, but creator of the entire earth. I love him. I care deeply about protecting his creation. I sustain and honor his chosen servants. I hope to prove worthy in whatever corner of his vineyard I am called upon to tend.

110   •

CHAPTER 12

A TESTIMONY OF THE PLAN OF
PROGRESSION AND ETERNAL LIFE

DANIEL H. LUDLOW
Emeritus Dean of Religious Education, Brigham Young University
Editor-in-chief, Encyclopedia of Mormonism

IT WAS A GREAT SURPRISE to me to be included as one of the LDS
scholars asked to contribute to this volume. As I contemplate the
great minds that have testified of the gospel of Jesus Christ in recent
decades, I certainly would not include myself among them. Thus, I
trust and hope the reader will accept this humble offering for what
it is—a personal testimony of the validity and importance of the plan
of progression and eternal life, coming from a fellow member of the
Church who has acquired a strong and firm testimony of the work
through considerable study, observation, and prayer.

I am firmly convinced that the greatest knowledge a person can
acquire in this life is the knowledge associated with the great plan of
progression and eternal life of our Heavenly Father, which we refer
to as the gospel of Jesus Christ. I am firmly convinced that this
knowledge or testimony is available to every person who has the ability to reason and who is willing to learn and obey the laws upon
which such knowledge is predicated. I deem it an honor to be asked
to share this testimony and these thoughts with you.

Throughout my seventy years upon the earth I have become

increasingly aware and convinced that, although all knowledge might be considered important, different types of knowledge are not equal in importance. Also, I have learned that there is a natural sequence or order to the acceptance of certain great truths—that is, the acceptance of some truths must precede the acceptance of other truths. These understandings led me to select early in my college education the goal of becoming a teacher of what I then thought, and now know, to be the "weightier matters" (Matthew 23:23) of life—those truths pertaining to our eternal lives and welfare.

It soon became obvious to me that the sources of truth pertaining to these "weightier matters" were primarily two: first, the scriptures (the will and mind and word of the Lord as revealed to earlier prophets) and second, the teachings of the prophets, seers, and revelators of this dispensation. This understanding led me to read and continually reread each of the books of scripture. It also led me to read all the available words of the prophets, seers, and revelators of this dispensation, particularly the words of the presidents of the Church. Major sources of these words were the publications of the Church, general conference reports, and books containing the major talks and teachings of the presidents of the Church. In the mid-1940s, when I was twenty years of age, these included such works as *Teachings of the Prophet Joseph Smith, Discourses of Brigham Young, The Gospel Kingdom* (John Taylor), *The Discourses of Wilford Woodruff, Gospel Doctrine* (Joseph F. Smith), and *Gospel Standards* (Heber J. Grant). Reading and studying these books and the talks and other writings of the presidents prompted my compilation and publication of selected statements in 1948 under the title *Latter-day Prophets Speak*. Since then, I have continued to carefully read the word of the Lord as he has revealed it through the prophets, seers, and revelators of his church.

From these two primary sources—the scriptures and the words of the prophets—I have obtained my testimony, realizing that such testimony can ultimately come only from the Holy Ghost as a result of asking, seeking, and knocking—that is, through prayer.

Obtaining a Testimony

A first question might be "What constitutes a testimony of the gospel?" A testimony of the plan of progression and eternal life might include different elements during different periods of history. But for me, a testimony of this plan in the dispensation of the fulness of times would include at least the following major elements:

1. *God exists as an eternal, omnipotent Being.* He is the Eternal Father of the spirit bodies of all of us who now live, who have lived, or who will yet live upon this earth. Thus, we are all either sons or daughters of God, and therefore we are brothers and sisters to each other.

2. *Jesus Christ is the firstborn Son of God in the spirit;* thus, he is our eldest brother in the spirit creation. Jesus Christ is the Only Begotten Son of God in the flesh. He is actually, physically, and biologically the Son of God in the flesh. He also is the foreordained Savior and Redeemer of all mankind. Through his infinite atonement, Jesus Christ became for all of us the Advocate and Mediator with the Father.

3. *God the Father and Jesus Christ the Son are separate and distinct from each other in being and in person.* However, they are one in doctrine, in testimony, in witness, in purpose, and in goals and ideals. The work and glory of the Father are also the work and glory of the Son.

4. *God reveals his mind and will through chosen prophets, who speak for him.* When a prophet is moved upon by the power of the Holy Ghost, he speaks the mind, the will, and the word of God (D&C 68:4). Thus, whether God speaks to mankind directly or through his Son or through his prophets, it is the same so far as mankind is concerned (D&C 1:38).

5. *God has a kingdom through which he administers his affairs in regard to mankind.* His Son holds the keys of that kingdom and administers the affairs of the kingdom in heaven. Christ has now and has had in the past a kingdom upon the earth over which he presides. This kingdom on the earth presently has the formal title of "The Church of Jesus Christ of Latter-day Saints"; it is the only true and living church upon the face of the earth today.

6. *Joseph Smith was the first prophet of the dispensation of the fulness of times.* His successors, the presidents of the Church, hold the keys of the kingdom under his direction, and Joseph Smith holds them under the direction of Jesus Christ. Thus, the living prophet on the

earth holds the keys of the kingdom and is directly responsible for administering the affairs of the kingdom.

7. *The Book of Mormon is indeed "Another Testament of Jesus Christ"*; it was prepared under his direction and was translated by his gift and power. This sacred volume contains an account of the Savior's dealings with his people in the Americas as well as his appearance to them as a resurrected being. The Book of Mormon is the word of God.

Other persons might include additional elements in their explanations of what constitutes a valid testimony of the gospel of Jesus Christ. But, to me, those listed above are the essential elements of such a testimony.

A second major question might be, "What must a person do to obtain a testimony of the gospel?" Elder Bruce R. McConkie has suggested the following steps:

> Any accountable person can gain a testimony of the gospel by obedience to that law upon which the receipt of such knowledge is predicated. This is the formula:
>
> 1. He must *desire* to know the truth of the gospel. . . .
> 2. He must *study* and learn the basic facts relative to the matter involved. . . .
> 3. He must *practice* the principles and truths learned, conforming his life to them. . . .
> 4. He must *pray* to the Father in the name of Christ, *in faith,* and the truth will then be made manifest by revelation "by the power of the Holy Ghost. And by the power of the Holy Ghost ye may know the truth of all things."[1]

This formula may appear to be almost too simple, but I believe it contains all the essential elements. Note that it involves the action of our innermost being—the hoping and the desiring, the studying and the learning, the determining to practice or live, and the praying. Thus, by the time we have acquired a testimony through the application of these steps (and I know of no shortcuts), we have internalized this knowledge. Therefore we are much more apt to conform our lives to these truths, and we are much more apt to receive the promised blessings. What a marvelous plan it is that in this life we acquire a testimony only through the power of our spirit, acting upon the principle of faith.

These definitions and explanations should help us arrive at two fundamental conclusions: First, it should be abundantly clear that the acquisition of a testimony does not require an education in a formal classroom setting, nor are testimonies limited to "scholars." A testimony must be acquired on a personal basis and comes only as an individual earnestly hopes, desires, studies, learns, lives, and prays about the basic truths upon which a testimony is based. Second, our total thinking or reasoning powers must be involved in acquiring a testimony.

This second conclusion prompts me to list a few attributes or characteristics of our spirits (the source of our thinking or reasoning powers) so we can better appreciate this power and also the eternal blessings that flow from a testimony of the gospel.

1. *Our spirits are the real eternal part of all of us.* They have always existed and will always exist. They can be neither created nor destroyed:

> Man was also in the beginning with God. Intelligence, or the light of truth, was not created or made, neither indeed can be. (D&C 93:29)

> The mind [spirit] or the intelligence which man possesses is coequal with God himself. . . .
> The intelligence of spirits had no beginning, neither will it have an end. . . .
> Intelligence is eternal and exists upon a self-existent principle. It is a spirit from age to age, and there is no creation about it.[2]

> We know . . . that there is something called intelligence which always existed. It is the real eternal part of man, which was not created or made. This intelligence combined with the spirit constitutes a spiritual identity or individual. . . .
> The spirit of man, then, is a combination of the intelligence and the spirit which is an entity begotten of God.[3]

2. *Our spirits are the part of our beings through which we gain knowledge.* Although theologians, philosophers, and social scientists may disagree on the name or title or description or extent of this power we have within ourselves (a few terms they have suggested are *ego, consciousness, will, intelligence,* and *mind*), it is the power by which we think and make conscious decisions. We acquire all our

knowledge, whether of a spiritual or physical nature, through the power of our spirits.

3. *The spirit has the power to learn, understand, and comprehend by itself, independent of the physical body.* Thus, before the spirit was clothed with a physical body, it could learn the spirit laws that governed its existence and thus could receive the consequences (blessings or punishments) associated with action in the realm of such law. Even though a veil of forgetfulness came upon us at the time of birth into a physical body, our spirits still possess the power to learn.

4. *When our spirits came into our physical bodies, we became living souls* (Genesis 2:7). The spirit gives life to the physical body. It is the spirit that enables the eyes to see, the ears to hear, the fingers to move.

5. *The spirit works with and through the physical body in obtaining further knowledge.* The senses of the physical body provide additional means by which the spirit may obtain knowledge:

> If I had time to enter into this subject alone I could show you upon scientific principles that man himself is a self-registering machine, his eyes, his ears, his nose, the touch, the taste, and all the various senses of the body, are so many media whereby man lays up for himself a record which perhaps nobody else is acquainted with but himself.[4]

6. *The spirit can obtain a testimony of the plan of progression and eternal life only through its own power, although the Holy Ghost will provide a confirming witness.* That is, each person must obtain a testimony by himself or herself; one person cannot give another person a testimony:

> By the power of the Holy Ghost ye may know the truth of all things. (Moroni 10:5)

> And the Spirit giveth light to every man that cometh into the world; and the Spirit enlighteneth every man through the world, that hearkeneth to the voice of the Spirit. (D&C 84:46)

During the fifty-two years I have been associated with institutions of higher education in our country and abroad, I have felt that a limiting factor in the growth of some intellectuals in spiritual matters is their unwillingness to accept these basic truths concerning the spirit and its powers. Thus, they have limited themselves because of their refusal to accept earlier verities upon which the latter truths are based. This self-limitation is imposed by members of the Church and non-members alike. It seems to me that part of the limitation has come to some through their reluctance to believe in any power greater than the power of man. A second limiting factor is their unwillingness to bestow on man the power to progress eternally. Perhaps a third limiting factor has been the inability or unwillingness of many to determine which of all the truths known to them are the most important.

Philosophers and others have debated the nature of truth throughout the centuries. Unfortunately, the world does not have the Savior's answer to Pilate's question, "What is truth?" (John 18:38). Fortunately, we have the Savior's response, as revealed to his prophet in modern times: "And truth is knowledge of things as they are, and as they were, and as they are to come" (D&C 93:24). In other times and places we have learned such verities as these: truth is eternal,[5] "truth embraceth truth" (D&C 88:40), all truth might be encompassed into one grand whole. Thus, one of our goals should be to search for truth wherever it might be found. It is in such a search for truth that a testimony might be obtained.

The acquisition of truths associated with a testimony of the plan of progression and eternal life would be a blessing indeed, and, as we have learned from modern scripture, is a blessing predicated upon obedience to law (D&C 130:21). Several experiences have helped convince me that a knowledge of the truths associated with a testimony of the gospel is the most important knowledge of all. In closing, let me share with you one of these experiences.

An Exercise in Priorities

Sister Ludlow and I have been blessed with nine children—one son and eight daughters. These children have blessed us with forty-one grandchildren. We have tried over the years to promote special activities that would help keep the larger family close together so that cousins, for instance, could feel a love and concern for each other.

Until recent years, most of the family would gather together for a bounteous and delicious Thanksgiving meal. Then after the meal, one by one, we would share with each other the blessings for which we were especially grateful during that year. One year I was particularly sensitive to the fact that most of us were mentioning material blessings as those of greatest significance—a new bicycle or car, a color TV, air-conditioning in the home, and so on. Very few blessings of a spiritual nature were mentioned.

So that year, after the family had completed their expressions of gratitude for their blessings and had dispersed into smaller groups for other activities, I went into a separate room, took several sheets of paper of various colors, and cut each sheet into eight pieces. Then I wrote on each small piece of paper one particular blessing. I placed blessings that seemed to be in the same category on the same color of paper. For instance, blessings of a material nature were written on goldenrod; blessings of a family nature were written on green; blessings of a community or educational nature were written on yellow; blessings of a physical nature were written on brown; and blessings of a religious or spiritual nature were written on blue.

I then mixed up all of the pieces of paper and placed them on a large table so each of the blessings could be easily read. The older members of our family (we decided to include those eight years of age and up) were then invited to arrange themselves around the table according to age so we could participate in a "Choose Your Blessings" activity. I explained that the purpose of the activity was to "prioritize" our blessings to determine which blessings were the most important. In order to do this, each person, in turn, had to decide which one of the blessings remaining on the table he or she would rather lose, remove from the table the piece of paper containing that blessing, and then explain why he or she felt that particular blessing was not as important as those remaining.

The activity proceeded rather quickly and smoothly for several rounds. Soon all blessings of a material nature were removed, while many of the other types of blessings (including all of those of a spiritual nature) remained. As the activity progressed, participants discovered that it became more and more difficult to decide which blessing should be discarded, as all the remaining blessings seemed important. This was the real soul-searching part of the activity, and we learned a great deal about each other.

Frankly, I had not thought beforehand what final ten or five or even two blessings might remain on the table near the end. My major purpose in preparing and suggesting the activity was simply to stimulate members of the family to realize that spiritual blessings—those that have eternal consequences—are infinitely more important than the material blessings many of them had mentioned earlier.

Finally, however, only a "tremendous ten" remained, then a "fabulous five," and at last only two blessings remained. They were "Having a Living Prophet" and "Having a Testimony of the Gospel." With only these two blessings remaining, it was my wife's turn to choose which blessing she would forfeit. After taking a few minutes to explain to all of us the extreme importance of a living prophet, Luene concluded, "But a testimony of the gospel is most important"—and she left that sole blessing on the table.

Luene and I have participated in this activity on numerous occasions since then, including with semester-abroad students in Jerusalem and with full-time missionaries in western Australia. Almost without exception, the results have been the same—the blessing remaining last of all, and hence the one considered to be most important, is "Having a Testimony of the Gospel."

I have pondered these results many times, and each time I become more convinced of the importance of a testimony. Without a testimony, we would not listen to the living prophet. What difference would it make whether or not we have the scriptures if we do not have a testimony? Without a testimony of the gospel, we would be unlikely to search the scriptures diligently. What difference would it make whether or not we have a temple nearby if we do not have a testimony of the gospel? Without a testimony, we would not be interested in receiving the blessings of the temple and extending them to our progenitors. The obvious conclusion is that a testimony of the gospel gives meaning, significance, and importance to all of our other blessings.

Shortly after Thanksgiving in 1985, Luene was invited to speak in our new home ward in Salt Lake City—the Canyon Road Ward. She told of our earlier experience with the family in the "Choosing Your Blessings" activity, including the fact that in the long run having a testimony of the gospel is more important to an individual than having a living prophet.

President Ezra Taft Benson was a member of our ward and happened to be present for that sacrament meeting. You can imagine

Luene's concern in delivering her talk, but she presented the facts just as they had occurred. As soon as the meeting was over, President Benson came over to Luene and greeted her with the words, "Sister Ludlow, you are absolutely right. A testimony of the gospel is the greatest knowledge a person can acquire in this life. I wish every member of the Church could have heard your talk and testimony today."

Later, President Benson prepared a First Presidency message in the *Ensign* on this subject, entitled "Valiant in the Testimony of Jesus."[6] His statement serves as a confirming witness that a testimony of the gospel is indeed the most important knowledge a person can acquire on this earth.

In his classic address at the October 1988 semiannual general conference of the Church entitled "I Testify," President Benson closed with this stirring testimony:

> I testify to you that a fulness of joy can only come through the atonement of Jesus Christ and by obedience to all of the laws and ordinances of the gospel, which are found only in The Church of Jesus Christ of Latter-day Saints (see Articles of Faith 1:3).
>
> To all these things I humbly testify and bear my solemn witness that they are true, and I do so in the name of Him who is the head of this church, even Jesus Christ, amen.[7]

This type of testimony is available to all who will keep the laws upon which such a blessing is predicated. I also bear humble witness that I know these things are true.

....

NOTES

1. Bruce R. McConkie, *Mormon Doctrine*, 2d ed. (Salt Lake City: Bookcraft, 1966), 786–87; emphasis in original.

2. *Teachings of the Prophet Joseph Smith*, comp. Joseph Fielding Smith (Salt Lake City: Deseret Book, 1961), 353–54.

3. Joseph Fielding Smith, *The Progress of Man* (Salt Lake City: Deseret Book, 1973), 11.

4. John Taylor, "Discourse," December 14, 1884, in *Journal of Discourses*, 26 vols. (Liverpool: Latter-day Saints' Book Depot, 1886), 26:31.

5. Smith, *The Progress of Man*, 325.

6. Ezra Taft Benson, "Valiant in the Testimony of Jesus," *Ensign*, February 1987, 2–3.

7. Ezra Taft Benson, in Conference Report, October 1988, 104; or "I Testify," *Ensign* (November 1988), 87.

CHAPTER 13

THE UNITY AND
THE POWER OF SCRIPTURE
An Experience

ROBERT J. MATTHEWS
Emeritus Dean of Religious Education, Brigham Young University

T HE SUBTITLE of this collection of writings is *Testimonies of Latter-
day Saint Scholars,* and while I am honored to be included in such a
distinguished group of persons, I have never been of a disposition to
call myself a scholar. However, there are things of which I am able
and willing to testify. I lay claim to being a believer in the holy scriptures or standard works of The Church of Jesus Christ of Latter-day
Saints. I am a believer in the principle of divine revelation both in
ancient times and in the present day. I also have an unqualified assurance that Jesus is the Christ, the Only Begotten of the Father in the
flesh on this earth, the only Savior of the world. Likewise, by the
spirit of revelation I know that this same Jesus has established his
church on the earth through the Prophet Joseph Smith and his successors, and I am completely confident that the church they established is "the only true and living church upon the face of the whole
earth" (D&C 1:30), having divine priesthood authority and a divine
commission to teach the gospel to all nations and administer the
ordinances to all who believe and obey.

To be a scholar of the scriptures in the finest sense, one must know that the holy scriptures are true; however, in and of itself that is not enough. One must also become informed about what the scriptures mean and be intimately acquainted with the instruction they contain on the principles of eternal life, as well as the facts of history, culture, and doctrine. It is essential also to experience the feeling, spirit, or particular flavor of the various scriptures. Such familiarity can be obtained only by reading, searching, comparing, praying, meditating thoughtfully, reflecting, and contemplating. To be a scripture scholar and to learn the facts, it is necessary to know the meaning of technical words and phrases, and it is also necessary to be aware of the context in which statements are made. One must apply a little common sense, especially in interpreting symbolic utterances, in order to recognize the intent of a scripture.

Finally, being a true scholar of the scriptures requires not only intellectual activity, but also the interaction of the Holy Spirit with one's natural senses. There must be feeling as well as facts. Feeling is part of knowing. Since the scriptures were written by holy men as they were moved upon by the Holy Ghost (2 Peter 1:20–21; see also D&C 68:3–4), inspiration from the same Holy Ghost is required in order for anyone else to perceive the true meaning and intention of a scripture (see Joseph Smith–History 1:73–74).

In every discipline, considerable energy and sustained effort must be expended in order for one to master the literature of that discipline and be able to move with ease through its pages. The same is true with learning the history, doctrinal content, and spirit of each of the books of scripture. It is not to be acquired in a few surface lessons and cannot be obtained without the assistance of the Holy Spirit. In this regard, becoming a scholar of the scriptures may be even more rigorous and demanding than would mastering other fields of learning because in the case of the scriptures, study must be accompanied by personal revelation and obedience to the moral precepts that are taught in the scriptures. One cannot be a true scripture scholar without believing what the scriptures say. The greater light of understanding is dependent on previous acceptance of the primary concepts. Perception in depth cannot come without obedience on the part of the learner, for the things of God can be known only by the Spirit of God and not by the intellect alone (see 1 Corinthians

2:12–14; D&C 76:116). The natural man or woman can read the words but cannot fathom the deeper meaning. Though it is probable that one could master the concepts of other disciplines without a moral and spiritual commitment, this is not possible in the matter of scripture. Nephi's discussion with Laman and Lemuel is a case in point:

> And it came to pass that I beheld my brethren, and they were disputing one with another concerning the things which my father had spoken unto them.
>
> For he truly spake many great things unto them, which were hard to be understood, save a man should inquire of the Lord; and they being hard in their hearts, therefore they did not look unto the Lord as they ought. . . .
>
> And . . . I spake unto my brethren, desiring to know of them the cause of their disputations.
>
> And they said: Behold, we cannot understand the words which our father hath spoken. . . .
>
> And I said unto them: Have ye inquired of the Lord?
>
> And they said unto me: We have not; for the Lord maketh no such thing known unto us.
>
> Behold, I said unto them: How is it that ye do not keep the commandments of the Lord? How is it that ye will perish, because of the hardness of your hearts? (1 Nephi 15:2–3, 6–10)

This same characteristic is later used to describe other people: "And now because of their unbelief they could not understand the word of God" (Mosiah 26:3). Similar passages from latter-day scriptures also illustrate the special commitment required to become a scripture scholar.

As in all disciplines, the more we learn, the more we are able to learn—and the more quickly that learning will come.

The Unity of Scripture

Four standard works currently compose the basic written documents of canonized scripture in the Church, and it is anticipated that in the future we will be given many additional documents, such as the sealed portion of the gold plates that came out of the Hill Cumorah, the 116 manuscript pages of the Book of Mormon that were stolen, the ancient record of the Ten Tribes (2 Nephi

29:13–14), the record of Enoch (D&C 107:57), the record of John (D&C 93:18; Ether 4:16), the plates of brass (1 Nephi 5:18–19; Alma 37:3–4), and numerous other sacred records that are not now available. In addition to the restoration of these ancient records, there will be a multitude of documents containing new revelations and items of instruction that have never been revealed or recorded on earth.

Among the extant records (so far as they are translated correctly), there is a basic unity of purpose and of concept. There are not substantive contradictions of doctrine, although there are numerous variations because some items are dealt with in greater clarity and detail in certain passages than in others.

Since a unity of purpose exists among the extant scriptures (the Bible, the Book of Mormon, the Doctrine and Covenants, and the Pearl of Great Price), there is ample reason to conclude that the same unity will exist in additional volumes and, that while they will greatly increase our understanding, they will not contradict the scripture we now have. Such unity exists and will continue to exist because there is only one Savior, one plan of salvation, one Lord, one faith, and one remedy for man's fallen condition; therefore, the Lord speaks "the same words unto one nation like unto another" (2 Nephi 29:8).

The unity of scripture can be quickly discovered in the Topical Guide that has been published in the LDS edition of the Bible since 1979. The Topical Guide was compiled by four men (of which I was not one) on assignment from the Scriptures Publications Committee of the Church. This 598–page document contains 3,495 subject entries arranged in alphabetical order, containing many thousands of references from the four standard works. Scripture citations accompanied by the principal words of each passage are arranged for each entry where applicable, beginning with those from the Old Testament, then those found in the New Testament, the Book of Mormon, the Doctrine and Covenants, and the Pearl of Great Price. Reading the citations of a few entries quickly demonstrates the orderly flow of information from each of the standard works, and the searcher is soon rewarded not only with an abundance of facts, but also with an awareness of the fundamental unity of all the scriptures. Because of the oneness of doctrine, there is a certain amount of duplication among the books of scripture cited within each entry, but each citation contributes something unique. Latter-day revelation is seen to be generally more complete and informative than biblical passages.

Researching Prayer

In the late summer of 1979, I was scheduled to give a lecture to an Education Week audience on the use of the new LDS edition of the Bible. To demonstrate how the Topical Guide can be used, I randomly selected the subject of prayer. This was just a few days after the "new" edition of the Bible had come from the press.

Although I was already aware that there is a unity and oneness among the standard works, the reality of it was drilled more fully into my consciousness when I analyzed the references under the "Prayer" heading. I did not have the unity aspect uppermost in my mind at the time, but it became very evident as the study progressed.

I began my study by reading each of the scripture references and concordance-like summaries in the Prayer category. (I discovered that there were 174 scriptures in this one topic alone—see the Topical Guide, pp. 380–82.) When I encountered any item that seemed particularly impressive or useful, I recorded that citation on a sheet of paper. By the time I had read all of the 174 citations, I had listed 20 of them. I then proceeded to read the entire text of these 20 passages from the scripture itself. During the reading I made notes of the particular concepts that I wished to present in the lecture. From this final list and the notes I had made, I then formulated in my mind the approach and the facts I would use. The whole process took about three hours.

Several things occurred during this analysis. First, I was treated to a cornucopia of statements about prayer—far more than I could use in one lecture. The Topical Guide proved to be an extremely fruitful source of information. Second, because I was obliged to make a selection of those passages that seemed to be most notable and impressive to me at the time, it was a refining and thought-provoking process. Third, I was impressed over and over with the similarity of ideas in all of the scriptures, which to me was an inescapable evidence of their unity. Fourth, it became evident that in latter-day revelation, concepts are usually more completely expressed than they are in the text of the Bible. Fifth, I felt that in using the Topical Guide I had been exposed to the most extensive collection of facts about prayer in the shortest period of time that I had ever experienced, even though I had studied the gospel all my adult life.

As to the greater clarity of latter-day revelation, the following is an example. In Matthew 18:19, Jesus states: "If two of you shall agree on earth as touching any thing that they shall ask, it shall be done for them of my Father which is in heaven." And in John 14:13–14, Jesus says: "And whatsoever ye shall ask in my name, that will I do. . . . If ye shall ask any thing in my name, I will do it." As contained in the New Testament, these promises are given without any qualifications or conditions.

By comparison, we find more complete recitations in the Book of Mormon and the Doctrine and Covenants. In 3 Nephi 18:20, Jesus says: "And whatsoever ye shall ask the Father in my name, *which is right,* believing that ye shall receive, behold it shall be given unto you" (emphasis added). In 2 Nephi 4:35, we find Nephi saying: "Yea, I know that God will give liberally to him that asketh. Yea, my God will give me, *if I ask not amiss*" (emphasis added). In Doctrine and Covenants 8:10, the Lord counsels: "Do not ask for that which you ought not." And in Doctrine and Covenants 50:29–30 the Lord promises: "Ye shall ask whatsoever you will in the name of Jesus and it shall be done. But know this, *it shall be given you what you shall ask*" (emphasis added).

Another example of the greater clarity of latter-day revelation as compared to the biblical text is found in the following analysis. In Matthew 6:22 we read of Jesus saying: "If therefore thine eye be single, thy whole body shall be full of light." Luke 11:34 presents essentially the same thought. However, the Joseph Smith Translation of Matthew 6:22 gives a more complete text: "If therefore thine eye be single *to the glory of God,* thy whole body shall be full of light" (emphasis added). Likewise, in Doctrine and Covenants 4:5 the Lord speaks of "an eye single *to the glory of God*" (emphasis added). A similar clarification is found in Doctrine and Covenants 27:2.

The mental accumulation of facts about prayer, the discovery of the unity of scripture, and the wealth of the Topical Guide as a source of spiritual information were all important, but the greatest reward of that afternoon of study was that as I searched the scriptures that spoke of prayer, there welled up within me an intense desire to pray. I wanted to pray like I had never wanted to pray before. I hungered with my heart as well as my head for communication with the Lord. I had known and felt those things before, but I knew it even better and felt it even stronger after a three-hour session with the scriptures concentrating on the subject of prayer alone.

I testify that there is a sacred power in the scriptures that we can draw upon, and that power can and will transform our lives, affect our attitude, and influence our behavior. Becoming scripturally literate is not an optional pursuit. Counsel from the Lord is that all should "treasure up," "feast upon," and "search" the written scriptures (Joseph Smith–Matthew 1:37; 2 Nephi 31:20; John 5:39; 3 Nephi 23:1–3). In so doing we not only come to know eternal spiritual truths from the scripture produced by former prophets, but we also become better prepared to recognize and obey the flow of scripture that emanates from the living prophets. An observation by President George Q. Cannon nearly one hundred years ago is still current:

> I have noticed . . . that where the people of God pay attention to the written word, they are always better prepared to hear the oral instructions of the servants of God . . . [and] they have greater interest in seeking to obtain instructions, than they have when they are careless about the written word of God.[1]

....

NOTE

1. George Q. Cannon, in Conference Report, October 1897, 38.

CHAPTER 14

"SHALL WE NOT GO
ON IN SO GREAT A CAUSE?"

DANIEL C. PETERSON
Associate Professor of Asian and Near Eastern Languages,
Brigham Young University

R AISED IN WHAT was then a part-member family in southern
California, I think I first felt some of the thrill of the gospel in connection with a novel by Nephi Anderson entitled *Added Upon.*[1] I
stayed home from school one day at about the age of eleven or
twelve. (I cannot recall, frankly, if I was really sick.) After a few hours,
as usually happens in such cases, I was deeply bored. For some reason, I picked up a copy of *Added Upon* that we had inherited from
my maternal grandmother, and I began to read. Nephi Anderson's
novel, a product of the "home literature" movement that flourished
in the Church early in the twentieth century, is certainly not a great
piece of writing by ordinary standards. But its scope caught my attention. In fact, I was entranced. I had thought of the gospel, up to this
point, as something rather conventional, indeed as little more than a
never-ending round of rather dull meetings.

   Added Upon depicts a small group of characters as they move from
the premortal existence through this life (where they come in contact with the gospel), into the spirit world, and beyond, into the resurrection and the millennium. I must have heard of such things
before, but I had never previously had any notion of the richness, the

sheer sweep and grandeur, of what we call "the plan of salvation." It was, I realized, the most exciting thing I had ever encountered, the most magnificent vision of human destiny imaginable. And this sense of excitement has never left me. Moreover, although I know that it disturbs some outside the Church, I have never felt that the idea of exaltation, properly understood, leads to arrogance or pride; it is, rather, profoundly humbling, and a very holy doctrine.

A few years later, while in high school, I attended a BYU Education Week that took place, as I recall, in West Covina. There I saw Truman Madsen pack the hall with discussions of such difficult topics as "existentialism" and "logical positivism," bringing them into dialogue with the gospel. I began to see Mormonism then, and I still do, as a "philosophy" that is easily as profound as any of its rivals. Subsequent studies and experience around the world have only confirmed that early impression. A few years ago, for example, I spent two months at a seminar in Berkeley, California, sponsored by the National Endowment for the Humanities. Under the leadership of the eminent comparative religionist Huston Smith, twelve of us— including a Jesuit process theologian, a couple of Buddhists, a Nietzsche scholar, a Platonist, a Hindu, a Catholic priest–Indologist, and a Mormon Islamicist (me)—researched, discussed, and debated several central issues in the comparative philosophy of religion. The seminar was an enjoyable experience, but one of the most important things that came out of it for me was a conviction that the insights revealed through Joseph Smith hold up quite well when compared with the world's great religious systems.

I arrived at Brigham Young University as a mathematics major. With a poster of Albert Einstein mounted on my wall, I was intent on becoming a theoretical physicist, a cosmologist. Not far into my first semester, though, I realized that this was not my calling. I had already been reading Hugh Nibley, and I soon came fully under his spell. So I changed my major to classical Greek (with a minor in philosophy). I am still a fan of Nibley's. While I may not always agree with him, and while he may in fact occasionally be wrong on this or that issue, I am firmly convinced by my own reading and thinking that his overall approach has been fundamentally (and brilliantly) sound. I like to think of him as someone who has investigated a vast abandoned building, running through it, shining his flashlight into this room and that, giving us a basic overview, despite his limited time, of the rooms and their contents. It now remains for us, a more plodding but larger group, to complete the systematic inventory of the rooms. Nibley has, for many, set the basic agenda and identified the basic issues. There will be modifications in various places, perhaps even in many places, but he has established the general features of a particular kind, my kind, of Mormon studies.

Following graduation from BYU, I switched over to Arabic studies, which continue to serve as my formal academic specialty, and went to the Middle East. While in Israel for the first time, early in 1978, I ran across John Tvedtnes's work on the feast of tabernacles among the Nephites.[2] Then just a typescript in a folder in the files of the Jerusalem Branch, his analysis was, for me, a dramatic discovery. At that time I conceived the idea of an organization that might serve as a kind of clearinghouse for such work, which otherwise had an unfortunate tendency to languish in undistributed obscurity. Fortunately, people with far more organizational ability and drive than I possess also saw the need and actually brought the idea to reality. Today, with its extensive publication program and its support for interesting investigations across many disciplines, the Foundation for Ancient Research and Mormon Studies (FARMS) probably exceeds anything that any one of us ever anticipated for it.

During the several years that I spent doing graduate work in history, language, and literature in Cairo, I had the privilege of studying for six months, one-on-one, with a Dominican priest who was one of the world's foremost authorities on Islamic philosophy. This was a fascinating and, in a number of ways, a challenging experience for me. Father Anawati represented the highly sophisticated, two-thousand-year-old intellectual tradition of Roman Catholicism, and at the same time was an eminent scholar of yet another sophisticated intellectual tradition, one that had fourteen centuries of deep thinking and a vast literature behind it. There were times, I confess, when it struck me as ridiculously improbable that a young and relatively tiny church, far off in the arid American West, could claim to be the uniquely authorized custodian of God's revealed truth. I never doubted what I had, in fact, come to know, but I became acutely aware of how our claims must seem to others. Yet this must be precisely how an early Christian would have felt, confronted with the power and glitz of Rome and the ancient sophistication of Athens. However things might appear, though, it is simply fact that God chose the Galilee, a backwater area of a rather unimportant Roman province, as the place in which his Son was to be raised, and that the resurrection of Christ occurred in Jerusalem, a relatively insignificant provincial town. So, too, I am convinced that God in our own day called Joseph Smith, a common New York farmer's son with an almost comically common name, to found a church of craftsmen and farmers and laborers that would someday fill the earth.

I eventually finished a doctorate in Near Eastern languages and cultures at the University of California at Los Angeles, writing my dissertation on an extremely obscure eleventh-century Arab Neoplatonic philosopher—obscure in every sense of the word. Along the way, too, I was offered and accepted a position teaching Arabic and Islamic studies at BYU. I have enjoyed my work at the university tremendously. I hear some critics of the Church claim that Mormonism is intellectually closed and stifling, but I have never, in even the slightest degree, found this to be the case. Quite the contrary. Mormonism has been an immensely useful lens through which to view the ancient world and Islam. It has supplied me with questions and with interesting, unusual perspectives that have greatly enriched my own scholarly life. At BYU, I have felt myself free to write not only on Islamic topics, but on Latter-day Saint topics as well. And, not infrequently, I have written in a very Latter-day Saint way on Islamic topics. I have, for instance, delivered and published papers on such topics as anthropomorphism in the Qur'an, ascension rituals and the story of Muhammad's heavenly journey (which I see as related to some of the ordinances of the temple), and the deliberate burial of sacred records. I got away with this sort of thing for years, until just a while ago, when, immediately after I had given a paper in Paris that related to the question of human deification, a friend in the audience came up to me and said, "I'll bet the leaders of your church would be interested in this sort of stuff." My friend teaches at a university in the eastern United States, and he and his wife often come out to Utah to ski. Clearly, he knows more about Mormonism than I had supposed. My cover has been blown.

While I was a graduate student in Cairo, I wrote a lengthy paper on two medieval Islamic groups: the *akhi* warrior organization among the early Ottoman Turks and the *futuwwa* guild, an organization with its own rituals that developed into what might be described as early Islamic labor movements. Much to my surprise, my professor, a notorious curmudgeon, really liked the paper. However, as we talked about the piece he demanded to know why I had chosen to devote so much time and attention to what he termed "the biggest non-subject in the history of Islam." I am afraid that I did not give him a fully adequate answer. I could not tell him of the echoes that I had found in the topic, echoes both of the Gadianton robbers of the Book of Mormon and, from another aspect, of the temple.[3] And my dissertation, which won a major award from the Middle East Studies Association of North America, was a prolonged meditation on themes of human deification in the thought of an eleventh-century Arab Neoplatonic philosopher. My interests as a scholar and my religious concerns as a Latter-day Saint have never, ever, clashed.

I have found Mormonism to be endlessly productive of interesting questions and hypotheses, and my only limitation is in the time to pursue all the fascinating pathways that it opens up to me. In this and other ways, one of the most intriguing features of the restored Church is temple worship. The temple has always been an important element in my testimony. From my first awareness of the temple, I have felt it to be precisely what it claims to be: a link between this world and the realm of God and angels. I have a strong sense of its holiness and power. Some of my deepest spiritual experiences have come in connection with the temple, and there have been times when I have seemed almost to see beyond it or through it into eternity. But the temple is also, in academic terms, a window upon antiquity, and one of the most powerful evidences of Joseph Smith's prophetic calling.

The Book of Mormon has similar power and is easier to talk about. The most remarkable thing to me about the Book of Mormon is that it reads like plausible history. I have read a great deal of history from a number of different cultures, including several in the ancient and medieval Near East. The Book of Mormon's account of the development and decline of several ancient peoples seems to me entirely reasonable and true to what I know.[4] Yet, if the book's critics are to be believed, it should not. The Book of Mormon should have collapsed decades ago as a transparent fraud, even without the rigorous and often hostile criticism to which it has constantly been subjected. Had this book merely been the work of an unlettered upstate New York yokel and charlatan, it would have collapsed. But it has not, and it fails to show any of the telltale signs of pretense. The Book of Mormon is, for example, sober and realistic, and never strains for effect. This is no small thing. As the British-born literary scholar Arthur Henry King observed in another, but related, context:

> When I was first brought to read Joseph Smith's story, I was deeply impressed. I wasn't inclined to be impressed. As a stylistician, I have spent my life being disinclined to be impressed. So when I read his story, I thought to myself, this is an extraordinary thing. This is an astonishingly matter-of-fact and cool account. This man is not trying to persuade me of anything. He doesn't feel the need to. He is stating what happened to him, and he is stating it, not enthusiastically, but in quite a matter-of-fact way. He is not trying to make me cry or feel ecstatic. That struck me, and that began to build my testimony, for I could see that this man was telling the truth.[5]

I, too, feel the presence of truth, of unfeigned sincerity, both in Joseph Smith and in the Book of Mormon. In a similar vein, when I first read John L. Sorenson's classic book, *An Ancient American Setting for the Book of Mormon,*[6] the thing that most impressed me was not that the Book of Mormon can believably be related to locations in pre-Columbian Mesoamerica, although it can, but that it yields a coherent and consistent geographical picture at all. Again, if the book's critics were correct, it would be a mere mass of confusion. (Fawn Brodie claimed that the Book of Mormon simply gushed forth "like a spring freshet" from the "marvelously fecund imagination" of an unreflective New York farmboy who had never really had a serious thought in his head.)[7]

I think familiarity with the Book of Mormon has, for many of us, dulled the sheer astonishment of it. Long before we worry about details of evidence for or against its authenticity as an ancient work of scripture, we should recognize that, on any account, it is a remarkable volume. For example, I once wrote a substantial book in a little more than two months. I was quite impressed with myself until I realized that the Book of Mormon, considerably longer, significantly more complex, and infinitely more important, had been dictated in its entirety and written by hand in just about the same length of time.[8] And whereas I was an academic with a doctorate, working on a sophisticated word processor by means of which I could (and frequently did) massively revise and rearrange my writing, what the semiliterate Joseph Smith dictated has had to stand with very, very few changes since Oliver Cowdery first put it on paper. (Those who think this would be easy to do simply have not tried it.) I find it far more believable that Joseph was translating an ancient document, and doing so with divine help, than that he was composing so complex a volume at so remarkable a speed.

But the Book of Mormon stands up amazingly well in the details, too. In recent years, to choose just a pair of examples, I have been deeply impressed by the research of Lynn and Hope Hilton and, more recently, by that of Warren and Michaela Aston, on Lehi's Arabian journey, and by the identification of likely modern sites for ancient Nahom and Old World Bountiful.[9] And my friend William Hamblin has been able to show that the widespread use of inscribed metal plates in antiquity, frequently mocked and denied by critics of the Book of Mormon, seems first to have occurred in the general area from which Lehi came, at precisely the right time.[10]

Not infrequently, even seeming liabilities or weaknesses in the Book of Mormon have turned out to be strengths. Certain anti-Mormons, for instance, have loudly mocked the name "Alma" as it occurs in the Book of Mormon. It is, they point out, a modern, Latin-based, woman's name, one hardly appropriate for an ancient Semitic man. But, in fact, as we have learned only in the second half of this century, "Alma" is an authentic ancient Semitic masculine name.[11] Joseph Smith could not have known this fact by any natural means, yet he knew it. Similarly, the prophetic declaration of Alma 7:10 that Christ would be born "at Jerusalem which is the land of our forefathers" has occasioned a great deal of laughter from opponents of the Church. "Every schoolchild," they point out, "knows that Jesus was born in Bethlehem." Just so. And Joseph Smith presumably knew it, too. Yet the Book of Mormon, we have learned only in the past few decades, includes Bethlehem within "the land of Jerusalem" in a way that is entirely, authentically ancient.[12]

The gospel as a whole has passed the test, even where I had not expected it to do so. For instance, for many years I thought that the doctrine of human deification was unlikely to receive much support from ancient Christian sources. Yes, there were some relatively ambiguous and scattered passages in the Bible, particularly in the New Testament, that seemed to support our position. But, although critics of the Church have found this notion especially irritating—we are the "God Makers," after all—I imagined that there was little we could do to support our position. This all changed, though, when I came across a fascinating doctoral dissertation written at Duke University by a Latter-day Saint graduate student.[13] Since then, I have learned that the doctrine of *theosis* or *theopoeisis,* as it is known, was widespread, in some form or another, throughout ancient Christianity. Again, what I had once thought to be something of a weakness has turned out to be a strength.

In fact, I have grown so accustomed to this sort of thing that I have come to expect it. Whenever I encounter a question that I cannot answer, I have learned to suspend judgment for a while, in the confidence, which has been rewarded many times, that an answer will eventually appear. I recommend this approach to any who may be troubled by attacks on the Church. Every field has unanswered questions. Students of Shakespeare and of Homer face unsolved riddles, as do scholars of Islam, and Mormon studies are no exception to the rule. But objections virtually always disappear with time and deeper knowledge, and my testimony, based on considerable experience, is that answers are always forthcoming.

I have always, also, been deeply impressed by the testimony of the witnesses to the Book of Mormon and by the failure of critics to deal with them. (Usually they simply ignore them or wave them aside with some witticism from Mark Twain.) The work of Richard Lloyd Anderson and others has established an extraordinarily strong case for the reliability of the witnesses' testimonies.[14] And the problems this creates for those who would dismiss the Book of Mormon as a product of the nineteenth century are huge: If Joseph Smith really had sixty pounds or so of engraved gold plates, and if there were no historical Nephites, where did he get them? Who made them? But if there were plates—and I think that the case for their existence is overwhelming—then it becomes very likely indeed that there were Nephites and that Joseph was actually visited by a real Moroni. I know from conversations with critics of the Book of Mormon that the physical reality of the plates constitutes a serious problem for them, one that many of them would prefer to ignore. But they can't.

Historical and other evidence for the truth of the scriptures and the authenticity of Joseph Smith's prophetic calling has its place. In more than a few cases, such information actually sheds light on the interpretation of the scriptures. (A prime example of this is the lengthy chiasm found in Alma 36, which represents a clear instance of the Christ-centeredness of the Book of Mormon.)[15] Yet ultimately, although there is, in my judgment, more than enough evidence to justify a decision to put faith and trust in the Lord as he has manifested himself through the prophets and scriptures of the Restoration, our testimonies must go beyond the shifting sands of academic fashions and the uncertainties of scholarly arguments. We must seek confirmation from God himself.

I can believe in prophecy and revelation because I have, on my own small scale, experienced them. I have known things about the future that I could not possibly have known from any natural reading of the situation. I have felt the Lord speak through me and pronounce things (including a remarkable healing) that I, a cautious fellow, would never have said on my own. Indeed, I have been astonished and more than a little bit shocked to hear the words of the Lord come out of my mouth. Yet they have been fulfilled. I have, on one or two occasions, found myself seeming to see the things that I was reading about in scripture. I have felt the power of the ordinances of the temple. I have enjoyed, in the various wards and branches on four continents in which I have participated, the same fellowship of the Saints that I read about in scripture. This strengthens my faith both in the contemporary Church and in the plausibility of the ancient books. It has been revealed to me, in ways that I can neither deny nor forget, that we are indeed led by prophets and apostles, authorized of God.

> *Some for the Glories of This World; and some*
> *Sigh for the Prophet's Paradise to come;*
>   *Ah, take the Cash, and let the Promise go,*
> *Nor heed the music of a distant Drum!*

So says Edward Fitzgerald's rendering of the verse of the medieval Persian poet Omar Khayyam. But I find the gospel wholly fulfilling in the here and now, and I do not dream only of the world to come, glorious as I believe that will be. And the dream of Zion, of which I have had some foretaste, ignites my imagination:

> The building up of Zion is a cause that has interested the people of God in every age; it is a theme upon which prophets, priests and kings have dwelt with peculiar delight; they have looked forward with joyful anticipation to the day in which we live; and fired with heavenly and joyful anticipations they have sung and written and prophesied of this our day; but they died without the sight; we are the favored people that God has made choice of to bring about the Latter-day glory; it is left for us to see, participate in and help to roll forward the Latter-day glory. . . . And whilst we are thus united in the one common cause, to roll forth the kingdom of God, the heavenly Priesthood are not idle spectators, the Spirit of God will be showered down from above, and it will dwell in our midst. The blessings of the Most High will rest upon our tabernacles, and our name will be handed down to future ages; our children will rise up and call us blessed; and generations yet unborn will dwell with peculiar delight upon the scenes that we have passed through, the privations that we have endured; the untiring zeal that we have manifested; the all but insurmountable difficulties that we have overcome in laying the foundation of a work that brought about the glory and blessing which they will realize; a work that God and angels have contemplated with delight for generations past; that fired the souls of the ancient patriarchs and prophets; a work that is destined to bring about the destruction of the powers of darkness, the renovation of the earth, the glory of God, and the salvation of the human family.[16]

And so, with Joseph Smith, I ask myself and others, "Brethren [and sisters], shall we not go on in so great a cause?" (D&C 128:22). I testify that the promises we have received are true. I cannot conceive of anything more worthy of our utmost efforts and loyalty.

NOTES

1. Nephi Anderson, *Added Upon: A Story* (Salt Lake City: Deseret News Press, 1939).

2. Now easily accessible as John A. Tvedtnes, "King Benjamin and the Feast of Tabernacles," in *By Study and Also by Faith,* ed. John M. Lundquist and Stephen D. Ricks (Salt Lake City: Deseret Book and FARMS, 1990), 2:197–237.

3. I hope, someday, to expand upon and to publish some of those early findings.

4. I have set out one of my reasons for this judgment in my article "The Gadianton Robbers as Guerrilla Warriors," in *Warfare in the Book of Mormon,* ed. Stephen D. Ricks and William J. Hamblin (Salt Lake City: Deseret Book and FARMS, 1990), 146–73.

5. Arthur Henry King, *The Abundance of the Heart* (Salt Lake City: Bookcraft, 1986), 200–201. This remarkable collection of essays, by the way, deserves a much wider readership than it has evidently received.

6. John L. Sorenson, *An Ancient American Setting for the Book of Mormon* (Salt Lake City: Deseret Book and FARMS, 1985).

7. Fawn M. Brodie, *No Man Knows My History: The Life of Joseph Smith,* 2d ed. (New York: Knopf, 1971), 27, 44. Incidentally, Brodie's portrayal of Joseph Smith as a charming con artist utterly devoid of serious ideas cannot be made to square with the demonstrable magnitude of his achievement. This is increasingly recognized even by skeptics. See, for instance, Heikki Räisänen, "Joseph Smith und die Bibel: Die Leistung des mormonischen Propheten in neuer Beleuchtung," *Theologische Literaturzeitung* 109 (February 1984): 81–92.

8. See John W. Welch and Tim Rathbone, "The Translation of the Book of Mormon: Basic Historical Information" (Provo, Utah: FARMS, 1986).

9. See Lynn M. Hilton and Hope Hilton, *In Search of Lehi's Trail* (Salt Lake City: Deseret Book, 1976); and Warren P. Aston and Michaela Knoth Aston, *In the Footsteps of Lehi: New Evidence for Lehi's Journey across Arabia to Bountiful* (Salt Lake City: Deseret Book, 1994).

10. William J. Hamblin, "Sacred Writings on Bronze Plates in the Ancient Mediterranean" (Provo, Utah: FARMS, 1994).

11. See Yigael Yadin, *Bar-Kokhba: The Rediscovery of the Legendary Hero of the Second Jewish Revolt against Rome* (New York: Random House, 1971), 176.

12. See the treatment of this issue in my review of John Ankerberg and John Weldon's *Everything You Ever Wanted to Know about Mormonism,* in *Review of Books on the Book of Mormon* 5 (1993): 62–78. But new evidence continues to appear, so my discussion should now be supplemented with a brief article in the FARMS newsletter, "Revisiting the Land of Jerusalem via the Dead Sea Scrolls," *Insights* (March 1994), 2.

13. Keith E. Norman, "Deification: The Content of Athanasian Soteriology" (Ph.D. dissertation, Duke University, 1980).

14. See particularly Richard Lloyd Anderson, *Investigating the Book of Mormon Witnesses,* corrected reprint (Salt Lake City: Deseret Book, 1989); and Lyndon W. Cook, ed., *David Whitmer Interviews: A Restoration Witness* (Orem, Utah: Grandin Book Co., 1991).

15. See the discussion of this and other passages in John W. Welch, "Chiasmus in the Book of Mormon," in *Chiasmus in Antiquity: Structures, Analyses, Exegesis,*

ed. John W. Welch (Hildesheim: Gerstenberg, 1981), 198–210; and in John W. Welch, "Chiasmus in the Book of Mormon," in *Book of Mormon Authorship: New Light on Ancient Origins,* ed. Noel B. Reynolds (Provo, Utah: BYU Religious Studies Center, 1982), 33–52.

16. Joseph Smith, *History of the Church of Jesus Christ of Latter-day Saints,* 7 vols. (Salt Lake City: Deseret Book, 1976), 4:609–10.

CHAPTER 15

NOT TO WORRY

HUGH W. NIBLEY
Emeritus Professor of Ancient Scripture, Brigham Young University

I HESITATE TO APPLAUD the idea of having schoolmen confront schoolmen to settle an issue. Terence and Galbungus debated for fourteen days and nights in a futile effort to decide whether the personal pronoun *ego* has a vocative case. That was a formal *disputatio*, a rhetorical exercise for showing off. As a disingenuous rustic at the Council of Nicaea observed just before the opening session, which was the more miraculous, to make a stone speak or a philosopher stop speaking? As usual, the Book of Mormon covers such contingencies: "There shall be no disputations among you, as there have hitherto been; neither shall there be disputations among you concerning the points of my doctrine. . . . He that hath the spirit of contention is not of me, but is of the devil" (3 Nephi 11:28–29).

Debating was a popular sport on the American frontier. I refer to George Caleb Bingham's famous painting, *Stump Speaking*, or to Joseph Smith's own childhood recollection of the babble of voices in his neighborhood. Where religion is concerned, its effects have not been to settle issues but to exacerbate things to a state of permanent factions and sects. Joseph recognized both the value and danger of debating lively issues; the last three months of 1835 brought the question to a head.

In his Ohio journal for October 29, 1835, the Prophet records: "Went to the Council. The Presidency arose and adjourned." The meeting thus happily curtailed, "Elder Boynton observed that long debates were bad. I replied that it was generally the case that too much altercation was indulged in on both sides, and their debates protracted to an unprofitable length."[1] For how many years now have the same issues been brought out in periodic outbreaks of scholarship, with scholars picking over the same old chestnuts and calling them startling new discoveries?

One evening a month later (November 18, 1835), Joseph, paying a convivial visit to his father's house, found that "some of the young Elders were about engaging in a debate on the subject of miracles. . . . After an interesting debate of three hours or more, during which time much talent was displayed," the judges pronounced their decision. But President Smith "discovered in this debate, much warmth displayed, too much zeal for mastery, too much of that enthusiasm that characterizes a lawyer at the bar, who is determined to defend his cause, right or wrong." Joseph told the young men that "they might improve their minds and cultivate their powers of intellect in a proper manner, that they might not incur the displeasure of heaven; that they should handle sacred things very sacredly, and with due deference to the opinions of others, and with an eye single to the glory of God."[2]

Almost exactly a month later, on December 16, 1835, the Prophet says he

> went to Brother William Smith's to take part in the debate that was commenced Saturday evening last. After the debate was concluded, . . . some altercation took place upon the propriety of continuing the school [debate] fearing that it would not result in good. Brother William Smith opposed these measures, and insisted on having another question proposed, and at length became much enraged, particularly at me, and used violence upon my person, and also upon Elder Jared Carter, and some others.[3]

Two days after the brawl, in a long letter to William, Joseph concluded that the debaters were "under the influence of a wicked spirit,"[4] that is, the spirit of contention, and "he that hath the spirit of contention is not of me, but is of the devil, who is the father of contention" (3 Nephi 11:29).

Going through the journals on both sides, it all seems like déjà vu, back to the *Patrologia* and Schools of the Sophists, where the arguments were already trite. What kept the doctors going for thousands of years? The inexhaustible fires of vanity. "Where is the man that is free from vanity?" said Joseph Smith.[5]

There are some very good articles in *Sunstone, Dialogue,* and other publications, including the Church magazines. But the general feeling in perusing many of those publications is that of walking on a treadmill: The scenery never changes. There are always legitimate boasts and grievances. I will admit that floods are bad, fires deplorable, plagues are awful, and the faults of one's leaders can be annoying. But what do you expect me to do about it? While I wait for the Millennium, I have full instructions: to do what the Saints should be doing under all conditions, good or bad. The commandments do not alter with circumstances or they would be hopelessly pliable. No matter what happens, I know exactly what to do: "If *any* of you lack wisdom, let him ask of God, that giveth to all men liberally, and upbraideth not; and it shall be given him" (James 1:5; emphasis added). This was the first revelation given to the boy Joseph.

What is happening today is nothing new. Joseph had no sooner prepared a banquet for the Saints than the cooks began crowding into the kitchen, each eager to improve the recipe. It has always been thus; it may even be salutary, this periodic shaking up, like the forest fires of Yellowstone.

Here is Brother Joseph home from Missouri, safe in the bosom of the Saints at last: "After a tedious journey from the midst of enemies, mobs, cholera, and excessively hot weather,"[6]

I found all well on my ar[r]ival, ... but found our common adv[er]sary had taken the advantage of our brothe[r] Sylvest[er] Smith and others who gave a false colloring to allmost every transaction from the time that we left Kirtland untill we returned, and thereby stirred up a great difficulty in the Church against me accordingly I was met in the face and eyes as soon as I had got home with a catalogue that was as black as the author [Satan] himself and the cry was Tyrant! Pope!! King!!! Usurper!!!! Abuser of men!!!!!

Ange[l]!!!!!! False prophet!!!!! Prophesying Lies in the name of the Lord and taking consecrated monies!!!!!!! and every other lie to fill up and complete the cattelogue that was necissary to perfect the Church to be meet for the devourer the shaft of the distroying Angel! . . . But that God . . . has given me power from the time that I was born (into this kingdom) to stand and I have succeeded in putting all gainsayers and enemies to flight unto the present time.[7]

He concludes the missive by remarking that "the church seems to be in a languid cold disconsolate state, and . . . we may look for revolutions among this wicked and perverse generation and also in the Church of Christ!"[8]

Two years later what is the situation?

The powers of Earth & hell seem combined to overthrow us and the church by causing a division in the family, and indeed the adversary is bring[ing] into requisition all his subtlety to prevent the Saints from being endowed, by causing division among the 12, also among the 70, and bickerings and jealousies among the Elders and official members of the church, and so the leaven of iniquity foments and spreads among the members of the church.[9]

Such was his New Year's greeting for January 1, 1836.

As Andrew Ehat and Lyndon Cook have pointed out, "Often throughout the remainder of his life [that is, after 1840], Joseph Smith would lament that many Saints were unwilling to accept the glorious things revealed to him from heaven."[10] In his own words, "I have tried for a number of years to get the minds of the Saints prepared to receive the things of God; but . . . [they] will fly to pieces like glass as soon as anything comes that is contrary to their traditions."[11] This, we are told, was a severe trial to him. Brigham Young would get so exasperated when the Saints failed to act on clear and sensible advice that he "could cry like a whipped child" in sheer frustration. For all his frustration, the Prophet Joseph gave no magisterial commands: "Did I not give [any man] the liberty of disbelieving any doctrine I have preached, if he saw fit?"[12] Nay, he said, "Every man has a natural, and, in our country, a constitutional right to be a false prophet, as well as a true prophet."[13] Advice and admonition were freely available, but without compulsion. Speaking to a throng of newly arrived immigrants in Nauvoo, Joseph "showed them that it was generally in consequence of the brethren disregarding or disobeying counsel that they became dissatisfied and murmured." But then Joseph's irrepressible charity and good nature shows through: "But if they would bear with my infirmities and the infirmities of the brethren, I would likewise bear with their infirmities." Concluding an exuberant welcome and wise counsel to newly arrived immigrants to Nauvoo, he observed almost casually that he would have to leave them and hide out in the woods for a while. Such is not the stuff of power-mad, image-conscious dictators.[14]

The Prophet was always aware of what was going on. "We have thieves among us, adulterers, liars, hypocrites. . . . As far as we degenerate from God, we descend to the devil and lose knowledge. . . . The Church must be cleansed."[15]

> There is a great deal of murmuring in the Church about me; but I don't care anything about it. . . .
>
> Well, be it so. If the stories about Joe Smith are true, then the stories of John C. Bennett are true about the ladies of Nauvoo; . . . that the Ladies' Relief Society are all organized of those who are to be the wives of Joe Smith. Ladies, you know whether this is true or not.[16]

Passages like this are still used today to support Bennett as an authentic source of Church history.

Recently, a new line of books has made available significant details of Joseph Smith's personal history. Now beside the *Teachings of the Prophet Joseph Smith*, your library should contain Ehat and Cook's *The Words of Joseph Smith*; Dean C. Jessee's *The Personal Writings of Joseph Smith* and *The Papers of Joseph Smith*; *Joseph Smith: The Prophet, the Man*, edited by Susan Black and Charles Tate; and *An American Prophet's Record: The Diaries and Journals of Joseph Smith*, compiled by Scott H. Faulring.[17] From such works we see how the Twelve kept a revolving door in motion as they left Joseph to tell vile stories to the papers and swear horrendous affidavits in court, only to return in a few weeks or months to ask for forgiveness and reinstatement, which were instantly granted, until presently for some new grievance they effected another departure and subsequent repentance. It seems that the revolving door has always been available and many Saints have had a way of blowing hot and cold, usually depending on business and politics.

When I was young I used to go to the bookstores that lined the dingy streets of lower Los Angeles. The stores had alcoves or whole walls lined with books labeled "Mormon." Anti-Mormon literature was a special genre in those days. To qualify as an author, one only had to have been a Mormon, the one unchallenged certificate of authenticity. False memory flourished as one writer supported another in a flood of clichés and purple prose. No one paid any attention to Joseph's own story; and this is a remarkable thing. From his day to the present, the Prophet's image has *never changed;* after all the study and research, there has been no revision because any concession at all would require a new reading of the whole story. Who would believe that a book entitled *Secret Ceremonies: A Mormon Woman's Intimate Diary on Marriage and Beyond* was not the product of hysterics of the proper 1880s or lurid early 1900s, but was published and sold in the year 1993?

Shining Armor

A common refrain of our learned Mormon critics is, "Why should anyone want to fight the *truth?*" Open-minded, detached, and informed, they only want to help, and their sensibilities are injured when the generous offer is not accepted. *"Truth* is what I believe—if it wasn't true, of course I wouldn't believe it." In the past, thousands have left the Church as individuals or in groups and gone their ways, which is the sensible thing to do if you no longer believe its message. But many have found out that when they are Mormon has-beens, the public loses all interest in them; those splinter groups that have so often broken from the Church inevitably fade and vanish or persist as forlorn little communities.

Joseph built the house—a colossal task—but others have always offered to make their own alterations. Are they qualified? It depends on how much they really know, since superior knowledge is what they would bring to the project. This takes us to the subject of scholarship. Socrates always told his disciples to test the knowledge of their Sophist teachers before following them. But that is a no-no in the profession; it is insidious and embarrassing, and it cost Socrates his life. The purpose of caps, gowns, processions, degrees, committees, offices, ranks, and so on is to deflect, discourage, and overawe any who would ask naive questions about the emperor's clothes. But we must ask just the same. What do these people have that the Saints have not had in the past? We are referred in our scholarly journals to the priceless ingredient—"scholarly methodologies." Since the mid-nineteenth century, the universal credo has been that to be valid at all, scholarship had to be scientific. It had to have its special methods. It was refined and sharpened methodology that converted mere guessing to science; in religion, specifically in biblical scholarship, it became Higher Criticism.

The scholastic philosophers laid down rules for God—what he could do and what he could not do, what he was and what he was not. In making their translations and commentaries of the scriptures, they added and subtracted to suit their fancy, thus doing what they strictly forbade God to do. From the early Renaissance, scholarship became a matter of restoring the wisdom of the ancients from a vast heap of newly discovered manuscripts. It was a matter of collecting, sorting, then reading, comparing, and classifying manuscripts, and afterwards forming one's own conclusions. The idea of modern "scholarly methodologies" imparting unlimited authority is high comedy; it fairly pleads for Gilbert and Sullivan: After the chorus has sung its welcoming praise, the Great Scholar steps forward to center stage and sings his aria, how in school and seminar he learned to intone in the correct voice, or drawl, wear the tweed or the cloth with equal deference, smoke the pipe, and follow the departmental line.

The actual method of these giants was surprisingly simple. A great scholar goes through the scriptures and every time he finds a passage proclaiming the miraculous, supernatural, or otherworldly, he simply expunges the offending words as obvious interpolations or corruption in the text. In the 1940s, Rudolf Bultmann and others called it "demythologizing." What remained after this learned exercise of casting out lingering remnants of dark superstition from the Bible was the pure original text, stripped of all supernatural accumulations.

In the 1920s and 1930s, a crowd of LDS graduate students went to the University of Chicago for a ministerial Ph.D. and returned to BYU as ardent disciples of Albert Schweitzer, Ernest Renan, Adolf von Harnack, and the rest. They demythologized Jesus on the authority of the immortal Goodspeed.[18] Despite the heated debates of the 1940s and 1950s, BYU weathered the Higher Criticism of Chicago rather well.

While teaching at Claremont in the 1930s, I shared a humanities class with Goodspeed, who had retired from Chicago. He insisted with great emphasis that the New Testament was a Greek document because not a single Hebrew manuscript was known to exist from Jesus' time. It was shortly after Dr. Goodspeed's death that the Dead Sea Scrolls were discovered—how could he have known? Here were ordinary Jews writing Hebrew with skill and confidence in the time of Christ. Which illustrates the first rule of scholarship: *You are never playing with a full deck.* You never know how much evidence you may be missing, what it is, or where it is hiding. What counters that and saves the day for scholarship is what I have called the "Gas Law of Learning," namely, that any amount of knowledge, no matter how small, will fill any vacuum of ignorance, no matter how large. He who knows one or two facts can honestly claim to know at least something about a subject, and nobody knows everything. So it is with the schoolmen who make the rules and move the goalposts.

Joseph Smith did not come before the world with a premise, or a proposition, or a hypothesis, or a special interpretation of the scriptures, any of which would have given logical grounds for endless discussion. He simply told a straight story to be accepted or rejected, leaving no room for argument. He could neither deny his story nor reach an accommodation with the ministers, and that explains a good deal of their implacable rage against him. "What is a Bible scholar anyway?" asks Harold Bloom. "A Bible scholar, so far as I can see, with very rare exceptions, is just a very bad literary critic."[19] The scholar is really doing what the literary critic does, giving his considered opinion, which is passed off as scientific fact on the helpless public awed by the mysteries of "scholarly methodology." Bloom continues (we may credit *Sunstone* for printing this), "[Joseph] Smith had found his way back, either by inspiration or by imagination . . . to certain elements in archaic Judaism [see the Books of Moses, Enoch, Abraham, Nephi, and so on] that normative Judaism and Christianity have abandoned."[20] That may, if you please, be fanciful stuff, but it is specific and amenable to careful checking against ancient sources, although few were available to anyone in Joseph's time and none were available to him. Others, scientists like Eric Paul, scholars like Eduard Meyer, and learned mystics like Manley P. Hall, have noted the same phenomenon in the case of Joseph: He had an inside track to something. But no one has followed up on it, and why should they? The Mormons have a vested interest in such a pursuit but find it too much trouble. When mere appointment to the office of group leader can give one authority or stature, why should anyone bother? To find the things that Joseph found, however, no one can "come unto Mount Zion . . . unless he becomes as a little child, and is taught by the Spirit of God. Wherefore, we again say, search the revelations of God: study the prophecies."[21] So said Joseph Smith, who declared that he was fearful to ask God, in behalf of others, "about things the knowledge of which men ought to obtain in all sincerity, before God, for themselves." And how for themselves? "In humility by the prayer of faith."[22]

Star Witness

The greatest scholarly work of modern times is undoubtedly that of Eduard Meyer. To this day, his *Geschichte des Altertums (History of Antiquity)* is considered to be "the most perfectly documented and soundly reasoned resume of what is actually known about the peoples of Antiquity."[23] "The project was not original, but never before had it been undertaken by anyone with a comparable preparation."[24] Nor will it ever be surpassed again for, as E. Hornung recently observed, "Egyptian Historiography reached its high water mark in Eduard Meyer."[25] No one else could master the vast weight and scope of the materials, which are now doubled and broken into a dozen specialties. Meyer had a special preference for the history of religions, which never left him from his dissertation (at the age of twenty) to the great work of his old age, *The Origin and Beginnings of Christianity*. He matched that with another work, *The Origin and Beginnings of the Mormons, with Reflections on the Beginnings of Islam and Christianity,* published in 1912. What a happy coincidence! The origins of religion were always his grand passion, and for him Joseph Smith held the key. "Mormonism excited interest at an early age," Meyer writes, "both because of its surprising analogy to Islam" and also because "Mormonism is one of the most instructive phenomena in the whole area of religious history. . . . Students of religions have kept themselves strictly aloof from Mormonism and disdained the rich instruction it has to offer."[26]

> It is not just another of countless sects, but a new revealed religion, [with] an exceptionally rich contemporary store of documents; . . . what in the study of other revealed religions can only be surmised after painful research is here directly accessible in reliable witnesses. Hence the origin and history of Mormonism possesses a great and unusual value to the students of Religious History.[27]

The common claim that Joseph Smith borrowed from the sects around him will not hold up, according to Meyer; for what it has in common with them anybody can find in the Bible.[28] In Joseph's revelations there is no sign of conscious deception or of outside influence.[29]

To say that he was simply a swindler no more explains Joseph Smith than it explains Amos, or Isaiah, or Mohammed, or Jeanne d'Arc. Many deserted Joseph Smith but never denied his prophetic calling; he expelled many from the Church, he never solicited the support of anyone or made any concessions in his message. It is the case of Joseph Smith that sheds light on all the others (Amos, Moses, Isaiah, Jeremiah, or Zoroaster and Hesiod) and not the other way around.[30]

But how about the Book of Mormon? The angel and the plates were for the Three Witnesses an "absolutely real experience."[31] But how to explain the Eight Witnesses? Meyer gives up on it. As a Higher Critic he cannot allow any taint of supernaturalism. Mormonism is not the correct view of Christianity because it does not accept the Christ of the Higher Critics:

> Jesus never appeared as a prophet. Certainly he feels the closest communication with God, who is his loving Father; the doctrine which Jesus preaches is God's truth, and hence Christ claims the authority to interpret the law autonomously and to teach religious truth and God's commandments with sovereign authority. But never did he claim a direct revelation which came to him in a moment, much less that he would have materialized such a revelation. Christ did not have visions, and he never predicted future events; he did not take any stand concerning the events of this world, nor did he give instructions concerning the world. His way was completely different from that of the prophets, including John the Baptist, Zoroaster,

Mohammed, or Joseph Smith; Christ is not a prophet, but a teacher like Buddha, who makes known religious truth in authoritative sayings and parables made convincing by their inner evidence.[32]

But how about John? "It goes without saying that the Gospel of John is utterly worthless as a source for the historical knowledge of Jesus."[33] So that need not annoy us. "Jesus never did predict future events." And Matthew 24? An obvious interpolation and invention, since such things just do not happen. The stories of Transfiguration and Ascension are mere fiction.[34] And so the Higher Critic has it all his own way. But, true or false, Mormonism parallels primitive Christianity: "During our historic presentation [of Mormonism] the thoughts of the reader . . . must often have strayed to the beginning of Christianity."[35]

As to the visions, angels, healings, casting out of devils, and other supernatural events, Jesus himself shared these beliefs; for him too, the constant intervention of the other world was something to be taken for granted. But the Book of Mormon? Forget it: "The style is clumsy and monotonous in the highest degree. . . . No one but a believer will ever bring himself to read it clear through."[36] From which it is evident that Meyer himself never gave it any intensive study. He dismisses it with the license of the Higher Critic. "There is no doubt at all that the golden plates, even though his mother and others say they were kept in a box in Smith's house, never existed in the real world."[37] "There is no doubt at all," claims the same absolute authority for rejecting the testimony of John, which, "it goes without saying," is worthless.

After displaying his prejudices, Meyer, backed by the full force of his matchless learning and insight, issues a confident prophecy for the Mormon Church as of 1912: "Though it has not been destroyed . . . still it has sunk from the position of a coming world religion to a sect something of the type of Judaism or the Parses." That is, a small, respectable, obscure, fading community. There is no more remarkable prophecy of Joseph Smith than his own unequivocal view of the future of the Church with its unstoppable progress. This is the thing that most impressed Eduard Meyer: All great religious founders have their moments of self-doubt, soul-searching, and agonizing—with the one single exception of Joseph Smith, who never for a moment betrayed the slightest sign of doubt or hesitation as to his calling or the future of Zion.

Meyer gives the clearest demonstrations of how critical methodology works. The resurrection story of the early Christians was an obvious fiction since it so perfectly matched the very story the early Christians *wanted* to believe.[38] They liked the story so much they *must* have made it up. The appearances of God to men in Genesis are exactly like those described by Paul and the early Christians, along with Moses and Joseph Smith—and what could be plainer proof, not that they are authentic, but that they are simply being copied down the line from the original in Genesis?[39] The many appearances of Christ after his resurrection are a cover-up, a conscious fabrication. Once assumed, this is "a neat [*huebsch*] illustration of how rationalistic criticism has always operated; the fact that the body has disappeared from the tomb is not questioned, but a logical explanation is sought."[40] *Credo quia absurdum . . . credible est guia impossible,* says Tertullian—if it is absurd, nobody has made it up; if it makes sense, somebody has been adjusting it.

The Big Question

The one purpose of religion is to answer the Terrible Question, which is also the one thing the clergy will not touch. Hans Kuehn's *Theology for the Third Millennium* contains not a single mention of death or the hereafter! The social gospel is the clergy's refuge from the question. As Ernest Becker put it, "When philosophy took over from religion it also took over religion's central problem, and death became the real 'muse of philosophy' from its beginning in Greece right through Heidegger and modern existentialism."[41] It was not until the late 1930s that the smart-aleck 1920s and early 1930s came face to face with a shocking realization brought home by depression and war that "to see the world as it really is is devastating and terrifying. . . . It places a trembling animal at the mercy of the entire cosmos and the problem of the meaning of it."[42] Soren Kierkegaard, a contemporary of Joseph Smith, became the flag bearer of the modern sophisticates. His "whole understanding of man's character is that it is a structure built up to avoid perception of the 'terror, perdition [and] annihilation [that] dwell next door to every man.'"[43]

On the very day that Joseph Smith renamed Commerce Town to make it a thing of beauty, Kierkegaard in his journal (May 12, 1839) cries out in hopeless despair: "The whole order of things fills me with a sense of anguish . . . all is entirely unintelligible to me, and particularly my own person. Great is my sorrow, without limits. None knows of it, except God in heaven, and He cannot have pity!" Becker writes, "This is the terror: to have emerged from nothing, to have a name, consciousness of self, deep inner feelings, an excruciating inner yearning for life, and self-expression—and with all this yet to die. It seems like a hoax."[44] So we try not to think of it, and instead, like Kierkegaard's Philistine, we tranquilize ourselves "in the trivial."[45] According to Neo-Freudianism, "*consciousness of death* is the primary repression, not sexuality. . . . *This* is the repression on which culture is built."[46] Freud, says his biographer, "had constantly before him the vision of man who is always unhappy, helpless, anxious, bitter, looking into nothingness with fright, and turning away from 'so-called posterity' in anticipatory . . . disgust."[47] This is the great revelation of the modern age.

But Joseph Smith had already stated the problem as clearly as anyone ever has, and done what no one else has done in giving us the solution. "What is the object of our coming into existence, then dying and falling away, to be here no more? . . . [This] is a subject *we ought to study more than any other*. We ought to study it day and night. . . . If we have any claim on our Heavenly Father for anything, it is for knowledge on *this important subject*."[48] And this is where religion has failed, turning to the social gospel and intellectual posturing to avoid the issue.

Joseph Smith not only states the problem, but he provides the prime clue to the answer on the same page: "Could you gaze into heaven five minutes, you would know more than you would by reading all that ever was written on the subject."[49] The answer must come from the outside, and that is recognized now. The term "breakthrough" that Eduard Meyer applied to the beginning of Christianity and Mormonism is today being widely used in theological journals to explain the divine origin of Christianity: It cannot be a human invention, our own imagining; to be real it must come from elsewhere. But of course the phenomenon is denied for modern times.

I ask LDS students what they would do with a thousand years of life, guaranteed, all expenses paid, and they give silly answers because they have been conditioned by the actuary to accept short lives with the prospect that all they will ever get is right here. They do not see the breakthrough. The great breakthroughs of 1820 and 1827, which changed everything, should settle the issue—but is it all real? Joseph shows us that it is: When solid plates pass between inhabitants of different worlds and visitors from above lay hands upon the heads of Joseph and his brethren, something is afoot. If it stopped there, we would be bemused, but Joseph kept his promise to tell us what was on the plates, to give us glimpses of things that lie beyond human reckoning.

Do you have the remotest inkling of an idea, my dear Galbungus, how much sheer mental effort it would take the smartest person to produce a book of Enoch, or Abraham, or Nephi, or Ether, or Helaman, or the first section of the Doctrine and Covenants? To lay it all out in order with the vast sweep and scope of the book of Moses, bridging great gaps in the human record? The Pearl of Great Price putting the whole into a cosmic setting in the manner of the ancients? The Book of Mormon with its ever-changing scenes of desert wanderers, luxury and danger in Jerusalem, migrations, wars, politics, ecology, trade and commerce, law and lawyers, paramilitary terrorists, youth gangs, strategy and tactics, natural disasters, organized crime, corrupt courts and politicians, dangerous opportunists, secret organizations, vain intellectuals, devout sectaries in the wilderness, prophets as near-death witnesses of the afterlife, great missionaries, dynastic feuds, and more, and with all this the doctrines of salvation set forth more fully than anywhere else, and in a setting not of Joseph Smith's rural America but of our own climactic age? It is no wonder Smith's most ambitious critics from Meyer to Fawn Brodie steer us away from the Book of Mormon and Pearl of Great Price, which leave them high and dry as critics.

So I see no reason why people should set themselves up as lights; I need not focus my feeble beam on the faults of others, in the Church or out, simply as a means of calling attention to myself. What remains is only "bearing down in pure testimony" (Alma 4:19).

NOTES

1. Joseph Smith, *History of the Church of Jesus Christ of Latter-day Saints,* 7 vols. (Salt Lake City: Deseret Book, 1976), 2:294.

2. Ibid., 2:317–18.

3. Ibid., 2:334–35.

4. Ibid., 2:341.

5. Ibid., 4:358.

6. *The Personal Writings of Joseph Smith,* comp. Dean C. Jessee (Salt Lake City: Deseret Book, 1984), 328.

7. Ibid., 329.

8. Ibid., 331.

9. Ibid., 121.

10. *The Words of Joseph Smith,* ed. Andrew F. Ehat and Lyndon W. Cook (Provo, Utah: BYU Religious Studies Center, 1980), 55.

11. *History of the Church,* 6:185.

12. Ibid., 6:273.

13. Ibid., 6:304.

14. Ibid., 5:181.

15. Ibid., 4:588.

16. Ibid., 5:285–86.

17. *Teachings of the Prophet Joseph Smith,* comp. Joseph Fielding Smith (Salt Lake City: Deseret Book, 1961); *The Words of Joseph Smith,* ed. Ehat and Cook; *The Personal Writings of Joseph Smith,* comp. Dean C. Jessee; *The Papers of Joseph Smith,* comp. Dean C. Jessee (Salt Lake City: Deseret Book, 1989, 1992); *Joseph Smith: The Prophet, the Man,* ed. Susan Easton Black and Charles D. Tate, Jr. (Provo, Utah: BYU Religious Studies Center, 1993); and *An American Prophet's Record: The Diaries and Journals of Joseph Smith,* comp. Scott H. Faulring (Salt Lake City: Signature Books, 1989).

18. Edgar Johnson Goodspeed, the prominent University of Chicago theologian.

19. Brett DelPorto, "Harold Bloom's Ironic, Female, Co-Author of the Bible," *Sunstone* 15, no. 1 (April 1991, issue 81): 57.

20. Ibid., 56.

21. *History of the Church,* 1:283.

22. Ibid., 1:339; see James 1:5.

23. *Enciclopedia Universal Illustrada,* ed. S. A. Espasa-Calpe (Madrid: Espasa-Calpe, 1907–1930), 34:1377.

24. *Enciclopedia Italiana di Scienze, Lettere ed Arti* (Rome: Instituto Della Enciclopedia Italiana, 1934), 23:140.

25. Erik Hornung, *Einführung in die Ägyptologie* (Darmstadt: Wissenschaftliche Buchgesellschaft, 1967), 121.

26. Eduard Meyer, *The Origin and History of the Mormons,* trans. Heinz F. Rahde and Eugene Seaich (Salt Lake City: University of Utah, 1961), i.

27. Ibid., i.

28. Ibid., 22–23.
29. Ibid., 10.
30. Ibid., vii–ix.
31. Ibid., 9.
32. Ibid., 199.
33. Ibid.
34. Ibid., 200–201.
35. Ibid., 198.
36. Ibid., 22–23, 25.
37. Ibid., 5.
38. Ibid., 202.
39. Ibid., 213–14.
40. Ibid., 207.
41. Ernest Becker, *The Denial of Death* (New York: Free Press, 1973), 12.
42. Ibid., 60.
43. Ibid., 70.
44. Ibid., 67, 87.
45. Ibid., 74.
46. Ibid., 96.
47. Ibid., 122.
48. *History of the Church*, 6:50; emphasis added.
49. Ibid.

CHAPTER 16

CHRISTIAN ETHICS IN
JOSEPH SMITH BIOGRAPHY

RICHARD LLOYD ANDERSON
Professor of Ancient Scripture, Brigham Young University

T HE DIVINITY and moral authority of Christ have been stressed by
every president of The Church of Jesus Christ of Latter-day Saints.
The message is to know the Lord, contemplate his principles, and
apply them persistently. Behind every exterior occupation is an
accountable individual, and Jesus teaches harmony of individual and
professional ethics. Can the Savior instruct the writer of history?
Historians aspire to recover important events and judge their ultimate significance. But Christ will make the final historical assessment:
"For the Son of man shall come in the glory of his Father with his
angels; and then he shall reward every man according to his works"
(Matthew 16:27).

In the meantime, the Lord left the Sermon on the Mount, with
its profound insights into motive, expression, and action, as the disciple's major moral guide. A historian's writing and its impact will be
divinely evaluated according to the Lord's principles. Christ's challenge for full righteousness certainly includes intellectual values.
Jesus' intense exposure of Jewish leaders who were plotting his
death (see Matthew 23) certainly has current applications: they could
venerate ancient prophets and obliterate those speaking to their own

generation (Matthew 23:29–31). How many of these leaders seriously considered Jesus' own story that he came with a mission from the Father, or the apostles' testimony that they were instructed by the resurrected Lord? As Mormonism expands, there will be more writers who let the Prophet tell his story of divine visions. But there are opposite trends that will no doubt also increase. Some scholars with Mormon roots are ashamed of the prophet of the Restoration, and some outside the Mormon tradition aim to destroy the Prophet's testimony with elaborate cultural explanations. Jesus said the quality of a person's religion is not measured by seating order or the width of design on his robes (Matthew 23:5–6). Neither is a scholar's accuracy easily apparent from the location of his training or the sheer mass of his footnotes.

Perhaps the greatest of Christian values is the will to believe. Jesus thanked the Father that what was scorned by "the wise and prudent" was revealed to those with childlike faith (Matthew 11:25). Skepticism by itself is sterile because it resists rather than reaches. In my experience, revelation adds an eternal dimension to all higher studies. I see few conflicts between the four standard works and my fields of study; tensions have been consistently resolved by patience combined with deeper inquiry. As an undergraduate in required science, I saw that the scientific method closely mirrored the process of my religious experience. The researcher frames a hypothesis consistent with known facts but beyond them, and then tests the validity of this theory. My testimony had earlier come in the same way. With reason, I had assumed that God was real and would answer prayers, and after I created the right conditions for answers, they came forcefully from time to time. My convictions of Christ's divinity and of divine communication to modern prophets are spiritual certainties.

Jesus reproved those creating religious rules without consistency, often in the context of rejecting him because he violated some preconceived notion about a prophet. After decades of teaching the New Testament, I remain puzzled by scholars who accept at least a core collection of Paul's writings (the Corinthian letters plus Romans and Galatians) and yet consider the Gospels to be formalized fables. In the view of many biblical scholars, Paul's letters from between A.D. 50 and 68 can be trusted, but the records of Christ originating about the same time enshrine mythology. But in 1 Corinthians Paul gave the historic essentials of the Christian message of the atonement and resurrection (15:3–7), as well as the institution of the sacrament at the last supper (11:23–25), insisting in both cases that this information came from eyewitnesses.[1] The entire first century of Roman history is alive and well in letter collections and in writings of quality historians and travelers, along with preserved inscriptions and coins. The Gospels and Acts fit into this world, as well as into the Jewish world of the Dead Sea scrolls in the first century and of Mishnaic traditions of the second century. Yet scholars read the first-century Jewish historian Josephus with minor corrections for bias and misinformation, while they feel that the Gospels may be largely dismissed.[2]

No substantial reason exists to reject traditional authorship that is supported in early manuscripts of the Gospels and by informed Christian writers of the second and third centuries. Thus I am confident that the four canonical Gospels come from apostles or those who relayed what they said or wrote about Jesus. Christ's words within this collection may be variously reported—nearly verbatim in several preserved discourses, paraphrased sometimes with equivalent meanings, evidently closely remembered at times. In all cases, those around Jesus should be more trusted for his teachings than current revisionists.

All this is not as far from Mormon history as it might seem. Today's overload of historical studies can be assimilated only by selective reading in secondary literature while focusing on firsthand documents. Except for the possibility of full sight-sound recording, there can be no true history without witnesses of events. Whether they write at the time, recall later, or are represented responsibly secondhand, observers are at the center of reconstructing the past. Beware of scholars mainly quoting scholars. A competent historian constantly quotes original sources. How many sources? No magic rule guarantees that two sources are enough. Reliable history is based on comparing all available sources, and not on gravitating to the unusual. Eyewitnesses normally agree on the essentials of an event, though irregular contemporary reports can arise from misinformation and bias.

The balance of this essay will illustrate the importance of relying on broad primary or eyewitness information. I highlight recent approaches to Joseph Smith that are deficient or careless to illustrate the dangers of ignoring or discounting firsthand accounts. I make candid observations in a sincere attempt to prevent major misunderstandings of the Prophet at the crucial beginning and end of his authoritative calling. I deliberately name specific books to illustrate marginal interpretations that too easily escape accountable review. I also probe moral decisions that confront all writers who deal with the lives of others, in the conviction that general attitudes determine particular decisions. Better perspectives could result in better methods.

Is Christ really relevant to the historian? My professor-friend, Kirk Hart, brings up challenging issues in his effective work on the ethics of public life. For businessmen, lawyers, and doctors, to name obvious professions, the problems are far more subtle than open dishonesty. How does personal reward affect daily gray areas, and what principles are more than token antidotes? What are the real reasons for self-serving actions? One's noble rationalization may be a facade. Like those in other occupations, historians may explain their vices as virtues. Here I believe deeply that the Sermon on the Mount contains remedial standards. Christ declares ideals for dealing with or even writing about others. Yet the code must be within the person, and real intent is everything. While I cannot cover all facets of historical ethics, I appeal to the conscience of historians, and to the conscience of the natural historian in every aware person. Ultimately, we each will answer for our responses to such appeals.

How many titles of books and articles begin with "A critical view"? Of course a critic is an evaluator, and may not primarily "criticize" in the normal sense of destructive evaluation. Yet Christ gave a severe warning here: "Judge not, that ye be not judged" (Matthew 7:1). The context tells what Jesus meant, for he follows with the illustration of one person's preoccupation with a tiny speck in another's eye. Thus, his point is not to avoid all judging, but to avoid being judgmental. The disciple is not warned against careful thinking, but he is told to avoid narrow condemnation without perspective of the whole. Thus Joseph Smith's clarifying translation is sound: "Judge not unrighteously, that ye be not judged: but judge righteous judgment" (JST Matthew 7:1). John's Gospel verifies such language from

Christ: "Judge not according to the appearance, but judge righteous judgment" (John 7:24).

"Warts and all" historians often violate this divine counsel. Chronicles of strange events or lists of supposed mistakes of Church leaders are lopsided and therefore amount to researched sensationalism. One could write a history of World War II cowardice, but stopping there would mask the massive sacrifices that brought Allied victory. Even mixing equal parts of cowardice and courage would be malformed history. Well-expressed negativism is sophisticated, which may be a warning sign. The great building in Lehi's vision represented the "pride of the world" (1 Nephi 11:36) and was filled with sophisticated critics—scoffing at those who fully accepted the testimony of the prophets and tasted of their experiences (1 Nephi 8:26–28; 15:24). Negativism in tone usually reflects that narrow viewpoint in selection. Using the double test of the courtroom oath, published research may tell the truth but not the whole truth. Hostile adjectives and faint praise mark the Joseph Smith biographer who lacks empathy with the subject. Ignoring Joseph's substantial achievements signals the inadequacy of the historian of the Prophet. Honesty demands relevant facts, but broad honesty is also sensitive to the problems and patterns of another era, including the Prophet's serious attempts to maintain civil rights in the face of unlawful aggression and midwestern programs of violence. Powerful positives are necessary to explain why Latter-day Saints expanded geometrically during the Prophet's life, and why they wept bitterly at his death, even when they knew his human faults better than any later historian.

Faith is the moral foundation for suspending judgment or judging only after a "righteous" investigation. The apostles' lives were at risk when the Lord stilled the sea and asked the piercing question: "Why are ye so fearful? how is it that ye have no faith?" (Mark 4:40). There are also storms of skepticism, academic fashion, and peer pressure. Can the religious historian write meaningfully about men of faith without experiencing and maintaining faith? Matthew 6, the middle third of the Sermon on the Mount, is devoted to the daily potential of faith. Trust God, Jesus told his disciples, for otherwise they would disseminate darkness, not light (Matthew 6:19–23).

Professions are in view in Christ's mandate: "Seek ye first the king-dom of God" (Matthew 6:33). Are many historians too skeptical? Bankers know how to balance faith and rational controls. While financial institutions are on guard for fraud, they are not preoccupied with it. National economies would deadlock without faith in repay-ment schedules of bonds and other obligations, nor could common currency exist without public trust. While tabloid history dwells on the Prophet's weaknesses, what is proved at most is his humanity. As an investigative historian, I am personally convinced of his honesty and the honesty of those associated with him in establishing the Lord's Church.

Joseph Smith testified of visions and lived a life of sacrifice for his beliefs, raising up a people who were not exploited by him and who testified of strong spiritual confirmations of his divine calling. He established a record of credibility well worthy of trust. Must he be perfect as a condition for us to have faith in his mission? By that unreasonable standard one could have faith in no prophet. I early had strong impressions of Joseph Smith's sincerity in describing the First Vision and the appearances of Moroni. Deep confirmations came as I read his fervent letters and spontaneous sermons and felt his urgency of mission. His conviction that he held authority from divine mes-sengers was sure. Like Paul, at pivotal points he was directed by clear visions of the Father and the Son. Moreover, selected companions shared crucial visions, just as there are multiple witnesses of the trans-figuration and resurrection in the New Testament. Oliver Cowdery was a most impressive person, and he consistently testified of being with the Prophet at both priesthood restorations. Oliver described these events while in the Church, out of the Church, and after returning to the Church.[3] Oliver is also one of the three who testi-fied that an angel appeared in a cloud of light at midday to show the plates of the Book of Mormon. Over decades I have collected scores of detailed interviews with the Three Witnesses, who repeatedly answered questions on an experience that they would neither deny nor allow to be explained away.[4] This supernatural event is in the his-torical field of vision, as plain as a radar screen with clear tracks of objects beyond eyesight but within reality.

One should approach Joseph Smith by reasonably assuming he

remembered his heavenly visitations and gave supplementing details on many unrehearsed occasions. Some writers adopt the skeptical approach to the First Vision and restoration of the priesthoods through divine messengers. They think what is left unsaid earlier was probably invented or "realized" later, and surface contradictions are more significant than correlations. Have we become academic pharisees in judging external forms while missing Joseph's sincere attempts to communicate overwhelming events in concise terms? Historians of deep faith have found far more correlations than conflicts in Joseph's accounts of his visions.

I personally see First Vision contradictions as occurring more in scholarly minds than in Joseph's accounts. Whether studying the Prophet or the Gospels, one can always make a speculative case for stories becoming bigger and better. But such explanations usually compare what Joseph Smith said later with what he failed to say earlier. This deceptive tool is the argument from silence—which takes nonmention of an event as proof that it did not happen. On the contrary, we all carry memories of vivid episodes that are not reduced to writing. Early and sustained abuse made the Prophet cautious about fully reporting his revelations (see Joseph Smith–History 1:21–22, 74–75). But as the one person most in a position to know, Joseph himself should define the compelling events of his career. When his visions are well understood, ordinary episodes of his life are interesting but secondary. When Paul faced personal attacks, he treated them as largely irrelevant. Instead, he reviewed divine visions that his detractors could not match: "Am I not an apostle? . . . have I not seen Jesus Christ our Lord?" (1 Corinthians 9:1). In the same manner, Joseph Smith insisted that his weaknesses were insignificant in the light of his latter-day call through the visible presence of God and Christ and angels.

What Joseph believed at the end and why he died are clear from his own words and contemporary reports of those closest to him. Though there is some historical clutter, my legal training has helped me to cut through such underbrush. The heart of law school is the "case method." Classwork is normally based on discussing opinions of appellate courts that determine a point of law. Two aspects of this process upgraded my historical reasoning. First, before each case was discussed, professors rigidly insisted on defining the issues and the procedure that brought the action before a higher court. Though I ultimately abandoned law, I retained an intense sense of context, a habit of not looking at a historical document without defining its background or setting. Second, classwork also stressed extracting precise judicial decisions from the discursive comments of judges. What becomes law is the judge's reasoning in deciding the case—what is said off the subject is not authoritative. This practice in separating court rulings from court philosophy has helped me separate firsthand information from mere opinions circulating without a known source. What is contemporary is not necessarily what is firsthand. The skeletal structure of history is what observers say or what is reliably reported from them. Yet many writing Mormon history are careless in applying this first principle of accurate reporting.

As a missionary, I read Fawn M. Brodie's *No Man Knows My History* to give inquirers an informed response, and from that experience I gained early lessons in slanted narrative. Some early reviewers noted that her product was much closer to fiction than history in its story line, imaginative drama, and easy access to the thoughts of her characters. I double-checked all of her references to discover that a great many were either atypical or quoted out of context. And these two habits in using sources also appear in several recent scholarly books that contribute to the historical tradition of misrepresenting Joseph Smith. What do sources from or near Joseph Smith say? Fortunately for an accurate picture, the full publication of the Prophet's letters, major papers, and journals is steadily making this important archival material more available.

The Nauvoo context or setting behind Joseph Smith's final speeches is crucial in understanding his closing confidence in his divine calling. Traditional law requires that there be witnesses to the signature of a will, to guard against fraudulent after-death claims. Soon after the martyrdom, James J. Strang produced a forged letter to prove that he was Joseph Smith's successor. Some others gave self-interested versions of private conversations with Joseph Smith before Carthage. But valid tests are available. What words of Joseph Smith are recorded just before martyrdom? Is this evidence supported by agreement among the Prophet's close associates, instead of by a single voice that contradicts them? The Prophet's late speeches regularly respond to the claim of dissenters that he was a fallen prophet. Early in 1844, Joseph's counselor, William Law, became the center of bitter opposition to the Prophet, culminating in Law's excommunication on April 18, followed by open meetings of his "Reformed Church."[5] In early June this group published its first and last issue of the *Nauvoo Expositor*, accusing Joseph of false teaching on the subjects of plurality of Gods and plural marriage. Since the latter practice violated the Illinois bigamy statute, the Prophet could say little publicly on that subject. But his insistent testimony that he was a true prophet is woven through the 1844 discourses, with the repeated themes of his authorization by revelation to institute temple ceremonies and declare the true nature of God.

This is the setting of Joseph Smith's phrase exploited by Fawn Brodie: "No man knows my history." To her, it suggested the Prophet had covered up his real story.[6] But in context Joseph meant that Latter-day Saints did not fully appreciate his encounters with God, even though they were informed about his early visions. The above phrase comes from his well-known King Follett discourse, given to the large conference meeting on April 7, 1844, on the nature of the Father and Son and the high destiny of mankind. In his long introduction Joseph referred to his revelations as the source of his knowledge of God, asking whether "any of you [have] seen him? heard him? communed with him?"[7] Joseph closed this speech with "No man knows my history," followed by the thought: "If I had not experienced what I have, I should not have known it myself."[8] This account, from Thomas Bullock's notes, is paralleled by that of official scribe Willard Richards: "I don't blame you for not believing my history—had I not experienced it, [I] could not believe it myself."[9] Joseph's point is the uniqueness of his being visited by God and his messengers. Giving the same message in the Adams funeral sermon, the Prophet said that a true knowledge of God could not come by "reading the experience of others, or the revelations given to them."[10] Thus, in the King Follett sermon, what Joseph Smith had "experienced" referred to his visual contacts with God and angels. Indeed, the Saints had been told of Joseph's visions, since he did not blame them "for not believing my history." Thus the "no man" comment, in context, is a reminder of known divine contacts, not an admission of untold secrets.

As opposition intensified, so did the Prophet's public replies, given with awareness that he could be assassinated at any time. On May 12, he again closed a sermon with personal testimony that God had spoken to him: "When did I ever teach anything wrong from this stand? . . . I never told you I was perfect, but there is no error in the revelations which I have taught."[11] And ten days before martyrdom he preached once more on the nature of the Father and Son, ending this last doctrinal discourse by insisting again that his knowledge of God came by direct divine encounters: "Did I build on another man's foundation but my own? I have got all the truth and an independent revelation in the bargain."[12] At the end, Joseph Smith insisted that there was no compromise on the reality of his visions.

These April and May sermons contain Joseph's own "last will and testament." His bravery in the face of strong forebodings of death is documented by the men who stayed with him in prison, as well as by the letter he wrote to Emma the morning of the martyrdom: "I am very much resigned to my lot, knowing I am justified and have done the best that could be done."[13] His clerk, William Clayton, pictured Joseph's "solemn and thoughtful" mood as he "rode down home to bid his family farewell," adding: "He expects nothing but to be massacred . . . but there appearing no alternative but he must either give himself up or the city be massacred by a lawless mob under the sanction of the governor."[14] As in Missouri, the Prophet saw himself as a hostage, endangering his own life rather than risking the safety of his people. So it is jarring to read in two indirect accounts that he gambled on massive bloodshed by sending for the Nauvoo Legion in his last hours.

But secondary sources may be quite wrong, and their continued use shows how prominent authors can be tempted by inferior data. Fawn Brodie created her melodrama of Joseph sending for the legion on his day of death, adding that commander Jonathan Dunham "pocketed the order and neglected to act upon it."[15] Her footnote explained: "This story is told by Allen J. Stout in his manuscript journal. . . . It is confirmed by T. B. H. Stenhouse in his *Rocky Mountain Saints* (New York, 1873)."[16] But these reports are simply quoted without evaluation. Stout tells that he was activated as a company commander when the Prophet's life was in danger, and he writes with intense frustration that the superior legion could not protect its leader: "And while they were in jail Brother Joseph wrote an official order to Jonathan Dunham to bring the legion and rescue him from being killed, but Dunham did not let a single man or mortal know that he had received such orders."[17] All late Nauvoo diaries and recollections lament the circumstances of Joseph's death, but only Stout is known to give the version of the aborted rescue order. Yet Stout was on duty in Nauvoo and had no personal knowledge of Joseph's actions at the jail. Did some demand a scapegoat in rage at the murder? Since Dunham died a year later on special assignment in Missouri, he is an unavailable witness. As for the Stenhouse version, he was converted in England after the martyrdom; later losing faith in Mormonism, he related the supposed command from Carthage in order to ridicule Joseph's martyrdom prophecies. Like Stout, he tells a story without a known pedigree, prefaced only by "it is understood."[18] But merely repeating a rumor does not confirm it.

Those with Joseph at Carthage are the only identifiable witnesses in this situation. A spirited and candid John Taylor tells how discussion on martyrdom day was "rather desultory" because there was no plan except to wait for a court hearing in two days. He adds that Joseph had already decided the question of using the legion. Taylor promised the Prophet freedom within five hours "if you will permit it, and say the word." Taylor added that he had planned to "go to Nauvoo, and collect a force sufficient," but "Brother Joseph refused."[19] In Taylor's more detailed version of the same conversation, Joseph ruled out a legion rescue, had considered repeating the Missouri escape, but was firm in waiting for legal release. Answering Taylor's offer of an armed force, Joseph said:

> That will not be the best way. It would be much better, if we contemplated escape, to call for a change of venue, and while passing from one place to another, to escape from the custody of the constable, and then claim our legal rights and protect ourselves until we obtain them.[20]

Enter Mark Hofmann. Interviewed according to his plea bargain, he told prosecuting attorneys that he created a Joseph command from Carthage after reading the above Brodie sources: "First let me say this is a very poor forgery and it was quickly done."[21] Forensic specialists examined this Dunham letter under the microscope and ultraviolet light and found the same ink cracks and light shifts that marked other Hofmann forgeries.[22] Before all this was known, the counterfeit order was included in *The Personal Writings of Joseph Smith*, on the basis of normal handwriting identification, though later editions listed Joseph's fictitious letter on an *errata* sheet as one of the fraudulent items mistakenly included in the collection.

A recent history, *The Mormon Hierarchy*, shows no knowledge of the above facts, a symptom of its preoccupation with sources claiming violence in the Mormon past. Yet ignorance of the fraudulent Joseph Smith order "in his own handwriting" is not my main point here.[23] In rigorous history, proving opportunity to know is not the same thing as proving knowledge. After quoting the forged rescue order, *Mormon Hierarchy* tells how Dunham disobeyed it, using the sentence quoted from the Allen Stout journal. "And while they were in jail Brother Joseph wrote an official order to Jonathan Dunham to bring the legion and rescue him from being killed, but Dunham did not let a single man or mortal know that he had received such orders." The one central issue is whether or not Stout spoke from personal knowledge, and he gives no clue that he did. Recreating the mob mentality at Carthage, Dan Jones tells how he was given a letter from Joseph at noontime on the day of martyrdom, an urgent request to attorney Orville H. Browning at Quincy to represent the Prophet in two days at a treason hearing. Just before Jones rode away, "News of the letter went throughout the mob like the wings of the breeze, and some claimed that it was orders for the Nauvoo Legion to come there to save the prisoners, and others claimed some other things."[24] It is irresponsible to quote Stout without showing that he had no better source than excited rumors. As discussed, John Taylor settles the issue by his firsthand report from the jail that Joseph Smith would not authorize use of force.

But *Mormon Hierarchy*'s skewed evaluation of Joseph is followed by another of Jonathan Dunham. In a Brodie-like disclosure, we are told that word of Dunham's disobedience spread, and "Nauvoo Mormons" seem to be divided into two groups: "Some called him a 'coward and traitor.' Others dismissed him as a 'fool and idiot.'"[25] Although these categories carry the weight of a total opinion poll, the sentence is copied from the 1873 comments of Stenhouse, a disaffected Mormon who never saw Joseph Smith's Nauvoo. The distortion is evident, since Nauvoo sources continue to show that Dunham was highly trusted after the martyrdom. The most obvious place to begin is a computer search of the *History of the Church* and Nauvoo periodicals, which indicate Dunham's involvement in significant events after Joseph's martyrdom: September 13, 1844, Dunham elected by the officers on the drill field as brigadier general of the second cohort of the legion, Brigham Young present; September 16, 1844, participated with the First Presidency and head legion officers in dedicating the arsenal site; January 15, 1845, his name published with about four dozen priesthood leaders authorized to collect tithing and donations for the Church, with approval of Bishops Whitney and Miller.[26]

Further evidence of Dunham's respect in the eyes of leading Mormons comes in his admission to the Council of Fifty, the body under the Twelve involved in managing Church secular interests, including the coming exodus. On March 1, 1845, William Clayton noted Dunham's initiation and appointment as assistant in a confidential mission to build Indian relationships, proceeding "from tribe to tribe to unite the Lamanites and find a home for the Saints." Designations were made "by unanimous vote of the Council." The mission had highest priority because it would help "fill Joseph's measures" for a western location from which a worldwide message could proceed. Assignments were modified on April 11, when "President Young appointed J. Dunham, C. Shumway, Lorenzo Young to go with Brother Dana on the Western Mission." This was Lewis Dana, whom Clayton called "a Lamanite of the Oneida nation." Four days later Phineas Young was substituted for Lorenzo, with an open-ended commission to go "to the Indian Council at Council Bluffs and thence if they think best to the Pacific Ocean."[27] Apparently general goodwill came from this diplomatic expedition, and Presidents Kimball and Young considered it important enough to record the setting apart and departure of the group, as well as intelligence that Dunham died on July 29, 1845.[28]

Dunham's record in the last year of his life does more than redeem his reputation. Had he disobeyed a Carthage order from Joseph, Brigham Young never would have trusted him to be third in command of the legion or to take tithes from the Saints or to accomplish a sensitive and dangerous mission. Dunham's post-martyrdom career proves that he was far from intellectually or morally bankrupt in the eyes of the Saints. Adopting these 1873 labels of Stenhouse is not responsible history.

Dozens of eyewitnesses report Joseph's farewells in leaving Nauvoo, as well as his discussions in the jail. They agree with Taylor that the Prophet was resigned to a probable martyrdom and was committed to leaving events in the hands of God. Several of Joseph's statements in his final four days show in fact that he retained the spirit of prophecy. John Taylor rode with Joseph to Carthage and soon published the Prophet's remarks on leaving Nauvoo—that he went innocent to the slaughter and would be murdered (D&C 135:4). In ancient history one might take a general report as indicative of public knowledge, but in Mormon history many correlating participants usually make historical hearsay unnecessary. Stout's untraceable claim of a rescue order sharply deviates from the norm established by direct observers. The resources for understanding the Prophet include official minutes, letter books, discourse reports, private journals, contemporary newspapers, and responsible recollections. These furnish a control on Joseph Smith's Nauvoo life, and a test and corrective for eccentric documents.

Revisionism, a major pattern in historical writing, may bring progress or a plague. I once read an interview in which Robert Frost said he would like to teach a course in slow reading, and my ideal history department would offer a seminar in deliberate publication. Joseph Smith history has more affinity with regional history than with the broad generalizations that are part of courses in world civilization and national history. Local historians and genealogists deal with highly specific data and careful standards of proof. On the other hand, Mormon periodicals and publishers heavily value reader interest and writing skills. But if quality evidence is not carefully considered, today's avalanche of writing in the Latter-day Saint cultural community will mix new ages of information and misinformation.

The answer is to have more awareness of what makes firsthand sources, more determination to gather all major ones, and more care in judging sources fairly on the basis of their broad agreements. The answer is also more author awareness of challenging Christian ethics. In my own private and professional life, I find these among Christ's most sobering words:

> But I say unto you, That every idle word that men shall speak, they shall give account thereof in the day of judgment. For by thy words thou shalt be justified, and by thy words thou shalt be condemned. (Matthew 12:36–37)

....

NOTES

1. See Richard Lloyd Anderson, "Paul's Witness to the Early History of Jesus' Ministry," in *The Apostle Paul,* Twenty-third Sidney B. Sperry Symposium, ed. Paul Y. Hoskisson (Salt Lake City: Deseret Book, 1994), 9, 31 n. 20.

2. See ibid., 4–8, for a survey of current theory that the Gospels were written by anonymous editors selecting stories about Christ that had already grown in the telling. As is known from current publicity, the Jesus Seminar group estimates a majority of information in the Gospels is not historically reliable. More conservative scholars throw considerable doubt on Christ's life and teachings in the Gospels. For instance, see Joseph A. Fitzmyer, *A Christological Catechism: New Testament Answers,* rev. ed. (New York: Paulist Press, 1991), 25: "The evangelists picked up traditional material and fashioned it into their accounts as they saw fit, and not necessarily with factual accuracy."

3. See Richard Lloyd Anderson, "The Second Witness of Priesthood Restoration," *Improvement Era,* September 1968, 15–24, with corrections that the priesthood restoration part of the Prophet's official history was written in 1838 or 1839 (15), and Oliver's patriarchal blessing book descriptions were written in 1835 instead of 1833 (20).

4. See Richard Lloyd Anderson, *Investigating the Book of Mormon Witnesses,* corrected reprint (Salt Lake City: Deseret Book, 1989).

5. Law's dissent and actions are recorded in his Nauvoo record, reprinted in Lyndon W. Cook, *William Law* (Orem, Utah: Grandin Book Company, 1994), 37–38, 54–55. For the group's Nauvoo label as the "Reformed Church," see Richard Lloyd Anderson, "Joseph Smith's Final Self-Appraisal," in *The Prophet Joseph Smith: Essays on the Life and Mission of Joseph Smith,* ed. Larry C. Porter and Susan Easton Black (Salt Lake City: Deseret Book, 1988), 322, n. 9.

6. Fawn M. Brodie, *No Man Knows My History,* 2d ed. (New York: Alfred A. Knopf, 1971), vii.

7. Afternoon discourse, April 7, 1844, William Clayton report, in *The Words of Joseph Smith,* ed. Andrew F. Ehat and Lyndon W. Cook (Provo, Utah: BYU Religious Studies Center, 1980), 356. Quotations of Joseph Smith and his contemporaries in this article are conservatively edited to standardize spelling, punctuation, and capitalization.

8. Afternoon discourse, April 7, 1844, Thomas Bullock report, in Ehat and Cook, 355.

9. Afternoon discourse, April 7, 1844, Joseph Smith diary entry by Willard Richards, in Ehat and Cook, 343.

10. Afternoon discourse, October 9, 1843, *Times and Seasons*, ed. John Taylor (Nauvoo, 1843), 4:331; also in Ehat and Cook, 253. Cf. Ehat and Cook, 254, for the equivalent thought in the official Richards diary.

11. Discourse, May 12, 1844, Thomas Bullock report, in Ehat and Cook, 369.

12. Morning discourse, June 16, 1844, Thomas Bullock report, in Ehat and Cook, 382. For the significance of the sermon, see Anderson, "Joseph Smith's Final Self-Appraisal," in Porter and Black.

13. Joseph Smith to Emma Smith, between 8:20 and 9:40 A.M., June 27, 1844, Carthage Jail, in *The Personal Writings of Joseph Smith*, comp. Dean C. Jessee (Salt Lake City: Deseret Book, 1984), 611.

14. William Clayton journal, June 24, 1844, in Richard Lloyd Anderson, "Joseph Smith's Prophecies of Martyrdom," in *A Sesquicentennial Look at Church History*, Sidney B. Sperry Symposium, January 26, 1980 (Provo, Utah: Religious Instruction, Brigham Young University, 1980), 10.

15. Brodie, 392.

16. Ibid.

17. Allen J. Stout autobiography, text following the original held by LDS Church Archives.

18. T. B. H. Stenhouse, *The Rocky Mountain Saints* (New York: D. Appleton and Company, 1873), 164 n.

19. John Taylor, "The Martyrdom of Joseph Smith," in Richard F. Burton, *The City of the Saints*, ed. Fawn M. Brodie (New York: Alfred A. Knopf, 1963), 614. Burton tells of visiting John Taylor in 1860 and "receiving from the apostle a manuscript account" of the martyrdom, which was printed "in its integrity." Quotations from Brodie's reprint agree with Burton's original 1861 edition and with Taylor's shorter recollection, found in *History of the Church of Jesus Christ of Latter-day Saints*, 7 vols., ed. B. H. Roberts (Salt Lake City: Deseret Book, 1976), 7:99–100.

20. John Taylor, Carthage Jail Memoirs, August 23, 1856, 45–46, LDS Church Archives ms.

21. Office of Salt Lake County Attorney, *Mark Hofmann Interviews* (North Salt Lake City: A.I.S.I. Publishers, 1987), 2:393. See also 2:390, where Hofmann remembered consulting Donna Hill's book, *Joseph Smith, the First Mormon* (Garden City, New York: Doubleday, 1977). However, Hill, 412 and 491 n. 16, cites only Brodie, *No Man Knows My History*, 392 n., where the Stenhouse story that Hofmann remembered seeing in a Joseph Smith biography appears.

22. George J. Throckmorton, "A Forensic Analysis of Twenty-one Hofmann Documents," in Linda Sillitoe and Allen D. Roberts, *Salamander: The Story of the Mormon Forgery Murders* (Salt Lake City: Signature Books, 1988), 547–48.

23. D. Michael Quinn, *The Mormon Hierarchy: Origins of Power* (Salt Lake City: Signature Books, 1994), 141.

24. Dan Jones, "The Martyrdom of Joseph Smith and His Brother Hyrum," a component of Jones's 1847 Welsh compilation, *History of the Latter-day Saints*,

translated by Ronald Dennis, in *BYU Studies* 24 (Winter 1984): 91, with Jones's 1855 recollection (103) that Joseph's letter was addressed to attorney Browning at Quincy. For the letter, which asked for "your professional services" for the coming treason hearing, see Jessee, 612.

25. Quinn, 179.

26. *History of the Church*, 7:270–71, with corresponding entries in the Brigham Young journal; *Times and Seasons* 6 (Jan. 15, 1845): 780–81.

27. Clayton entries are transcribed in Andrew F. Ehat, "'It Seems Like Heaven Began on Earth': Joseph Smith and the Constitution of the Kingdom of God," *BYU Studies* 20 (Spring 1980): 269, 271.

28. See the Kimball entries in Stan Kimball, *On the Potter's Wheel: The Diaries of Heber C. Kimball* (Salt Lake City: Signature Books, 1987), 164, for setting apart on April 20 and departure April 23, 1845, the latter date postponed a day in *History of the Church* 7:401. The entry in *History of the Church* 7:437 about Dunham's death is based on the Brigham Young journal for Sept. 1, 1845, which reports "a letter announcing the death of Bro. Jonathan Dunham, which to[ok] place the 28th of July a little before daylight at the house of Joseph Rogers, Newton Co., Mo." According to Clayton's journal of Sept. 1 and 9, 1845, Daniel Spencer was the one who brought the letter—he had found Dana and reported that Dunham "died of a fever." These contemporary reports to Church authorities contradict a later story that Quinn quotes and prefers, citing the Seymour B. Young diary for May 23, 1903, which reported Oliver B. Huntington's version—that Dunham was despondent over the martyrdom and "'persuaded a friendly Indian' (Dana) 'to kill and bury him'" (Quinn, 180, 404, n. 188). Dunham's early death no doubt contributed to curiosity and mythology about him.

Chapter 17

Fides Quaerens Intellectum
The Scholar as Disciple

Stephen D. Ricks
*Associate Dean of General Education and Honors, Professor of Hebrew
and Semitic Languages, Brigham Young University
Chairman of the Board, Foundation for Ancient Research
and Mormon Studies*

Half a lifetime ago, as an eager undergraduate at Brigham Young University, I volunteered my services as an aide to the university's student vice-president of academics. One of our areas of responsibility was the "Last Lecture" series, where invited speakers would present addresses as though they were the final lectures they would give. Topics of these lectures were remarkably uniform: Zion, discipleship, saintliness. In view of a recent "significant life event," in which my life was providentially spared, my contribution to this volume is much like a "Last Lecture": an appeal to discipleship coupled with scholarship, an affirmation of belief seeking a context, of "faith seeking reason" (Latin: *fides quaerens intellectum*).

What is the role of the disciple-scholar? To provide the historical context for understanding the faith, to furnish a backdrop for further discussion. Writing about C. S. Lewis, Austin Farrer noted: "Though argument does not create conviction, the lack of it destroys belief. What seems to be proved may not be embraced; but what no one shows the ability to defend is quickly abandoned. Rational argument does not create belief, but it maintains a climate in which belief may flourish."[1] The glorious burden of the disciple-scholar is *fides quaerens intellectum*, faith seeking—and finding—"a reason of the hope that is in [us]" (1 Peter 3:15).

This volume was proposed as a collection of "testimonies of scholars." Why not "testimonies of intellectuals"? After all, are we who engage in the adventure of ideas, who live the life of the mind, not "intellectuals"? Perhaps, but perhaps not. A writer for the *Salt Lake Tribune* quoted one LDS writer who self-assuredly claimed that "the LDS intellectual community is almost unanimously outraged at the censure of some of its own."[2] But as BYU professor Ralph Hancock states, "Mormon 'intellectuals' . . . are those who are embarrassed by the Church's resistance to what they regard as progressive trends in the larger society." Further, Hancock points out, this "intellectual" is a foster child of Enlightenment philosophies: "This new intellectual ambition, characterized in the philosophical and social movement known as the 'Enlightenment,' discarded the time-honored belief that man is subject to law ordained by a source higher than his own understanding."[3] While the "intellectuals" define themselves into an informal community, others "head for the exits." A well-known Latter-day Saint writer, addressing a group of freshman students in BYU's Honors Program, insightfully stated that the "intellectuals" who were recently disciplined were not "the smartest, just the proudest."[4] Scholarly research should be done with insight and care, but also with humility and a sense of humor. At the crossroads of mind and spirit, the path of discipleship should be followed. Adventurousness in the realms of mind is not an invitation to adventurism.

In my green and zealous youth, I developed a passion for understanding languages and history. I wanted desperately to learn Latin, but was obliged to wait until my eighth year in school to begin. Before entering the university as a freshman, I started studying classical Greek at the University of California at Berkeley, only a few blocks away from my high school. My mind was set on fire by reading some of the works of Hugh Nibley (who has remained a profound influence in my life), including *Lehi in the Desert* and *The*

World and the Prophets. In the former volume, Nibley outlines and demonstrates an ancient Near Eastern setting for the Book of Mormon. In the latter, he revisits the setting of the early Christian church and shows how the doctrines of the Restoration are redolent of the first Christian teachings. If time has vindicated the prophets (the original popular title of Nibley's Sunday evening presentations on KSL radio), it has also vindicated Nibley's thesis in a number of different and important ways.

In what follows, I contrast the teachings of normative Christianity with doctrines of the Restoration and compare them with the teachings of the ancient Church. My colleague Daniel Peterson and I addressed some of these issues—the doctrine of the Trinity, the belief in anthropomorphism, teachings on human deification, the doctrine of creation and belief in prophets—in a book about how anti-Mormons play word games to attack Latter-day Saints.[5] These concepts also form the basis of a longer forthcoming study on the relationship between teachings of the restored Church and the doctrines of ancient Christianity.

Trinitarianism

Traditional Christianity's belief in the Trinity is summarized in the first part of the Nicene Creed:

> We believe in one God, the Father almighty, maker of all things visible and invisible;
> And in one Lord, Jesus Christ, the Son of God, begotten from the Father, only-begotten, that is, from the substance of the Father, God from God, light from light, true God from true God, begotten not made, of one substance with the Father, through Whom all things came into being, . . .
> And in the Holy Spirit.[6]

By contrast, Joseph Smith expressed the Restoration's radical departure from normative Christianity's doctrine of the Trinity in his history: "I saw two Personages, whose brightness and glory defy all description, standing above me in the air" (Joseph Smith–History 1:17).

According to biblical commentator J. R. Dummelow,

> although the exact theological definition of the doctrine of the Trinity was the result of a long process of development, which was not com-

plete till the fifth century or even later, the doctrine itself underlies the whole New Testament, which everywhere attributes divinity to the Father, the Son, and the Spirit, and assigns to them distinct functions in the economy of human redemption.[7]

Many of the early church fathers—including Justin Martyr, Clement of Alexandria, and Hippolytus—held views that the Father and the Son were separate and equally divine.[8] The period of transition from a belief in three separate and equal deities to orthodox trinitarianism was long and painful. In the view of Maurice Wiles, Dean of Clare College, Cambridge:

> To generations of Christians the description of the Son as "of one substance" with the Father has served as a joyous affirmation of the faith in a creed sung at one of the highest moments of Christian worship. Yet that is very far from being the way in which it found entrance into the vocabulary of Christian doctrine. Rather, it was admitted with reluctance as being the only available means of excluding Arianism.[9] [Arianism was a heretical Christian movement named after the Alexandrian priest Arius, who maintained that Christ was of like substance (Greek: *homoiousios*) with the Father and subordinate to him.]

Anthropomorphism

Related to the doctrine of the Trinity are the concepts of anthropomorphism and anthropopathism—the teachings that Deity is endowed with parts (anthropo*morph*ism) and passions (anthropo*path*ism) similar to those of man. In contrast to the view of historical Christianity, the Doctrine and Covenants asserts that "the Father has a body of flesh and bones as tangible as man's; the Son also; but the Holy Ghost has not a body of flesh and bones, but is a personage of Spirit. Were it not so, the Holy Ghost could not dwell in us" (D&C 130:22).

In fact, the early Christians believed in a corporeal deity, as the German church historian Adolf Harnack notes: "God was naturally conceived and represented as corporeal by uncultured Christians, though not by these alone, as the later controversies prove (*e.g.*, Orig[en] contra Melito; see also Tertull[ian] De Anima)."[10]

The church father Melito also accepted an embodied God, which Origen notes with some dismay.[11] Origen and Augustine reluctantly admit that before Platonic thought was introduced to Christianity, belief in a corporeal God was widespread. Origen wrote, "I am aware that there are some who will try to maintain that even according to our scriptures God has a body," and they had maintained it for generations before his own time.[12] Christianity, made "finer and nobler" with a Platonic overlay, would brook no such anthropomorphic crudities (anthropomorphism, by the way, is generally modified with adjectives such as *crude, crass, vulgar,* and *primitive*). The result of Origen's "rigorous investigation" was that Deity is incorporeal. His conclusions permit his critique of the Platonist Celsus's second-century attack on Christianity. In Celsus's view, in comparison with the assumptions of Plato's philosophical theology, the corporeal Deity of Christianity was found wanting. Seven decades later, when Origen responded to Celsus (whose Platonic assumptions he had accepted), rather than defend Christianity's anthropomorphic God, he claimed that no one else he knew believed it, either.   ·

Augustine, the man most deeply influenced by Platonism, felt himself nearly convinced by arguments for the corporeality of Deity until, "under the influence of Bishop Ambrose, he became acquainted with Latin translations of Platonist writings and with the possibility of God's being a purely 'spiritual,' i.e., totally immaterial, invisible and incorporeal being."[13] Greatly relieved that this "stumbling block" to his faith was now removed, Augustine accepted baptism in A.D. 386, at age thirty-two. But with the conversion of Augustine the hinge of fate had turned, with disastrous consequences for the development of Christian doctrine. Augustine represented the reconciliation of Classical Antiquity and Christianity.[14] In fact, however, this "reconciliation" meant the refraction of the doctrines of earliest Christianity through the distorting lens of Platonism— Christianity had thus been Platonized. Thereafter, nothing was to be the same again.

While the church accepted and incorporated Augustine's teachings with relief, they were a cause of distress to individual Christians. Typical of this was the experience of the fourth-century Christian monk Abba Sarapion. According to John Cassian, Abba Sarapion believed God to be like a man; since Adam was created in his image, he pictured an embodied God as he prayed. When the deacon

Photinus visited, he was asked concerning the teaching that Adam was created in the image of God. Photinus replied by saying that this was to be interpreted "spiritually" and not "literally" (*"non secundum humilem litterae sonum, sed spiritualiter"*). Sarapion was eventually persuaded to give up imagining an anthropomorphic Deity during his devotions. Yet he was devastated. Sarapion exclaimed despairingly that "they have taken my God from me, and I have now none to behold, and whom to worship and address I know not."[15]

Human Deification: Theopoiesis

Shortly before Joseph Smith introduced him to the doctrine of human deification in Nauvoo, a verse couplet came to Lorenzo Snow's mind intimating this doctrine:

> *As man is now, God once was,*
> *As God is now, man may become.*

Teachings in the Doctrine and Covenants join celestial marriage with deification: Abraham, Isaac, and Jacob "have entered into their exaltation, according to the promises, and sit upon thrones, and are not angels but are gods" (D&C 132:37). Further, at the end of his life Joseph "seems to have regarded himself as revealing a wonderful mystery" in teaching that God was once a man:[16] "God himself was once as we are now, and is an exalted man, and sits enthroned in yonder heavens! That is the great secret. . . . We have imagined and supposed that God was God from all eternity. I will refute that idea, and take away the veil, so that you may see."[17] No other teaching of the Restoration has been more repugnant to normative Christianity than the belief that man can attain to God's glory. And yet it is richly attested in earliest Christianity. Christ taught his disciples in the Sermon on the Mount, "Be ye therefore perfect, even as your Father which is in heaven is perfect" (Matthew 5:48). "The Spirit itself beareth witness with our spirit," Paul wrote to the Romans, "that we are the children of God: And if children, then heirs; heirs of God, and joint-heirs with Christ; if so be that we suffer with him, that we may be also glorified together" (Romans 8:16–17). Irenaeus (d. A.D. 180) wrote, "For we cast blame upon Him, because we have not been made gods from the beginning, but at first merely men, then at length gods."[18] In the view of Clement of Alexandria, who died in A.D. 215, "By thus receiving the Lord's power, the soul studies to be God."[19] The idea of deification is vital to Athanasius.[20] According to the German Protestant church historian Ernst Benz:

> One can think what one wants of this doctrine of progressive deifi-
> cation, but one thing is certain: with this anthropology Joseph Smith
> is closer to the view of man held by the Ancient Church than the pre-
> cursors of the Augustinian doctrine of original sin were, who consid-
> ered the thought of such a substantial connection between God and
> man as *the* heresy, par excellence.[21]

Creation Ex Nihilo

The teaching of normative Christianity affirms creation *ex nihilo*. By implication, the Hebrew verb *bārā'* refers to *ex nihilo* creation as well. Not so the teachings of the Restoration. The Doctrine and Covenants affirms that "the elements are eternal" (D&C 93:33). Joseph Smith, in his sermon at the funeral of King Follett, stated:

> You ask the learned doctors why they say the world was made out
> of nothing; and they will answer, "Doesn't the Bible say He *created*
> the world?" And they infer, from the word create, that it must have
> been made out of nothing. Now, the word create came from the word
> *baurau* which does not mean to create out of nothing; it means to
> organize; the same as a man would organize materials and build a
> ship. Hence, we infer that God had materials to organize the world
> out of chaos—chaotic matter, which is element, and in which dwells
> all the glory. Element had an existence from the time he had. The
> pure principles of element are principles which can never be
> destroyed; they may be organized and re-organized, but not
> destroyed. They had no beginning, and can have no end.[22]

The doctrine of *creatio ex nihilo* was not so in the beginning of Christianity. According to Jonathan Goldstein, "medieval Jewish thinkers . . . held that the account of creation in Genesis could be interpreted to mean that God created from pre-existing formless matter, and ancient Jewish texts state that he did so."[23] Indeed, again according to Goldstein, "We have to wait until the second half of the second century to find unambiguous Christian statements of creation *ex nihilo*."[24] In his history of the Christian teaching concerning *ex nihilo* creation, Gerhard May notes with some surprise (and dismay) that this doctrine was introduced only at the end of the second century, and only then by the Gnostic Basilides.[25] At root, this orthodox Christian doctrine may have been a Gnostic heresy! Indeed, in recent years many scholars have begun reassessing their position on *ex nihilo* creation. "The verb *br'* used in the very first sentence of the creation story," states Assyriologist Shalom M. Paul, "does not imply, as most traditional commentators believed, *creatio ex nihilo*, a concept that first appears in II Maccabees 7:28, but denotes, as it does throughout the Bible, a divine activity that is effortlessly effected."[26]

Prophets

In explaining "why prophecy ceased," a distinguished Jewish scholar recently showed that the rabbis claimed that prophecy ended with Malachi at the close of the Old Testament. This claim was intended to, first, undercut Christian claims to prophetic authority and, second, support the claims to authority by the rabbis themselves.[27] The fate of the early church was the same: when the prophets disappeared after the apostolic era, the prophetic office was placed "under restraint" by the religious authorities (the famous *Amt/Geist* "Office/Spirit" controversy in the early church), and the mantle was transferred to the schools—the "driving engines of the apostasy"—which Platonized Christianity. The prophets succumbed, and self-perpetuating schools rose, insisting that students be trained in *their* philosophical theology to gain their seal of approval. Augustine is an outstanding example of the perils that result from the loss of the prophets, as Nibley points out:

> We couldn't ask for a better case to prove it than that of St. Augustine, precisely because he is such a good and great man. The better man he is, the better he illustrates the point, which is that *no* man, no matter how good, wise, hard-working, devoted, and well-educated he may be, can give us certainty without revelation. In Father Bligh's opinion, time has not vindicated Augustine's opinions. It has shown that we can trust only the prophets.[28]

In the final analysis, the loss of the prophets was truly fateful for the ancient Church. Without prophets—without authority—the gates were unbolted and thrown open to the whirlwinds of scholarly second-guessing and one-upsmanship. Without prophets, scholars assumed for themselves the mantle of authority, creating a trajectory of their own choosing. The Protestant Reformation was a revolution in church organization and in the matter of personal accountability and "grace," but nothing changed—even to the present—in the Reformation's views of the doctrines I have just discussed. Recapturing the teachings of the earliest church required a restoration, not a reformation.

Joseph Smith's visions shattered the distorting lens of Platonized Christianity and again blazed the trail to the beginnings of the Church in the meridian of time. The LDS disciple-scholar gifted with such faith *(fides)* and endowed with such insights is to seek—and share—an understanding *(quaerens intellectum)*, a reason, a link, a context for what was so in the beginning: to seek—and find—"a reason of the hope that is in [us]" (1 Peter 3:15).

NOTES

1. Austin Farrer, "The Christian Apologist," in *Light on C. S. Lewis,* ed. Jocelyn Gibb (New York: Harcourt, Brace & World, 1965), 26.

2. Peggy Fletcher Stack in *Salt Lake Tribune,* September 1993; cited by Ralph C. Hancock in "What Is a 'Mormon Intellectual?'" *This People* (Fall 1994): 21.

3. Ibid., 23, 25.

4. Orson Scott Card, an address delivered in the spring of 1994.

5. Daniel C. Peterson and Stephen D. Ricks, *Offenders for a Word* (Salt Lake City: Aspen Books, 1992).

6. Cited by J. N. D. Kelly, *Early Christian Creeds* (New York: David McKay Company, 1972), 215–16.

7. *Commentary on the Holy Bible,* ed. J. R. Dummelow (New York: Macmillan, 1927), cxiii.

8. Justo L. Gonzales, *A History of Christian Thought* (Nashville: Abingdon Press, 1970), 1:108, 205–6, 239–40; W. H. C. Frend, *Martyrdom and Persecution in the Early Church* (Grand Rapids, Michigan: Baker, 1981), 358, 376.

9. Maurice Wiles, *The Making of Christian Doctrine* (Cambridge: Cambridge University Press, 1967), 33.

10. Adolf von Harnack, *History of Dogma* (New York: Dover, 1961), 1:180 n. 1.

11. Origen, *Selecta in Genesim,* in J. P. Migne, *Patrologiae Graecae* (Paris: Garnier, 1857–66), 12:94; cf. Origen, *Commentarius in Epistolam b. Pauli ad Romanos,* I, 19, in *Patrologiae Graecae* 14:870–71.

12. Origen, *De Principiis* II, 4, 3.

13. David L. Paulsen, "Early Christian Belief in a Corporeal Deity: Origen and Augustine as Reluctant Witnesses," *Harvard Theological Review* 83, no. 2 (April 1990): 115.

14. Charles Norris Cochrane, *Christianity and Classical Culture: A Study of Thought and Action from Augustus to Augustine* (New York: Oxford University Press, 1977), 376–84.

15. Cited in "The Anthropomorphites in the Egyptian Desert," in Georges Florovsky, *Aspects of Church History*, vol. 4 of *Collected Works of Georges Florovsky* (Belmont, Massachusetts: Nordland, 1975), 89, 96, cited in Paulsen, 116.

16. Peterson and Ricks, *Offenders for a Word*, 89.

17. *Teachings of the Prophet Joseph Smith*, comp. Joseph Fielding Smith (Salt Lake City: Deseret Book, 1961), 345.

18. Irenaeus, *Against Heresies* IV, 38, 4, in *The Ante-Nicene Fathers*, ed. Alexander Roberts and James Donaldson (Grand Rapids, Michigan: Eerdmans, 1981), 1:522.

19. Clement of Alexandria, *The Stromata*, VI, 14, in *The Ante-Nicene Fathers*, 2:506; cf. Philip L. Barlow, "Unorthodox Orthodoxy: The Idea of Deification in Christian History," *Sunstone* 8 (September–October 1983): 13–18.

20. Keith Norman, "Deification: The Content of Athanasian Soteriology" (Ph.D. dissertation, Duke University, 1980), 77–106.

21. Ernst W. Benz, "Imago Dei: Man in the Image of God," in *Reflections on Mormonism: Judaeo-Christian Parallels*, ed. Truman G. Madsen (Provo, Utah: BYU Religious Studies Center, 1978), 215–16.

22. Joseph Smith, "King Follett Discourse," in *Teachings of the Prophet Joseph Smith*, 350–52.

23. Jonathan Goldstein, "The Origins of the Doctrine of Creation Ex Nihilo," *Journal of Jewish Studies* 35 (1984): 127.

24. Ibid., 132.

25. Gerhard May, *Schöpfung aus dem Nichts: Die Entstehung der Lehre von der Creatio Ex Nihilo* (New York: Walter de Gruyter, 1978), 53–55.

26. Shalom M. Paul, "Creation and Cosmogony in the Bible," *Encyclopaedia Judaica* (Jerusalem: Encyclopaedia Judaica, 1972), 5:1059.

27. Frederick E. Greenspahn, "Why Prophecy Ceased," *Journal of Biblical Literature* 108, no. 1 (Spring 1989): 37–49.

28. Hugh W. Nibley, *The World and the Prophets* (Salt Lake City: Deseret Book and FARMS, 1987), 97; Father John Bligh is a learned Jesuit theologian.

CHAPTER 18

QUESTIONS, BUT NO DOUBTS

RICHARD NEITZEL HOLZAPFEL
Assistant Professor of Church History and Doctrine,
   Brigham Young University

DURING MY graduate school experience, I met a bright and articulate Christian fundamentalist who assumed that since I was an active
Latter-day Saint, I was neither a committed disciple of the *real* Jesus
nor a believer that the Bible was the word of God. As we approached
the end of our studies together she made an interesting observation
and asked an important question. Although I do not remember her
exact words on that occasion, this is the substance:

"When I started my graduate work, I firmly believed in the infallibility and inerrancy of the Bible. Now, after several years of study, I
no longer believe in the Bible and have stopped attending my church.
You, however, are still committed to your faith and still believe in the
inspiration of scripture. How is that possible after all you have been
exposed to in graduate school?"

I have thought about this situation and similar circumstances
many times during the past few years. On such occasions, I often
recall what Peter told the early Christian Saints: "Be ready always to
give an answer to every man that asketh you a reason of the hope that
is in you with meekness and fear" (1 Peter 3:15). I have found "a reason" for the hope that is in me and for why I continue to be a committed disciple after years of study and thought.

I observed friends and classmates coming to terms with their own beliefs and commitments during the strenuous period of graduate school. The transition to a different understanding of the scriptures was a time of uncertainty and often a period of severe personal anguish for them. It affected not only their own lives but the lives of loved ones and friends as well. As they attempted to find a new way of understanding their own faith and tradition, many came to feel that religious fundamentalism was deeply inadequate, while others gave up religion altogether.

Normally, people do not become fundamentalists—and by fundamentalists I mean those who hold the Bible to be both infallible and inerrant—if they are already well informed about scripture, doctrine, and history. While fundamentalists are not necessarily unintelligent or ill informed, people characteristically become fundamentalists before they know much about scripture, doctrine, or history.

Graduate school is not only a rigorous experience but also an intellectual adventure. For fundamentalists, graduate studies can have devastating results. Their fundamentalism usually arises from the practice of reading single texts in isolation from context. In fundamentalism, more than in any other tradition, the warning of 2 Peter is disregarded and disobeyed: "No prophecy of the scripture is of any private interpretation. For the prophecy came not in old time by the will of man: but holy men of God spake as they were moved by the Holy Ghost" (2 Peter 1:20–21).

My response to the question of why I still have hope is that I escaped fundamentalism long before entering graduate school. I did not believe in the infallibility or inerrancy of the Bible. My faith in its value and inspiration was never under attack during my studies because I viewed the text in a different way than my fundamentalist friends did. Therefore, I approach study without fear and view my efforts in this field as ultimately in harmony with what I believe the gospel demands of disciples.

The Place of Academic Inquiry

I have come to believe that the acquisition of the simplest of academic tools is necessary for a mature understanding of the message of the gospel. That is not to say, however, that individuals who cannot read or write are somehow unable to develop a deep and committed discipleship. I know of such cases and believe that salvation comes to all of God's children without a price (including the price of an educational degree). Yet, in the context of my world, an environment where access to education is available, I believe the Lord expects me to progress—not only by learning to read and write, but also by thinking clearly and deeply.

In a certain and limited sense, academic training is by and large the acquisition of tools. Whether we learn to read and write English so we can read the Book of Mormon or learn to read Hebrew and Greek so we can read the Bible, we are acquiring proficiency in a language—a tool. Tools are not inherently good or bad; how one uses them is what matters.

For example, when the 1830 Book of Mormon was published, it was printed on a press at E. B. Grandin's print shop on Palmyra's Main Street. The press was a tool to make the translation available to the public. That same printing press was used at the same time to publish a Palmyra weekly entitled *The Reflector.* In this newspaper, Abner Cole published pirated extracts of the Book of Mormon and, in some cases, criticism of the work. Cole worked on the paper on Sundays when the press was free. The point is that the same tool was used in publishing both the Book of Mormon and the pirated extracts and criticisms of the work. Each individual used this tool for his own purpose.

Likewise, academic training is simply the acquisition of scholarly tools. Almost everyone in North America has learned how to use some tools of scholarship. The very act of learning to read, write, and think is the basis of all academic training. Those who write critically of the foundation of Christianity or modern Mormonism use the same tools as those who write with an eye of faith about Jesus of Nazareth and Joseph Smith.

However, academic pursuit alone is insufficient to lead one to a testimony of God's power and interest in us. Even the study of sacred and inspired scripture will leave us spiritually empty, emotionally hollow, and doctrinally unsound unless we draw inspiration and strength from the Author of holy scripture. I am reminded that British social critic Malcolm Muggeridge once said: "Future historians . . . are likely to conclude that the more we knew about Jesus the less we knew him, and the more precisely his words were translated the less we understood or heeded them."[1]

In brief, academic tools have a role in our pursuit of eternal truth—but not a dominant one. Sheer historical research can, in fact, turn out to be a way of avoiding the real drama and the essential issues raised by the gospel of Jesus Christ. The question we all face is "Am I willing to put my whole life with all its unanswered questions and hopes into the hands of the resurrected Christ?" Any academic research that prevents this challenge from being heard is both playing false to the nature of the message of the living Christ and substituting scholarly idols for the two important questions Jesus asks each of us: "What seek ye?" and "Lovest thou me?" (John 1:38; 21:15).

The scriptures remind us sharply that we are not saved by academic pursuit alone. Yet the scriptures and the prophets encourage us to consider our faith thoughtfully through the acquisition of academic tools. I recognize the constant tension that exists between finding Jesus through academic study and finding him through service to the least, the last, and the lost—through service to the world's poor; through worship with the Saints of God; and, more important, through personal expressions of worship such as fasting and prayer.

Joseph Smith's Example

I have carefully studied the life of Joseph Smith, who both relied upon inspiration from the Lord and dedicated himself to serious and thoughtful study. No one was more determined to expand his vision by study than the Prophet. While exposed to incredible outpourings of the Spirit, he nevertheless spent time and money in an effort to learn Hebrew and German so he could read the scriptures in languages he felt could help him. Joseph records: "My soul delights in reading the word of the Lord in the original, and I am determined to pursue the study of the languages, until I shall become master of them, if I am permitted to live long enough."[2] Joseph Smith demonstrated the necessary balance between seeking the Lord through private, personal experiences with God and seeking the Lord through study.

The Church follows Joseph Smith's lead as we expand our literacy program so all Saints may benefit from the acquisition of the simplest of academic tools—reading and writing. At our institutions of learning (including seminaries and institutes of religion), we use the latest tools to teach students the scriptures. We want students not only to feel but also to think about the gospel they have received. Our missionaries are exposed to the very latest academic tools to acquire a proficiency in foreign languages; teachers who have been well trained in their fields of study are employed to help prepare these ambassadors to preach the gospel to the world. The stream of thoughtful talks, discourses, essays, and books by Church leaders suggests a commitment to the proposition that one's testimony can be strengthened and confirmed by study as well as by faith.

I begin my religious education classes at the university with a statement something like this: "I want you to know that there is nothing wrong in saying 'I do not know the answer.' I will try to answer your questions honestly and will, on occasion say, 'I do not know.' I have many questions myself about the glorious gospel we have received, but I have no doubts about the message of hope in Christ and the trust in the prophetic leadership of the Church."

I found a story in Camilla Eyring Kimball's biography that has been very useful to me in dealing with unanswered questions:

> Camilla had a philosophy about religious problems that helped her children. She said that when things troubled her, she put them on the shelf; later when she looked at them again, some were answered, some seemed no longer important, and some needed to go back on the shelf for another time.[3]

We cannot answer all the questions of life, let alone academic issues raised in the debate of the so-called marketplace of ideas. We must trust in the Lord with a mature faith that someday we will know the answers to the right questions. Yet, from time to time, we find an answer to a burning question that we may have put on the shelf earlier. These answers confirm our faith and our appreciation for the profound nature of the gospel.

One question I was able to answer by putting it on the shelf for a while concerned boat building in the ancient world. During my graduate training, I took courses in ancient history, including a seminar dealing with Mediterranean Sea commerce. Although the emphasis in this field has been, for the most part, on the economic and political aspects of ancient commerce, during the past twenty years scholars have become increasingly interested in the ships themselves.

Although many cargo ships sailed the ancient Mediterranean for thousands of years, underwater archaeologists have only recently discovered and excavated their remains. A major breakthrough in understanding the ancient art of building ships came when a Greek merchant ship was discovered in 1967 off the north coast of Cyprus, near the small town of Kyrenia.[4]

The shipbuilders of the *Kyrenia* used hull-first construction—a labor- and material-intensive construction technique. The keel was laid first, but instead of adding the frames next, as in modern wooden shipbuilding, the builders added hull planks. These planks were held together by mortise-and-tenon joints. The frames were then added as buttresses only after the hull was completed. The contents of the cargo indicate that the ship may have sailed from Samos to Nisiros to Rhodes before being sunk by pirates around 300 B.C.

With the information gleaned from this important discovery, George F. Bass was able to piece together the story of shipbuilding practices in the Mediterranean Sea. He had already reconstructed another ship, this one from the seventh century A.D. It was a merchant ship uncovered near Yassi Ada, Turkey, during the summers of 1961 through 1964.[5] Comparing the Yassi Ada shipwreck with the *Kyrenia,* Bass discovered that both ancient and modern techniques were used to construct the Yassi Ada ship. With their construction techniques, these shipbuilders were laying the groundwork for the eventual emergence of the skeleton-first system of hull construction, the most widely followed method of wooden-hull construction in the world today.

Finally, Bass worked on another Mediterranean shipwreck inside Serce Liman, a natural harbor on the southern Turkish coast opposite Rhodes.[6] The ship is dated from the first half of the eleventh century A.D. and demonstrates the final evolutionary step of modern wooden-ship construction. With a rigid skeleton of frames, the ships from this time period on were stronger than the earlier ships—strong enough to leave the Mediterranean Sea and to cross the oceans for India, Asia, and America.

It did not require much time to understand the implication of the work of these nautical archaeologists: Nephi could not have built a ship strong enough to cross the ocean in 600 B.C. because the techniques necessary for such an undertaking were not available to him. Like most Latter-day Saints, I was aware that attempts had been made to prove that a raft could have made such a trip.[7] Nearly everyone has heard of Thor Heyerdahl's efforts to prove that people could have "floated" to the Western Hemisphere. Yet the evidence from the Mediterranean suggested another interpretation of the data. Because I had no doubts about my foundation—the Book of Mormon is an ancient text—I decided to put this question on the shelf.

Sometime later, I took the question down from my shelf after reading the Book of Mormon and paying closer attention to what the text actually said:

> We did work timbers of curious workmanship. And the Lord did show me from time to time after what manner I should work the timbers of the ship.
>
> Now I, Nephi, did not work the timbers after the manner which was learned by men, neither did I build the ship after the manner of men; but I did build it after the manner which the Lord had shown unto me; wherefore, it was not after the manner of men. (1 Nephi 18:1–2)

Nephi apparently did not use the shipbuilding techniques of his day. He says clearly that the "timbers" were used in a way that was unfamiliar to him and to others who built ships at the time. The ship was, in fact, built according to what the Lord showed Nephi. Modern nautical archaeology appears to confirm the historical setting of this story—no one during this period of history had the knowledge to build a wooden ship strong enough to cross the ocean. The Lord has left us, through Nephi's writings, a significant clue—a precious gem that may now shine and enlighten our appreciation for this marvelous text.

External Evidences

Some may question the need or even the desire to find external evidences for the Book of Mormon—especially using tentative academic tools such as archaeology, as in the case above. Yet readers of the Book of Mormon are exposed to the testimonies of witnesses printed in the front of the book, themselves external evidences. Interestingly enough, the two testimonies are essentially different from one another. The first, signed by three men, is a "spiritual" witness—the witnesses saw an angel and heard a heavenly voice declare the translation was correct. The second testimony, signed by eight men, is a physical witness. The men saw and hefted the plates—no divine voice and no angelic appearance, just the plates.

The New Testament has similar testimony contained in its pages. The witness of Jesus Christ is based on two separate and distinct experiences—the spiritual testimony and the physical testimony. Peter came to know who Jesus really was through the Spirit (see Matthew 16:16–17). The resurrected Lord stood before the disciples on several occasions and, by "infallible proofs," showed himself alive (see Acts 1:3). Some touched him and others saw him eat—physical evidences of the resurrection.

The fact that the Lord has provided both types of witnesses suggests that, in his eyes, we cannot make the choice between spiritual testimony and physical testimony an either/or proposition. Both are valid and essential to his divine purposes. The acquisition of academic tools that may provide a physical witness to our central beliefs through archaeology, linguistic studies, and cultural background is an important part of our testimony.

In this respect, students of the scriptures add their witnesses to those of others who have gained a spiritual witness of the Restoration without the acquisition of academic tools (they may not even know how to read or write). Each witness is valid and essential to the proclamation of the message that God lives, that Jesus is the Christ, that Joseph Smith was a chosen servant of the Lord to bring forth the Book of Mormon, and that we have a divinely appointed leadership today.

I believe, passionately, that I must use every faculty within me—my whole soul, that is, my mind and my heart—to find God, to search out his ways, and to praise and worship him and his Son. My worship then becomes complete as I sing praises to his name, pray and fast, attend to the divinely appointed ordinances in sacred places, and, finally, worship him with my mind through study and contemplation.

Although I still have a shelf full of questions, like Camilla Kimball, I have no doubt that in time all these questions will be answered. On another level, I have no doubt about the foundation of my faith and hope in Christ and the glorious future that awaits his faithful disciples beyond death. Like Paul, I believe that "for now we see through a glass, darkly; but then face to face: now I know in part; but then shall I know even as also I am known" (1 Corinthians 13:12).

NOTES

1. Malcolm Muggeridge, *Jesus: The Man Who Lives* (New York: Harper & Row, 1975), 8.

2. Joseph Smith, *History of the Church of Jesus Christ of Latter-day Saints,* 7 vols. (Salt Lake City: Deseret Book, 1976), 2:396.

3. Caroline Eyring Miner and Edward L. Kimball, *Camilla: A Biography of Camilla Eyring Kimball* (Salt Lake City: Deseret Book, 1980), 110.

4. George F. Bass, *A History of Seafaring Based on Underwater Archaeology* (New York: Walker and Company, 1972), 38–41, 48–52, 62–64, 69.

5. George F. Bass and Frederick H. Van Doorninck, Jr., *Yassi Ada: A Seventh-Century Byzantine Shipwreck* (College Station: Texas A&M University Press, 1982).

6. George F. Bass and Frederick H. van Doorninck, Jr., "An Eleventh Century Shipwreck at Serce Liman, Turkey," *The International Journal of Nautical Archaeology and Underwater Exploration* 7 (1978): 119–32.

7. See also John L. Sorenson, "Transoceanic Crossings," in *The Book of Mormon: First Nephi, The Doctrinal Foundation,* ed. Monte S. Nyman and Charles D. Tate, Jr. (Provo, Utah: BYU Religious Studies Center, 1988), 251–70.

PART 3

FAITH AND THE BOOK OF MORMON

CHAPTER 19

UNLOCKING THE SACRED TEXT

MARILYN ARNOLD
Emeritus Professor of English, Brigham Young University

UNLIKE THE SCIENTIST of faith, who studies the work of the Creator every time he or she enters the laboratory or the field, the English teacher studies the product of the human mind, relentlessly pursuing meaning and delight in the written word. To the onlooker there may seem to be little connection between literary studies and religious faith; but to me there is an almost inseparable bond. In fact, it was not until I began to read sacred texts with the skills I had acquired in studying nonsacred texts that the eyes of my understanding truly began to open. Most assuredly, my training in literary analysis has enhanced my reading of scripture and my testimony of its divine origin.

Of the many hundreds of texts I have read, none has touched me more profoundly than the Book of Mormon. Without question, it is the greatest book I have ever encountered. The near-perfect blend of poetry and truth is, in my view, simply unequaled. I confess, however, that I have not always appreciated its greatness, and for too many years my reading was sporadic and merely dutiful. I knew that the Book of Mormon contained some splendid passages, but as a whole it had not grabbed me and shaken me into a realization of its unparalleled magnificence. Three things transformed the book for me, though it was not I that changed the book, but the book that changed me. The first transforming event was my decision to read the Book of Mormon in earnest, from cover to cover, investing the same concentrated energy that I would accord a complex and masterful literary text. The second transforming event grew out of the first: it was the decisive entrance of the Spirit into my study of the book, and hence into my life, with unprecedented intensity and constancy. The third transforming event also grew out of the first: it was the prayerful desire to experience the great change of heart described by King Benjamin and Alma, to be more than an "active Mormon," to be spiritually born as a child of Christ.

These three events, in concert, permanently transformed my inner life. They implanted in my soul an indescribable love of the Book of Mormon, of the gospel of Jesus Christ, and of his church. At the time this change was occurring, my friends may have recognized the same lengthy frame and the same silly grin they had always known, but I knew I was not the person they had charitably tolerated all those years. It was as if I harbored a sweet secret that I was too shy to talk about. I now wanted desperately to live more purely, to correct my innumerable character flaws, to abandon my sins. What happened to me during that period of intense study, prayer, and self-assessment remains with me still.

Since that time, I have undertaken a yet more concentrated study of the Book of Mormon, and with each reading it almost magically expands to meet my increased ability to comprehend it. Truly, this is no ordinary book, and I am grateful that the practice of literary analysis, though anything but an exact science, has given me useful tools in the study of sacred texts. Then, too, the Book of Mormon has its parallels with good fiction, for both contain narratives that offer insight into human experience. And while fiction is not true in a literal sense, it can most surely be true in an absolute sense. But the Book of Mormon is much more than fiction, for it is factually true as well as philosophically and morally true. The Book of Mormon is more than history, too.

All readers, specialists or not, have much in common, and like most, I am drawn to great texts out of love. Consequently, emotion, positive or negative, to some extent shapes my reading and accompanies my objective responses to the written word. We should not be embarrassed by an emotional response to genuine greatness. The emotion that overwhelms me when I read an exceptional text like the Book of Mormon bears no resemblance to the cheap tears that are the stock in trade of tasteless popular literature. Such tears are induced by shallow notions, stereotypical characters, and shopworn images rather than by truth and artistry. Countless years of studying written texts have, I hope, fixed in me some small ability to distinguish between the good and the bad, the true and the false, the genuine and the spurious, the original and the imitative. When I read a book, I no longer have to ask with Hamlet, "Is this an honest ghost?"

In my experience, the first few pages of a book are critical; if a book is deceitful, its opening pages will betray it. I challenge anyone to apply that test to the Book of Mormon. Can an honest reader of the following lines doubt that Nephi is who he says he is and that he writes what he knows to be absolute truth?

> I, Nephi, having been born of goodly parents, . . . and having seen many afflictions in the course of my days, nevertheless, having been highly favored of the Lord in all my days; yea, having had a great knowledge of the goodness and the mysteries of God, therefore I make a record of my proceedings in my days. . . .
>
> And I know that the record which I make is true; and I make it with mine own hand; and I make it according to my knowledge. (1 Nephi 1:1, 3)

Nephi's forthrightness is apparent in every line. He opens by naming himself, paying homage to his parents and his God, and bearing testimony about his record. Thus, we learn immediately that the narrative voice belongs to someone who is candid, respectful, dutiful, and grateful, someone who is likely to cut a very straight course. No hedging, no circumventing, no embroidering the truth. In fact, the very structure of verse three projects Nephi's sincerity through the use of three sturdy parallel clauses, all beginning with the words "And I" followed by a single syllable verb: "And I know," "and I make," "and I make." That same sincerity is also conveyed through word repetition. The first sentence contains a subordinate clause that introduces the words "I make," words that Nephi deliberately repeats in the two independent clauses that follow. Nephi's prompt self-introduction takes on added significance, too, as we come to realize that throughout the Book of Mormon the Lord and his servants almost invariably announce who they are, while Satan and his servants rarely do. The honest have nothing to hide; the devious have everything to hide. By immediately announcing his identity and fealty, therefore, Nephi serves reliable notice that he is who he says he is and that he intends to prepare a true record.

Although I consider other factors, my preference in approaching a text is to appraise its value by examining the internal evidence the text itself presents. History, biography, critical theory, and literary fashion are all legitimate and interesting doors through which to enter and interpret a piece of literature. But to limit analysis to one or more of those approaches is, I think, to remain in the foyer rather than to enter the living quarters of the work. It is to assess, merely, and never possess. Whatever frustrations the Book of Mormon presents to the historian or the anthropologist, it lends itself particularly well to my brand of close textual reading. In fact, external information about the record's creation and its cultural setting is so sparse that the words on the page are very nearly the reader's only tangible resource. Except for concurrent biblical history and archaeological findings in Mesoamerica, we are largely ignorant of the world that engendered the Book of Mormon.

Coincidentally, because the Book of Mormon arrives with so few cultural trappings, the diligent, spiritually attuned seeker can study and appreciate it with no specialized academic preparation for the task, no extensive historical background, and no external biographical data. Even so, I regard it as a great personal blessing that my formal training is of the sort that adds significantly to my study of the Book of Mormon. Possibly I "see more" because I am trained to see more. Most certainly, the Spirit finds me a readier pupil than I might otherwise have been.

Perhaps I can illustrate briefly how my academic preparation translates into "seeing." Obviously, even inexperienced readers of the Book of Mormon readily perceive the opposition between Nephi and his brothers Laman and Lemuel because the narrative openly and repeatedly alludes to it. But while many readers might overlook the conflict's deeper significance, I see in this wrenching polarization a striking proof of Lehi's powerful discourse on the necessity of opposition in all things. Furthermore, readers might not notice the aptness in the positioning of Lehi's discourse; it is delivered in the patriarchal blessing pronounced upon Jacob, a younger son who has painfully witnessed firsthand the opposition between Nephi and his older brothers. Indeed, Jacob's whole existence has been marked by opposition; I think Lehi wants him to understand that, despite its concomitant pain, opposition makes possible the exercise of agency and is therefore a vital aspect of the plan of salvation.

As if echoing itself, but in much subtler tones, the text also reveals a contrast (though not a conflict) between Nephi and Jacob, thereby creating a kind of benign subtext on the theme of opposition. Although Jacob is gifted in language and solid in his testimony, to me he seems unusually tender, even a bit fragile, in his emotional makeup. Clearly, Jacob is no Nephi, nor need he be, but in a written text, as in life, he can serve as a complementary foil to his physically and spiritually imposing brother. Just who is this Jacob? One of the consummate pleasures of studying literature is the discovery of character. Whereas in real life, the essential person, the inner self, is carefully hidden from public gaze, in literature the very soul of a character can be opened, exposing a multitude of buried thoughts and anxieties. Jacob is a case in point. We often rush past Jacob because his hour on the stage is short and because Nephi quite naturally overshadows his more reticent younger brother. But under scrutiny the text actually reveals more than a little about Jacob.

Although Nephi's narrative is many times the length of Jacob's, we seldom see Nephi's inner self, the individual behind the courageous and faithful son, the undaunted prophet and the mighty leader. As narrator, he selects what will be told, and he chooses not to include his own sermons to his people or much personal musing. A notable exception, of course, is the lovely "psalm" that comprises verses 16–35 of 2 Nephi 4. But even then, Nephi formalizes the expression and distances himself from self-revelation by employing the overtly personal, but rhetorically impersonal, frame of the psalm. Conversely, the textual imprints of Jacob's character, and their replication in the hidden chambers of our own souls, are readily descried by the alert eye.

Any consideration of Jacob must take into account the matter of Nephi's influence. In literary studies, giants like Shakespeare can be seen as massive watersheds of influence, changing what successive writers do ever afterward. As southern fictionist Flannery O'Connor wryly observed, "The presence alone of Faulkner in our midst makes a great difference in what the writer can and cannot permit himself to do. Nobody wants his mule and wagon stalled on the same track the Dixie Limited is roaring down."[1] Nephi is just this sort of irrepressible human locomotive, and Jacob is sure to measure himself against Nephi and his achievement. Jacob himself is dutiful and conscientious in the extreme, but to what extent is that aspect of his character attributable to the presence and the enduring expectations of Nephi? Furthermore, does Nephi's death leave Jacob feeling abandoned and inadequate to the task ahead? More pronounced still is the distinct strain of melancholy that stamps Jacob's character, but it probably derives from another source. Consider this: Jacob was born in the wilderness and transported as a youngster on a long and arduous sea voyage, a voyage filled with terrifying cosmic and family tumult and ending in a strange, seemingly uninhabited land. And unlike his older brothers, who at least had roots and memory in civilized society, Jacob lived under the menace of bitter conflict and imminent annihilation most of his life.

The text does not make an issue of Jacob's suffering, but it provides enough indicators to offer a window into his character. For instance, Lehi shows his awareness of Jacob's situation and nature when he begins Jacob's patriarchal blessing with these words: "And now, Jacob, . . . Thou art my first-born in the days of my tribulation in the wilderness. And behold, in thy childhood thou hast suffered afflictions and much sorrow, because of the rudeness of thy brethren" (2 Nephi 2:1). Earlier, at sea, when Laman's and Lemuel's brutality toward Nephi heaps agony on the heads of Lehi and Sariah, the record notes that "Jacob and Joseph also, being young, having need of much nourishment, were grieved because of the afflictions of their mother" (1 Nephi 18:19).

It appears from the text, too, that conflict and grief have engendered in Jacob an intense empathy toward the suffering of others. Jacob's compassion is particularly evident in an emotional sermon he delivers after Nephi's death, a sermon quite different in tone and content from the earlier one recorded by Nephi (see 2 Nephi 6–10). In the later sermon, although painfully reluctant to harrow the already injured feelings of the women and children in the congregation, Jacob chastises the Nephite men for marital infidelity. Their wives and children, and others too, he declares, have come to hear the word of God, but will instead "have daggers placed to pierce their souls and wound their delicate minds" (Jacob 2:9). Jacob reiterates his concern in verse 35 of chapter 2, where he speaks of the "sobbings" of the broken hearts of the Nephite women and children over their husbands' and fathers' iniquities. Indeed, he says, "many hearts died, pierced with deep wounds."

The sensitivity and compassion I see in Jacob seem almost to spring from the melancholy begotten by exile and isolation. In public, and prior to Nephi's death, Jacob tries to put a positive cast on his people's circumstances, but his statement nonetheless reveals a deep-seated sense of their exile: "Let us . . . not hang down our heads, for we are not cast off; nevertheless, we have been driven out of the land of our inheritance; but we have been led to a better land, for the Lord has made the sea our path, and we are upon an isle of the sea" (2 Nephi 10:20). In private, speaking not to his people but to future generations, an older Jacob does not mask his feelings:

> The time passed away with us, and also our lives passed away like as it were unto us a dream, we being a lonesome and a solemn people, wanderers, cast out from Jerusalem, born in tribulation, in a wilderness, and hated of our brethren, which caused wars and contentions; wherefore, we did mourn out our days. (Jacob 7:26)

To skim that passage and miss its tone of heartbreak, its revelation of Jacob's character and his perception of his circumstances, is to miss a rich opportunity for human understanding. Most certainly, Jacob, like Nephi, paid dearly for his faith. The text also affirms that he was beloved of the Lord, for even when Nephi was alive, Jacob was visited by Christ and by angels. Moreover, Jacob was first among the Nephites to learn—from an angel—that the name of the Holy One of Israel would be *Christ* (see 2 Nephi 10:3). And anyone uninitiated to Jacob's rhetorical gifts need only study in detail the sermon fragment that Nephi elects to copy into his own chronicle.

My point is simply this: The Book of Mormon is an inspired text whose possibilities could not be exhausted in a lifetime of study, much less a lifetime of pulling isolated passages for Sunday lessons and talks. I am particularly blessed to be a student of literary texts, for my academic pursuits have enriched, even prompted, my study of scripture. More than that, the Spirit that sometimes illuminates sacred texts for me also seems to lend insight and discernment to my reading of nonsacred texts. In all, the felicitous merging of these two important strands of my study and my life has immeasurably increased my understanding and appreciation, not only of books, but of the very essence of study and life.

NOTE

1. Flannery O'Connor, *Mystery and Manners: Occasional Prose,* ed. Sally and Robert Fitzgerald (New York: Farrar, Straus & Giroux, 1969), 45.

Chapter 20

Not Merely an Ancient Book

C. Wilfred Griggs
Professor of Ancient Studies, Brigham Young University

Acceptance of the Book of Mormon is a spiritual, not an academic, matter. It is, of course, interesting to look into whatever materials are available from the past, such as documents and archaeological artifacts, to enhance one's understanding of the Book of Mormon, but such things cannot be an adequate substitute for a spiritual witness from God concerning the divine origin and message of the book. This observation is elementary to anyone who compares the limited and changing nature of scholarly activity with the infinite and eternal perspective of God that is transmitted when one is taught by the Holy Ghost.

Many years ago, when I was serving as a young missionary and had just been assigned to a particular city in Alberta, Canada, my companion took me to the home of an elderly member who was a constant source of referrals for future missionary visits. As I became acquainted with that plainspoken and strong-willed sister, I learned that she was a convert to the Church of some twenty years. In response to my request to learn some details of her conversion experience, she related her first encounter with two young missionaries from a church with which she was totally unacquainted. She accepted a book from them, even though she knew nothing of its contents.

Not long afterward, driven by curiosity to know more of the young men and the book they had given her, she opened the book to the first page of the text, which all readers of the Book of Mormon know contains a title, an italicized paragraph of summary material relating to 1 Nephi, and only four and a half verses of the text. It was an unforgettable experience for me to hear her declare that before she had turned that page with its limited amount of textual material, she had received a witness from God that the book was true and that it came from him.

From that time her reading was for a new purpose. She no longer wanted or needed to know if the book was true, but she desired and felt it necessary to learn all she could about the book that she then knew to be heavenly in origin and content. Her testimony had nothing to do with a knowledge of ancient history, languages, or literature, nor was it founded upon an analysis of the internal consistency or doctrinal orthodoxy of the text. She had not read enough of the work to know the characters, the plot, or the style of writing. Whatever she subsequently learned of such matters would have been worthwhile and interesting, no doubt, but she would have considered all else incidental and perhaps even superfluous when compared with the spiritual witness she had received from heaven. That witness set the course for her life, and no amount of discussion or dispute over the book would have dissuaded her from remaining faithful to God and his book.

A study of ancient cultures is both rewarding and instructive, not only because one gains increased understanding about human history and experience, but also because one can better appreciate the contexts in which prophets received and recorded revelations. One should not overestimate the value or accuracy of our knowledge of antiquity, however, for sources of information relating to the past were imperfectly recorded, have been very unevenly preserved and rediscovered, and are rarely interpreted with unity and certainty by modern scholars. Evidence that is persuasive to some scholars as establishing a point of view is often seen by others as leading to quite a different conclusion. Every student of the past encounters ongoing disputes over such fundamental questions as the relationship of the *Iliad* and the *Odyssey* to historical and archaeological sources, the connection (if any) between Socrates and the material written about him by Plato, Aristophanes, and Xenophon, and the difficulty in determining how and when Christianity was taken into countries and regions not discussed in the book of Acts. Where there is evidence relating to such questions, it is not seen or accepted by all scholars in the same way, and the lack of evidence does not invalidate the question or keep one from guessing at or searching for answers.

When Joseph Smith translated and published the Book of Mormon, most available scholarship relating to the ancient world focused on the Classical civilizations of the Greeks and the Romans. Much of the ancient Near East, including Egypt, the Mesopotamian cultures, the Hittites, and even the Minoans and Mycenaeans, was either virtually unknown or just barely coming to light by the middle of the nineteenth century. Courses on those subjects could not have been taught then, whereas entire departments devoted to them exist in universities at the end of the twentieth century. Even so, contemporary scholars do not teach courses with precisely the same contents or interpretations as those taught a half century earlier, so rapidly do things change. Even in such a hackneyed subject as the Athenian Empire of the fifth century B.C., Russell Meiggs, an acknowledged authority on the subject, could say in 1972: "When I studied Greek history as an undergraduate at Oxford nearly fifty years ago it was reasonable to think that nothing significantly new could be written about the Athenian Empire."[1] After chronicling some of the discoveries and advances in the scholarship during the twentieth century relating to that subject, Meiggs presented a magisterial work of more than six hundred pages. In the quarter of a century that has followed, further advances have made his work incomplete or obsolete in a number of instances, and it is doubtful that any current Greek historian believes we have final answers for many questions concerning fifth-century Athenian history.

If continuing discovery and change regularly require new and revised thinking about Classical and ancient Near Eastern cultures, where the history of scholarship is relatively long and where excellent conditions exist for continuing archaeological discovery, one ought not to be hasty in passing final judgment on the place of the Book of Mormon in ancient New World cultures, where the history of scholarship is still in its early and progressing stages, and where conditions for archaeological work (in Central America, at least) are much more difficult than in the Mediterranean basin. That is not to say that connections should not be sought or cannot possibly be made; but one should not be unduly concerned if the book's proper placement in both culture and geography remains the work of some future time. People read the *Iliad* for centuries before even an insecure relationship to the Mycenaean World, discovered toward the close of the nineteenth century, was proposed in modern times. It is worth repeating that acceptance of the Book of Mormon is a spiritual, not an academic, matter.

Because of my study of ancient history in the Mediterranean world, I have given some consideration to the Book of Mormon's origins in the early sixth century B.C. in the ancient Near East. Despite the changing landscape of scholarship about that region and time period, I am satisfied that the early part of the Book of Mormon is very much at home in that cultural milieu. Others, such as Professor Hugh Nibley and numerous researchers affiliated with the Foundation for Ancient Research and Mormon Studies, have been doing similar (and even more concentrated and detailed) work during recent decades, and they have come to similar conclusions. If there remain areas in which knowledge is lacking or disagreements continue, one needs only to be reminded that information is increasing and consensus does not exist for much pertaining to the ancient Near East at that time. The pervasiveness of Egyptian culture in the Levant and the advent of Greeks into Egypt (by way of both land and sea, most likely) during the seventh century B.C., to give two examples, are both widely acknowledged but imperfectly understood. The first would explain much that is Egyptian in the Book of Mormon (as Nibley and others have observed), and the second would account for Greek names and fundamental issues of so-called Greek pre-Socratic philosophy in the Book of Mormon (which has not yet received any attention). I find such studies interesting and worthwhile within the context of a spiritual testimony that the book is true, but I would not expect that one would base acceptance of the book on such studies.

In a similar context but for a different subject, discoveries of manuscripts and artifacts relating to the ancient church have been very interesting and useful to me in studying the New Testament and the growth of Christianity during the succeeding centuries. It is fascinating to observe the trends of scholarship in the last one hundred years, a time in which a veritable flood of such materials has been recovered. Hundreds of New Testament manuscripts have been found in the last century, bringing the total number to more than five thousand,[2] but such discoveries do not appear to have increased faith in the message of the writings. Those who believe in the inspired messages of the Bible, however, find satisfaction in studying the newly recovered writings to enhance their understanding of the biblical and related texts.

Likewise, those who have faith in the historical accuracy of the New Testament writings see their faith enhanced by the careful and thorough excavations of many sites in Israel, such as Sepphoris, Caesarea Philippi, and Caesarea (on the coast). There is no indication, however, that the excavation projects have brought skeptics to believe in Jesus or the historical accuracy of the New Testament events relating to those sites. At the same time, non–New Testament texts that suggest a more widespread missionary effort and a less-stringently defined doctrine in the Church than was found later by church fathers have nearly all been rejected from canonical consideration. The reasons presented for calling them apocryphal and pseudepigraphical have more to do with the opinions and definitions of the later church fathers than with historical and archaeological considerations.

Confronted with the mass of both New Testament manuscripts and the growing collection of noncanonical writings, a group of scholars calling themselves the Jesus Seminar, for example, determined to identify the authentic sayings of Jesus in all these sources.[3] After years of meetings and deliberations, these critical scholars, basing their decisions on the process of making "empirical, factual evidence—evidence open to confirmation by independent, neutral observers—the controlling factor in historical judgments,"[4] concluded that "eighty-two percent of the words ascribed to Jesus in the Gospels were not actually spoken by him."[5] Three sayings of Jesus found in the Gospel of Thomas, a postresurrection text found in Egypt in 1947, were considered authentic by the Jesus Seminar.[6]

From this example, provided by the more than two hundred voting fellows of the seminar, it is obvious that the evidences of newly discovered manuscripts and archaeological information do not result in increased faith or confidence in the scriptures. For those who have faith and confidence, scholarship can enhance and enlighten, but it can never be an adequate substitute for a spiritual witness from God concerning the truths found among the prophets and their writings. Those truths touch the hearts and minds of people of every age and culture, and they appear to be contemporary to readers of every period.

Most of the ancient writings known as classics that have been preserved and passed on through the centuries are not read as quaint but irrelevant relics from the past. True classics speak to people of every age, regardless of differences in culture or geography. Even though classics are always contemporary in their relevance to human hopes and concerns, some people may wonder how works that reflect concerns and issues of their time could have been written so long ago. Such attitudes reflect a cultural arrogance, based on the mistaken notion that the fundamental needs, interests, beliefs, hopes, and even problems of the people of today are different from those in the great civilizations of the past. The subjects that fill the front pages of daily newspapers or occupy much of the time on news programs—such as wars and threats of wars, religious freedom and persecution, family relations, questions and proposed solutions relating to the size and location of populations, corruption in government, educational concerns, limitations on government control in society and private interests, problems in both public and private morality, and numerous others—are all found as the primary focus of one or more ancient writings. Although the works from the past that have survived represent a relatively small percentage of what once existed, they illustrate that we have much more in common with ancient people than is often realized or acknowledged. That is why works that address universal issues, even in different historical contexts, sound contemporary in every age.

It is not the antiquity of the Book of Mormon but its timelessness that makes it attractive to its readers all over the world today. The age of a work does not alone guarantee its value, for there are some old writings that have survived despite their having little to recommend them. If the Book of Mormon were *merely* an ancient work, it would command attention only as a relic, an object worthy of respect for its age and venerability. Some critics have pointed to the Book of Mormon's contemporaneity with the nineteenth century as disproving its antiquity, yet it is that very quality of contemporaneity—a quality that could be attributed to many ancient writings—that makes the book not merely a curiosity from the past, but a relevant and compelling work for the present.

Prophets, inspired by the Lord in his eternal perspective, are able to address matters that are of concern to all of God's children. Without that perspective, whether obtained directly through revelation or from keen observation or experience, authors may produce manuscripts that enjoy temporary popularity, but that are read thereafter only by historians and literary critics. That is not the situation with the Book of Mormon. No other major literary work published in the nineteenth century has had such a continuing, and even expanding, influence through the twentieth century. The influence is not only to be measured temporally, but geographically and culturally as well, spreading to peoples of virtually every cultural background and tradition on the earth. Even if one did not accept the divine origin and inspired message of the Book of Mormon, the impact the book has had and continues to have in the world justifies giving it a place among the literary classics of human history.

Millions of readers would not be content with simply calling the Book of Mormon a classic, however, any more than they would be with thinking of the Bible as a great literary treasure. Among those who believe that the Bible's greatest worth derives from messages it contains, more than from its literary qualities, there are many who make the same claim on behalf of the Book of Mormon. People who accept these works as scripture given through prophets by inspiration may also study them for their literary qualities and in their ancient settings for historical insights, but they see them as keys to a better understanding of God and his ways, as well as guides for all who wish to return to God's presence. Believers aver that acceptance of the scriptures, including the Book of Mormon, is a spiritual, not an academic, matter.

NOTES

1. Russell Meiggs, *The Athenian Empire* (Oxford: Oxford University Press, 1972), vii.

2. Jack Finegan, *Encountering New Testament Manuscripts* (Grand Rapids, Michigan: Eerdmans Publishing Company, 1974), 52.

3. Robert W. Funk, *The Five Gospels: The Search for the Authentic Words of Jesus* (New York: Macmillan, 1993), 16–34.

4. Ibid., 34.

5. Ibid., 5.

6. Ibid., 474ff.

CHAPTER 21

THE BOOK OF MORMON
Integrity and Internal Consistency

DONALD W. PARRY
Assistant Professor of Hebrew, Brigham Young University

T HE SETTING was a midsized university town in Europe, in May of 1994. I was a dinner guest in the home of a world-renowned Dead Sea Scrolls scholar. Also present were the scholar's wife and two sons. (To protect their privacy, I will not provide their names.) As the evening began, we discussed such comparatively insignificant topics as the dictionary meaning of the name of a nearby street and the progress of the painting of a bedroom in the house.

After we'd enjoyed dinner together, my hosts inquired about my religious beliefs, and the course of the conversation turned to Mormonism and the Book of Mormon. I provided a brief overview of the contents of the Book of Mormon, answering their questions along the way. The scholar responded by observing that the story of the Book of Mormon resembles, in many details, the experiences of the ancient community affiliated with the Dead Sea Scrolls.

The entire evening was delightful. I enjoyed every moment with my hosts. I also had time to pause and once again appreciate the antiquity and correctness of the Book of Mormon. In this context, I desire to share a few of my feelings regarding the Book of Mormon— particularly concerning its complexity and its internal consistency.

The internal framework of the Book of Mormon is indeed complex. The events identified in the book cover a time span of approximately 2,600 years[1] and occur in both the Old and New Worlds. The book was written by more than twenty authors, edited and redacted by inspired editors, and translated by a prophet some 1,400 years after the final Nephite prophet hid the gold plates. The work contains the words of both prophet and false prophet, Christ and antichrist, hero and villain. Several languages have influenced the final product, including Adamic, Egyptian, Hebrew, reformed Egyptian, and English. The work contains many literary types—including historical narrative, poetic parallelism, biography, allegory, law code, judgment speech, lamentation, blessing and cursing, prayer, epistle, psalm, and parable. It contains such symbolic figures as metaphor, simile, synecdoche, metonymy, implication, and personification. As in the Bible, prophetic speech forms of various types appear throughout the Book of Mormon. These include the Messenger Formula, Proclamation Formula, Woe Oracle, Oath Formula, Revelation Formula, and Announcement Formula. The final composition of the book as translated by Joseph Smith is a product of several earlier sources, including the brass plates, the record of Lehi, the large plates of Nephi, the small plates of Nephi, the plates of Mormon, and the twenty-four gold plates of Ether. Although the book's goals and purposes are religious, the work treats many of the political, social, geographical, historical, and cultural elements that make up any civilization.

Yet with all of its complexities, the internal consistency of the book is remarkable. Unlike the Bible, which contains literally hundreds of changes made by scribes and copyists,[2] the Book of Mormon was transmitted directly from an ancient prophet (Moroni) to a modern prophet (Joseph Smith) and therefore lacks such a large number of errors. That is not to say that the Book of Mormon is free of errors or the mistakes of humanity, but certainly Joseph Smith's statement concerning the Book of Mormon is appropriate here: "I told the brethren that the Book of Mormon was the *most correct* of any book on earth."[3]

This article will seek to demonstrate the manner in which the book possesses a textual consistency—the agreement, harmony, uniformity, and logical coherence that are present in the Book of Mormon text.[4] Because of space limitations, I will discuss only three examples: First, I will demonstrate that, while the work presents a multitude of names and personalities, its presentation is logical and uniform; second, I will show the harmony that exists in the book's internal history, with special regard to wars and warfare; third, and most significantly, I will examine the book's focus on Christ and show how all references to Jesus Christ are textually consistent.

Unity of Names and Characters

The Book of Mormon "contains 337 proper names and 21 gentilics (or analogous forms) based on proper names."[5] Of the 337 proper names, "188 are unique to the Book of Mormon": for example, Abinadi, Amalickiah, Amulek, Morianton, Mormon, Moronihah, Kishkumen, Helaman, Hagoth, Gadianton, Omni, and Riplakish; 149 of the 337 proper names are common to both the Bible and the Book of Mormon: for example, Samuel, Isaiah, Gideon, Benjamin, Aaron, Noah, Shem, Timothy, and Jacob. Typical of the ancient Semitic languages from which the Nephite record is derived, the Book of Mormon does not use surnames[6] or attach modern titles to its names, such as Mr., Mrs., Dr., Professor, Reverend, Count, or Earl.[7] The names, as transcribed into the English language, do not use the letters *q, x,* or *w,*[8] nor do the names begin with either the characters *W* or *F,*[9] a fact shared with the names of the Old Testament. Much can be learned from a study of the names, as Paul Hoskisson has shown, for they may provide an indication of the types of languages used by the Nephites, Jaredites, and Lamanites; present a picture of Book of Mormon civilizations and cultures; and provide external clues about when the Book of Mormon record developed in the ancient world.[10]

George Reynolds[11] and Hugh Nibley[12] have conducted a number of studies of the history of Book of Mormon names and have shown that some have Hebrew and Egyptian roots and relationships. B. H. Roberts pointed out that there is a "quite marked distinction between Nephite and Jaredite proper names."[13] With few exceptions, Jaredite names "end in consonants, while very many of the Nephite names end in a vowel."[14]

Robert J. Matthews has created a serviceable who's who of Book of Mormon personalities, wherein he lists several social, political, and religious groupings[15] present in the book. He places personalities into categories and lists the following numbers of individuals within each group: four antichrists, twenty-seven Nephite military leaders, two Jaredite prophets, two priests of Noah listed by name, twelve disciples of Christ, four robbers, seven explorers, one harlot, twelve heads of the Church, two leaders of the Jews, twelve judges, eight Lamanite kings, one lawyer, thirty-one Jaredite kings, two Jaredite military leaders, six Lamanite military leaders, eleven missionaries, two Mulekite leaders, nine Nephite kings, a number of Nephite and Lamanite prophets, twenty Nephite record keepers, three ship-builders, five spies, and ten villains.

Several other characters or groups listed by Matthews,[16] who are unnamed in the record, include the Amalekite who contended with Aaron, the individual who attempted to slay Ammon, the brother of Jared, the brother of Shiblom, the daughter of Ishmael, the wife of Ishmael, the daughter of Jared, the daughters of the Lamanites, the daughters of Lehi, the five men mentioned in Helaman 9:1–39, the freemen, the Gadianton robbers, the high priests of King Gilead, three Lamanite kings, the Lamanite guards at Gid, the leader of the Zarahemla expedition, the forty-three men of King Limhi who went on the scouting expedition, two mighty Jaredite men, Morianton's maid servant, two queens of the Lamanites, the wife of Lamoni, the wife of Amalickiah, the second king of the Nephites, the servant of Ammoron, the servant of Helaman, the servants of the king of the Lamanites, the three Nephites, the twenty-four Nephites, and the two thousand sons of Helaman.

The record provides thousands of implicit and explicit facts and items about these individuals, both named and unnamed. Yet these facts are always kept straight. Never is an individual described in one way at one point and in another way later, unless the change is explained. The record never mistakenly assigns facts about one indi-vidual to another individual. For example, consider the way the record treats the Nephite character Helaman.[17] Helaman was the oldest son of Alma, was given instructions by his father, and was given the Nephite records, the plates of brass, the twenty-four

Jaredite plates, the interpreters, and the Liahona. He received his father's prophecy of the Nephite destruction, was blessed by his father, ordained priests and teachers in the Church, was rejected by the rich and the proud, became a high priest in the Church, preached repentance, maintained peace for a period of four years, baptized and ministered to the people, persuaded the converted Lamanites to keep their oaths, wrote an epistle to Moroni stating the affairs of the people, encouraged the people of Ammon not to break the covenant, joined forces with Antipus against the Lamanites, maintained with Antipus a constant vigil over the movements of the Lamanites, gathered and commanded an army of ten thousand men, led two thousand young men to decoy Lamanites from the city of Antiparah, captured many Lamanite prisoners and sent them to the land of Zarahemla, and corresponded with Ammoron about prisoner exchange.

Helaman also obtained the city of Antiparah from the Lamanites without a fight, captured the city of Cumeni by cutting off the food supply, sent part of the army to conduct Lamanite prisoners to Zarahemla, won a severe battle with the Lamanites, received a report from Gid about the escape of the Lamanite prisoners, praised God for his mercy and deliverance to the Nephites, captured the Lamanite city of Manti without the shedding of blood, obtained a release of many Nephite prisoners, again praised God for protection and deliverance, received six thousand men and provisions because of Moroni's intervention, returned to the land of Zarahemla with Moroni, began a preaching tour to regulate the Church, preached with power and authority, safeguarded the sacred things with which he had been entrusted, and died in 57 B.C. during the thirty-fifth year of the judges. In addition to these explicit, straightforward expressions about the life and activities of Helaman, a careful reader may also be able to glean items that are implied or alluded to in the text regarding the spiritual character of Helaman, his philosophy towards life, religious standing, physical prowess, emotional demeanor, and social standing.

Although Helaman is but one of the hundreds of named and unnamed characters identified in the Book of Mormon, not once does the record attribute to him an exact characteristic, familial tie, habit, personality trait, physical description, genealogical affiliation, vocational skill, political office, religious calling, occupation, spiritual or intellectual aptitude, military affiliation, contemporary historical event, or biographical deed that it explicitly attaches to another Book of Mormon personality to the point that there is a discrepancy or contradiction in the text. For example, in Alma 37, Alma anoints his son Helaman to be his successor and entrusts the accumulated plates and the Liahona to him. From that point until the end of Alma 62, where Helaman's death is recorded, this fact remains consistent: no one else is mistakenly described as holding the responsibilities Alma had given to Helaman. Further, the record does not confuse implied statements that are attached to Helaman and his world with another individual, nor does it ever accidentally place him in the wrong geographic locale or historical time frame. As I have set up Helaman as an example, so, too, could other personalities of the Book of Mormon be examined by a careful student, and never would that student discover an inconsistency or lack of agreement in the text. In view of this, it may be stated that the Book of Mormon demonstrates an internal consistency and coherence.

Historical Unity of Warfare

The Book of Mormon recalls historical situations, characters, and places that are external to the chronological and geographic setting of the Jaredites, Nephites, and Mulekites. Abraham, Joseph, Moses, Solomon, the building of Solomon's temple, Isaiah, Jeremiah, Zedekiah, the exodus from Egypt, and the great tower are mentioned in the book but do not belong to its immediate setting. Genealogical references presented in the record make solid connections between the house of Israel in the Old World and the family of Joseph in the New World. The family of Jared is directly linked with the era of the great tower, and the family of Lehi is shown to belong to the setting of Jerusalem shortly before its destruction by Babylon.

The Book of Mormon also sets forth a host of historical references, characters, and circumstances that so far are found only within its pages. Consider, for example, the treatment of wars and warfare in the work. The book features fifteen major conflicts, including the "Early Tribal Wars," the "Wars of King Laman's Son," the "War of

Amlici," the "Destruction of Ammonihah," the "War of the Ammonite Secession," the "Zoramite War," the "First and Second Amalickiahite Wars," the "Rebellion of Paanchi," the "War of Tubaloth," the "War of Moronihah," the "War of Gadianton and Kishkumen," the "War of Giddianhi and Zemnarihah," the "Rebellion of Jacob," and the three phases of the "Final Nephite Wars."[18] The Book of Mormon writers and editors dedicated anywhere from a few verses (Rebellion of Paanchi, Helaman 1:1–13) to twelve chapters (Second Amalickiahite War, Alma 51–62) to each of the major conflicts.

Students of the Book of Mormon can attach to many of the fifteen major wars approximate dates or seasons, geographical locales, underlying causes, battle tactics, military maneuvers, and final outcomes. Further, individual campaigns and engagements existed within each major war. Within the framework of the fifteen major wars mentioned above, John L. Sorenson has identified more than one hundred distinct conflicts in the record.[19] His identification includes the Lamanite, Nephite, and Zeniffite initiatives; Nephite versus Nephite conflicts; and confrontations between the Lamanites and the Anti-Nephi-Lehies. Further, we find in the book references to attacks and counterattacks; army pursuing or fleeing from army; strategies and political maneuvers; violent contentions; defeats and victories; mobilization of groups; preparations for war; marching armies; captives and prisoners of war; deployment, redeployment, and the positioning of troops; military spies; dissident forces; fortifications of cities and sites; the capture, loss, and recapture of cities; descriptions of combat, guerrilla movement, the flanking of troops, and other tactics; the raising of armies and recruitment of soldiers; strategic offenses and defenses; descriptions of military leaders and dissenters; the reinforcement of troops; armies against organized robbers; slaughter; bloodshed; and the extermination of entire peoples. In addition, the record identifies many of the weapons and armor used by different warriors at various times, including the sword, cimeter, bow and arrow, breastplate, shield, head-plate, arm-shield, club, sling, and "all manner of weapons of war" (Alma 2:12).

Yet with all these details, the presentation of wars and warfare in the Book of Mormon contains a textually consistent account that both recalls historical reality and lacks contradictory elements. From the first battle mentioned in 2 Nephi 5:34 to the final Nephite battle at Cumorah (Mormon 6:5–15), all of the wars and battles are interwoven into the Book of Mormon text to create a harmonious narrative. The connection between warfare and textual consistency in the Book of Mormon serves as an example of the book's integrity and correctness. Similar arguments could be made about all other historical references in the Book of Mormon.

Unity of Focus on Christ

Years ago, Susan Easton Black tabulated all of the occurrences of the names and titles of Jesus in the Book of Mormon.[20] Though Black's goals were different from those of this article, the results of her findings are quite instructive. According to Black, 101 names or titles of Christ are presented in the Book of Mormon. These include the names/titles Lord God Omnipotent, Redeemer of Israel, Shepherd, and Son of the Living God, each of which is found once in the work. The names/titles Stone, True Messiah, Mighty One of Jacob, and Great Creator are each found twice; the names/titles Holy One of Israel, Lamb of God, Lord Jesus Christ, Redeemer, and Messiah each appear 10 or more times; and the names/titles Christ, God, Jesus, Lord, and Lord God are each found at least 100 times in the book. In all, the 101 names/titles of Christ are collectively presented 3,925 times in 6,607 Book of Mormon verses.[21] Black's tabulation of the names and titles shows that on average, one name or title of Christ appears once every 1.7 verses.

The names and titles are used by the various Book of Mormon prophets to teach of Jesus' prebirth affiliations with the world, his earthly ministry, his atoning sacrifice (including his sufferings in Gethsemane, his death on the cross, and his resurrection from the garden tomb), his workings among American civilizations, his ministry to other peoples, his future mission with the latter-day church, his judgments upon the world, and his Second Coming to the inhabitants of the earth. By way of example, a number of names/titles of Jesus deal especially with the Atonement. These include Christ, Christ Jesus, Christ the Son, Creator, Eternal Father, Everlasting Father, Father of Heaven, Holy Messiah, Jesus, Jesus Christ, Lamb,

Lamb of God, Lord Jesus Christ, Mediator, Messiah, Only Begotten of the Father, Only Begotten Son, Redeemer, Redeemer of Israel, Savior, Savior of the World, Shepherd, and True Redeemer. Note also that Jesus serves in the capacity of an advocate, a fact that is explicitly mentioned in the Doctrine and Covenants (D&C 29:5; 32:3; 45:3; 62:1). Several statements imply this idea: the Holy Messiah "shall make intercession for all . . . men" (2 Nephi 2:9), "the Lord and thy God pleadeth the cause of his people" (2 Nephi 8:22), "the Lord standeth up to plead, and standeth to judge the people" (2 Nephi 13:13), God "will plead your cause" (Jacob 3:1), and Christ "advocateth the cause of the children of men" (Moroni 7:28).

The Book of Mormon contains not only a great variety of names and titles for Jesus, but also many thousands of personal pronouns that refer to him. Book of Mormon pronouns that have reference to Christ include *I, me, you, he, him;* the possessive (adjective) pronouns *my, your,* and *his;* and the relative pronoun *who.* Note the three appearances of the third-person pronoun in Mosiah 15:12, all of which refer to Jesus. I have italicized the pronouns for emphasis: "For these are they whose sins *he* has borne; these are they for whom *he* has died, to redeem them from their transgressions. And now, are they not *his* seed?" Note also the first-person pronouns found in 3 Nephi 11:11, again italicized: "And behold, *I* am the light and the life of the world; and *I* have drunk out of that bitter cup which the Father hath given *me,* and have glorified the Father in taking upon *me* the sins of the world, in the which *I* have suffered the will of the Father in all things from the beginning." The pronouns that have reference to God are interspersed throughout the Book of Mormon text, mingled with his 101 names and titles.

Beyond the use of deific names, titles, and pronouns in the Nephite record, witnesses of Jesus appear in the form of symbols, presented through such figures of speech as metaphor, simile, synecdoche, metonymy, implication, and personification. Metaphors of Christ, for example, are common in the book and include Moses' brazen serpent (1 Nephi 17:41; Helaman 8:14–15), "keeper of the gate" (2 Nephi 9:41), "Lamb of God" (1 Nephi 10:10), "the light and the life of the world" (3 Nephi 9:18), "Son of Righteousness"

(3 Nephi 25:2), foundation stone (Jacob 4:15–16), "the truth of the world" (Ether 4:12), and "rock" and "true vine" (1 Nephi 15:15).

First and foremost, the goal of the Book of Mormon is religious, with an emphasis and encouragement for individuals to come unto Christ (Jacob 1:7; Omni 1:26; Moroni 10:30, 32). Black's study on the frequent occurrence of the names of Christ in the work reveals that the book has a definite focus on Christ. Obviously, if one of his names or titles appears on average once every 1.7 verses (and such a tabulation does not include pronominal references to Christ), then the entire Book of Mormon is built around him, including its socio-logical, political, economical, theological, and historical parts. Yet if serious readers study the book contextually, they will discover that each occurrence of a deific name or title, personal pronoun, or sym-bolic reference shows an evenness, integrity, and lack of contradic-tion with all other parts of the book.

Not once does the book confuse a work or teaching of Jesus that belongs to another personality; never in all the references to Jesus, both explicit and implicit, does the work attach to a human either a power or a quality that belongs to God alone, nor does it attach a worldly, profane, or humanistic quality to the resurrected Jesus. Prophetic descriptions of Jesus Christ do not portray any member of the Godhead as possessing a human frailty, a sinful or fallen nature, an imperfection, or a corruption. Neither is God confused with other supernatural beings, either angels or evil spirits. Rather, the Book of Mormon clearly defines the roles of all three members of the Godhead—the Father, the Son, and the Holy Ghost. Every single reference to God, whether it be pronoun, name, title, or symbolic reference, is consistent and harmonious with every other reference. If confusion or contradiction appears to exist in the Book of Mormon, it is because of the limitations of the finite reader, who is attempting to understand things pertaining to the infinite.

As noted, by far the most significant personality identified in the book is Jesus Christ, and the weightiest topics pertain to his charac-ter, divine mission, and eternal goals. References to Christ serve as an adhesive, binding every verse of the work into a single, integral unit. All other parts of the book serve as appendages to this focus. The topic of Jesus and his mission fits squarely with the stated purpose of the book as listed on the title page and elsewhere in the book. The purpose of the record is, in part, "to show unto the remnant of the House of Israel what great things the Lord hath done for their fathers; and that they may know the covenants of the Lord, that they are not cast off forever—And also to the convincing of the Jew and Gentile that Jesus is the Christ, the Eternal God, manifesting himself unto all nations" (title page).

From the opening phrase, "I, Nephi, having been born of goodly parents," to the concluding expression, "the great Jehovah, the Eternal Judge of both quick and dead. Amen," the Book of Mormon is textually consistent, internally concordant, and written with integrity. If the reader follows the proper prescriptions, the Holy Ghost will bear witness of the book's truthfulness, and the reader will draw closer to God through reading it and applying its principles.

My testimony of the divinity and Sonship of Jesus Christ, the calling of the seer Joseph Smith, and the truthfulness of the Book of Mormon is based upon the Spirit-to-spirit relaying of truth that comes through the operations of the Holy Ghost. This testimony, however, is coupled with a number of internal evidences that convince me of the book's historicity and divinity. The record's textually consistent testimony is but one internal evidence of its truthfulness.

....

NOTES

1. Placing the Tower of Babel (Ether 1) at 2200 B.C. See Bible Dictionary, LDS edition of Holy Bible, 635.

2. On the textual problems with the Bible, see P. Kyle McCarter, *Textual Criticism: Recovering the Text of the Hebrew Bible* (Philadelphia: Fortress Press, 1986), and Emanuel Tov, *Textual Criticism of the Hebrew Bible* (Minneapolis: Fortress Press, 1992). This is neither an attack upon the Bible nor an argument that the Bible lacks integrity, internal unity, or textual consistency. Neither do I attempt to prove that the Book of Mormon lacks scribal or other transmissional errors. I do believe, however, that if the Book of Mormon contains errors, "they are the mistakes of men" (title page).

3. Joseph Smith, *History of the Church of Jesus Christ of Latter-day Saints*, 7 vols. (Salt Lake City: Deseret Book, 1976), 4:461; emphasis added.

4. Several authors have directly or indirectly touched upon the subject of textual consistency. For a look at the book's typological unity, see Richard D. Rust, "'All Things Which Have Been Given of God . . . Are the Typifying of Him': Typology in the Book of Mormon," in *Literature of Belief: Sacred Scripture and Religious Experience*, ed. Neal E. Lambert (Provo, Utah: BYU Religious Studies Center, 1981), 233–43; Eugene England, "A Second Witness for the *Logos*: The Book of Mormon and Contemporary Literary Criticism," in *By Study and Also By Faith*,

ed. John M. Lundquist and Stephen D. Ricks (Salt Lake City: Deseret Book and FARMS, 1990), 2:91–125; Bruce W. Jorgensen, "The Dark Way to the Tree: Typological Unity in the Book of Mormon," in *The Literature of Belief,* 218–30. John A. Tvedtnes, "Mormon's Editorial Promises," in *Rediscovering the Book of Mormon,* ed. John L. Sorenson and Melvin J. Thorne (Salt Lake City: Deseret Book and FARMS, 1991), 29–31, shows that the work possesses editorial integrity. John W. Welch, "Textual Consistency," in *Reexploring the Book of Mormon,* ed. John W. Welch (Salt Lake City: Deseret Book and FARMS, 1992), 21–23, states that "passages tie together precisely and accurately though separated from each other by hundreds of pages of text and dictated weeks apart." Welch provides four examples of textual consistency.

5. Paul Y. Hoskisson, "Book of Mormon Names," in *Encyclopedia of Mormonism,* ed. Daniel H. Ludlow (New York: Macmillan, 1992), 1:186. The names are listed in an appendix of *Book of Mormon Critical Text: A Tool for Scholarly Reference,* ed. Robert F. Smith (Provo, Utah: FARMS, 1987), 3:1218–24; John S. Turnbull, *A Dictionary of the Book of Mormon* (Salt Lake City: n.p., 1946); Alvin Knisley, *Dictionary of All Proper Names in the Book of Mormon* (Independence, Missouri: Ensign Publishing House, 1909); Robert J. Matthews, *Who's Who in the Book of Mormon?* (Salt Lake City: Deseret Book, 1976); and George Reynolds, *Dictionary of the Book of Mormon; Comprising Its Biographical, Geographical, and Other Proper Names; Together with Appendices by Janne M. Sjodahl* (Salt Lake City: Joseph Hyrum Parry, 1891).

6. A fact pointed out by Melvin R. Brooks, "Book of Mormon," in *LDS Reference Encyclopedia* (Salt Lake City: Bookcraft, 1960), 52–54. Brooks presents a list of twenty-eight peculiarities of the Book of Mormon. His list is adapted from Thomas W. Brookbank, "Pitfalls Avoided by the Translator of the Book of Mormon," *Millennial Star* 71 (1909): 273–79, 289–93. B. H. Roberts also pointed out that the Jaredites and Nephites attached only a single name to each person. This is similar to the ancient Hebrew custom of attaching one name only to an individual, but unlike the custom of the present era of giving two or more names to a person. See B. H. Roberts, *New Witnesses for God* (Salt Lake City: Deseret News, 1951), 3:134.

7. Brookbank, "Pitfalls," 292. The book does contain such ancient titles as priest, king, and judge.

8. Arthur G. Pledger, "The *W* and I," *Ensign,* September 1976, 24–25.

9. Ibid.

10. Paul Y. Hoskisson, "An Introduction to the Relevance of and a Methodology for a Study of the Proper Names of the Book of Mormon," in *By Study and Also By Faith,* 2:126–35. Hoskisson's methodology is helpful and presents a number of cautions to those who study proper names of the Book of Mormon.

11. George Reynolds, "Nephite Proper Names," *Juvenile Instructor,* September 15, 1880, 207–8.

12. Hugh W. Nibley, "Book of Mormon as a Mirror of the East," *Improvement Era,* April 1948, 202–4, 249–51. Reprinted, without illustrations, in *Improvement Era,* November 1970, 115–20, 122–25. See also Nibley, "The Lachish Letters: Documents from Lehi's Day," *Ensign,* December 1981, 48–54.

13. B. H. Roberts, *New Witnesses for God* (Salt Lake City: Deseret News, 1951), 3:134.

14. Ibid., 3:135.

15. Matthews, *Who's Who,* 73–75.

16. Ibid., 58–66.

17. Ibid., 18–19.

18. As identified and named by John W. Welch, "Why Study Warfare in the Book of Mormon," in *Warfare in the Book of Mormon,* ed. Stephen D. Ricks and William J. Hamblin (Salt Lake City: Deseret Book and FARMS, 1990), 3–24.

19. John L. Sorenson, appendix to "Seasonality of Warfare in the Book of Mormon and in Mesoamerica," in *Warfare in the Book of Mormon,* 445–77.

20. Susan Easton Black, *Finding Christ through the Book of Mormon* (Salt Lake City: Deseret Book, 1987); Susan Ward Easton [Black], "Names of Christ in the Book of Mormon," *Ensign,* July 1978, 60–61.

21. Black, *Finding Christ,* 5.

Chapter 22

Questions Answered
My Study and Teaching of American Literature and the Book of Mormon

Richard Dilworth Rust
Professor of English, University of North Carolina

If there is anything virtuous, lovely, or of good report or praiseworthy, we seek after these things.

—Articles of Faith 1:13

Faith added to study is like "seeing" a three-dimensional stereo-gram for the first time. When one of my sons-in-law first showed me a stereogram, all I could see initially was a flat surface with meaning-less small patterns. Through his coaching, though, I eventually learned to see a third dimension in the stereogram, and what at first appeared random took on meaning as I could identify the objects in the picture. The exhilarating feeling I had in finally "seeing" the stereogram immediately reminded me of the spiritual dimension to life. The movement into this deeper dimension is like the revelatory breakthroughs I have received after applying my best thoughts or tal-ents to a matter. In this, I have followed models of others who, like my son-in-law with the stereogram, have shown that their kind of spiritual experience is verifiable by one who is guided to "see" the same way.

Here is an instance of one of my spiritual three-dimensional experiences: One evening I was admiring the beautiful sunset-touched clouds in the sky, when in a way I had not emotionally realized before, I saw the hand of God in this glorious scene before me. Intellectually, I had known since I was a child that Heavenly Father through Jesus Christ created the world, and I was well familiar with Alma's affirmation to Korihor that "all things denote there is a God; yea, even the earth, and all things that are upon the face of it" (Alma 30:44), but at that moment there was something more. An inner voice spoke to my soul, confirming that the Creator acknowledged his artistry. I had a similar experience on an airline flight to Puerto Rico during which I viewed in awe and appreciation the beauty of the variegated clouds, including a brilliant phoenix-like shape, knowing that this was a manifestation of God's handiwork. Another time, I was stunned by the emotional and spiritual feeling I had in viewing bare trees silhouetted against a brilliant sunset. The trees were all different, just as each person on earth is different, and in their similarities yet differences of pattern they testified of conscious creation by a higher being.

These are just a few of the many experiences that confirm to me the reality of Deity. While with Nephi, "I do not know the meaning of all things" (1 Nephi 11:17), I do know with a certainty that there is a God, that Jesus Christ is the Redeemer, and that Joseph Smith, like Jeremiah, was chosen before he was born to be a prophet.

In the spirit of the thirteenth Article of Faith, I love to learn about and to experience the true, the good, and the beautiful. My chosen profession of literary studies has helped facilitate my seeking after that which is lovely and of good report, and the restored gospel of Jesus Christ has provided a sure framework for my understanding.

With Ralph Waldo Emerson, I have found that literature

is the record of the best thoughts. Every attainment and discipline which increases a man's acquaintance with the invisible world lifts his being. Everything that gives him a new perception of beauty multiplies his pure enjoyments. A river of thought is always running out of the invisible world into the mind of man. Shall not they who received the largest streams spread abroad the healing waters?

. . . Now if you can kindle the imagination by a new thought, by heroic histories, by uplifting poetry, instantly you expand,—are cheered, inspired, and become wise, and even prophetic.[1]

There is much truth in the world of literature. Indeed, one of the paradoxes of great writers is that they often get closer to the truth through fiction than they could through direct expression of reality. "Tell all the Truth but tell it slant," Emily Dickinson wrote.[2] The word "fiction" derives from the same word as "fictive," referring to the shaping imagination. A similar fictive process is used in great literature as in great portraiture. It comes from the qualities Nathaniel Hawthorne defines in a character whom Herman Melville identified as a self-portrait of Hawthorne. As Hawthorne described him, the man had a face "full of sturdy vigor, with some finer and keener attribute beneath; though harsh at first, it was tempered with the glow of a large, warm heart, which had force enough to heat his powerful intellect through and through." His bold declaration was "I seek for Truth."[3] A truth seeker himself, Melville loved "all men who *dive*," and believed that "all truth is profound."[4] Another truth seeker, Emily Dickinson, wrote: "Truth—is as old as God— / His Twin identity / And will endure as long as He / A Co-Eternity."[5] Henry David Thoreau said, "Rather than love, than money, than fame, give me truth."[6]

Yet with all the truth and beauty they provide, great writers are better at asking questions than finding answers. Who are we? they ask. How should we live? What is the purpose of life? Are we free to act, and if so, to what extent? What is man's place in the universe? Why is there evil, and why must people experience sorrow and suffering? What is beyond this life? In Melville's words through Ishmael, "Where lies the final harbor, whence we unmoor no more? In what rapt ether sails the world, of which the weariest will never weary?"[7]

The answers authors do provide may be limited or contradictory. For example, Emerson on the one hand says, "Is not prayer also a study of truth,—a sally of the soul into the unfound infinite?"[8] Another time, however, he says, "As men's prayers are a disease of the will, so are their creeds a disease of the intellect."[9] For his part, Melville was like Hawthorne in being "a seeker, not a finder yet."[10] He mused about "time and eternity, things of this world and of the next."[11] Yet he despaired of definitive answers. As Hawthorne reported about Melville's visit with him near Liverpool in 1856, Melville,

> as he always does, began to reason of Providence and futurity, and of everything that lies beyond human ken, and informed me that he had "pretty much made up his mind to be annihilated"; but still he does not seem to rest in that anticipation; and, I think, will never rest until he gets hold of a definite belief. . . . He can neither believe, nor be comfortable in his unbelief; and he is too honest and courageous not to try to do one or the other.[12]

While the reasoning of Melville and others like him "of Providence and futurity" may not bring them fully satisfying answers, my study of these writers has strengthened my testimony. How? They stir me into exploring avenues of thought and feeling. As just one example, they have led me into a decades-long study of the initiation theme in literature—which in turn has further enlightened, and been enlightened by, my understanding of the temple. Most of all, my testimony has been strengthened by revelation that comes in seeking answers to the hard questions these authors ask and also in confirming the answers they get.

It is as though writers of great literature give widening circles of response to truths about man and God, and the gospel provides the circumference. Put another way, the gospel provides a center for my life and allows means for proving all things and holding fast that which is good (1 Thessalonians 5:21). These answers, found through study and faith, have been confirmed to me by the power of the Holy Ghost. It is possible, as Jacob says, to know by means of the Spirit "of things as they really are" (Jacob 4:13). The gospel, in T. S. Eliot's words, places me "at the still point of the turning world."[13] Especially through temple ordinances, I am enabled (in Eliot's words) "to apprehend / The point of intersection of the timeless / With time."[14] With the aid of the temple experience, "the end of all our exploring," again in Eliot's words, "Will be to arrive where we started / And know the place for the first time."[15]

My practice of feasting daily from the Book of Mormon in conjunction with the other scriptures is a great help to me in orienting my life to eternal truths. Following the principles contained in the Book of Mormon helps me see "life steadily, and [see] it whole."[16]

With revelatory guidance, the book answers in a deeply satisfying way many of life's most challenging questions. This was reinforced for me by an experience I had speaking about the Book of Mormon with forty-five seminarians, most of them ministers, from the Southeastern Baptist Theological Seminary. While I had spoken to similar groups in previous years and had prepared for my part many weeks in advance, this time the approach I was to take was made clear to me only the day before I was to meet the group. This is what I was impressed to do: After describing the basic nature of the Book of Mormon (a copy of which I had put in each person's hands), I asked the seminarians to assume that the lost ten tribes had received God's word by way of prophets and to imagine that the ten tribes had now returned with scriptures. What fundamental questions of mankind, I asked, would be addressed in those scriptures? Rather than present the questions myself, I wanted the seminarians to formulate them. The questions, which I listed on the chalkboard, were profound, and I sensed they were ones that concerned these ministers personally. During the next twenty-five minutes, I called up each question in turn, and then we read together answers found in the Book of Mormon. As these answers were given me in the very moment when I needed them (see D&C 24:6), I marveled at how incisive, convincing, and penetrating they were. I could tell the seminarians were touched as well.

Here are the seven questions the seminarians came up with, together with parenthetical references to some of the scriptures we read together:

What is God like? (3 Nephi 11)

What evidence is there of the existence of God? (Alma 30, especially verse 44)

What is the purpose of life? (2 Nephi 2; Mosiah 2–3)

Why is there suffering and evil in the world? (2 Nephi 2:11; Alma 20:29)

What is the relationship of man to God? (Mosiah 2–3)

What happens after death? (Alma 40–42, especially 40:11–14)

What are the proofs of a true prophet? (Jacob 4, especially verse 6)

Just as the Book of Mormon contributes to my understanding of life's challenging questions found in literature and elsewhere, so my literary studies contribute to my understanding of the Book of Mormon. A number of years ago, I was approached by a colleague who proposed that we join together in writing a book about the Book of Mormon as literature. When he first mentioned this, it had not occurred to me to look at the Book of Mormon in those terms. While the collaboration did not continue beyond sending out a prospectus to a couple of major New York publishers, I pursued the project with increasing enthusiasm. The words of the Primary song, "search, ponder, and pray," described my daily involvement in engaging the Book of Mormon rigorously.

Learning from American Puritan and other treatments of typology, I recognized typology in the Book of Mormon.[17] Years of study of poetry, including Hebraic poetry in translation, helped open up to me the poetic nature of many passages in the Book of Mormon. This is likewise true for my studies of imagery in the book. Overall, my appreciation of literature and my testimony of the saving principles of the gospel of Jesus Christ converged in my seeing the Book of Mormon as a literary testimony of Christ. Almost on a daily basis, my inquiries into the book, enriched by writings of others and aided by the Holy Ghost, helped me to admire its varied styles and to discover in the book complex poetry, epic elements, vivid imagery, and memorable sermons and narratives.[18] I came to see how the impact of what the Book of Mormon says is often created through how it is said. Its interconnection of beauty, truth, and goodness woos us to Christ. In its literary richness, it is like what Ezekiel called "a very lovely song of one that hath a pleasant voice, and can play well on an instrument. . . . And when this cometh to pass, . . . then shall they know that a prophet hath been among them" (Ezekiel 33:32–33).

In my study of the Book of Mormon's literary aspects, I have been amazed at how beautifully designed the book is. As closer scrutiny of a rose or a butterfly wing shows even more its complexity and beauty, so with the Book of Mormon. Through aid of the Spirit, I am constantly finding new and remarkable aspects about the book the more intensely I look at it. And the Book of Mormon invites such scrutiny. "Ask, inquire, knock, pray, question, seek," the book says (see the Book of Mormon index under these words). Questioning can be an active affirmation of faith. The critical point is to ask like a humbled

Zeezrom who "began to inquire of them diligently, that he might know more concerning the kingdom of God" and then was open to the evidence of spiritual feelings, and not like an Antionah who asked questions only to be able to trap Alma (Alma 12:8, 20–21).

As my scholarship contributes to my faith, so my faith contributes to my teaching and scholarship. One of my favorite scriptural thoughts is "it is by grace that we are saved, after all we can do" (2 Nephi 25:23). I have some private variations of this, including "It is by grace that a kind Heavenly Father helps us along, after all we can do." This has been true many times in my professional life when I have met what seemed a dead end. Through prayer and humility (after I had done what I could do), and seemingly just at the point when I saw no way out, I have been given a solution.

For example, a decade ago I was presented with what seemed an insurmountable problem. The publisher of *The Complete Works of Washington Irving*, of which I was the general editor, decided to call in at once all the remaining manuscripts of volumes for the Irving edition. No doubt the publisher was expecting that a number of the volumes would not be completed in the two or three months they gave us, and if we missed their deadline, we would be providing them with the justification to close out a costly endeavor. Yet through immediate hard work on everyone's part, including that of a couple of scholars who had been involved with their volume for ten years, and through my prayers (and most likely through others' prayers as well), the manuscripts were delivered on schedule.

All except one volume, that is—Irving's *Tales of a Traveller.* It was so far from completion that we saw no way it could meet the new deadline. I earnestly sought help for this from my Heavenly Father, since I believed I should "let all [my] doings be unto the Lord" and should not "perform any thing unto the Lord save in the first place [I should] pray unto the Father in the name of Christ, that he [would] consecrate [my] performance" (Alma 37:36; 2 Nephi 32:9). The inspired solution that came from my thought and prayer was to find a cost-effective way to use computer technology to supply machine-readable text to the publisher. The volume editor and I consequently learned to use a mainframe computer and, later, personal computers to do this, and were successful in persuading the editor-in-chief to publish the volume. (*The Complete Works of Washington Irving*, I should add, now justifies its title.)

As for my teaching, I have made it a habit over the years to pray before every class I teach. My classes are my flocks and fields (see Alma 34:20); with Nephi, "I know that the Lord God will consecrate my prayers for the gain of my people" (2 Nephi 33:4). In each class I receive some evidence of divine help, often in the form of being guided to turn to the very passage I need in order to respond effectively to a question or to make a point.

The essence of my experience and conviction concerning the relationship of study and faith can be summed up in this scripture, which speaks both of diligently seeking and of learning the mysteries of God through the power of the Holy Ghost: "For he that diligently seeketh shall find; and the mysteries of God shall be unfolded unto them, by the power of the Holy Ghost, as well in these times as in times of old, and as well in times of old as in times to come; wherefore, the course of the Lord is one eternal round" (1 Nephi 10:19; also see Alma 12:9–12). In the "eternal round" of the Lord, "to be learned is good" if one hearkens to the counsels of God and despises not the revelations of God (2 Nephi 9:29; Jacob 4:8; also see Jacob 4:10). While I am continually humbled by a recognition of what I do not yet know, my confidence in God is constantly growing. I know through experience that the integration of the spiritual and the intellectual is the most expansive way to learn "of things both in heaven and in the earth" (D&C 88:79).

....
NOTES

1. Ralph Waldo Emerson, "Address at the Opening of the Concord Free Public Library," in *Miscellanies*, vol. 11 of *The Complete Works of Ralph Waldo Emerson* (Boston: Houghton Mifflin, 1911), 501–3.

2. *The Complete Poems of Emily Dickinson*, ed. Thomas H. Johnson (Boston: Little, Brown and Company, 1960), J:1129.

3. Nathaniel Hawthorne, "The Intelligence Office," in *Mosses from an Old Manse*, vol. 10 of *The Centenary Edition of the Works of Nathaniel Hawthorne*, ed. William Charvat, Roy Harvey Pearce, and Claude M. Simpson (Columbus: Ohio State University Press, 1962), 335.

4. Herman Melville, *Correspondence*, ed. Lynn Horth, vol. 14 of *The Writings of Herman Melville*, ed. Harrison Hayford et al. (Evanston and Chicago, Illinois: Northwestern University Press and the Newberry Library, 1993), 121 (italics in

original); *Moby-Dick*, ed. Harrison Hayford, Hershel Parker, and G. Thomas Tanselle, vol. 6 of *The Writings of Herman Melville* (1988), 185.

5. *Complete Poems of Emily Dickinson*, J:836.

6. Henry David Thoreau, *Walden* (Princeton: Princeton University Press, 1973), 330.

7. Melville, *Moby-Dick*, 492.

8. Emerson, *Nature*, in *The Portable Emerson*, ed. Carl Bode (New York: Viking Penguin, 1981), 49.

9. Emerson, "Self-Reliance," in *Portable Emerson*, 158. Still, Emerson allowed himself the latitude that "a foolish consistency is the hobgoblin of little minds" (145).

10. Melville, "Hawthorne and His Mosses," in *The Piazza Tales and Other Prose Pieces, 1839–1860*, ed. Harrison Hayford et al., vol. 9 of *The Writings of Herman Melville* (1987), 250.

11. Hawthorne, journal entry, August 1, 1851, *The American Notebooks*, ed. Claude M. Simpson, vol. 8 of *The Centenary Edition of the Works of Nathaniel Hawthorne* (1972), 448.

12. Hawthorne, journal entry, November 20, 1856, *English Notebooks*, in *The Portable Hawthorne*, ed. Malcolm Cowley (New York: Viking Press, 1948), 588–89.

13. T. S. Eliot, "Burnt Norton" from *Four Quartets* (New York: Harcourt, Brace & World, 1943), 3–8.

14. Eliot, "The Dry Salvages" from *Four Quartets*, 21–28.

15. Eliot, "Little Gidding" from *Four Quartets*, 31–39.

16. Matthew Arnold, "To a Friend," *Matthew Arnold*, ed. Miriam Allott and Robert H. Super, *The Oxford Authors Series* (New York: Oxford University Press, 1986), 53.

17. See Richard Dilworth Rust, "'All Things Which Have Been Given of God . . . Are the Typifying of Him': Typology in the Book of Mormon," in *Literature of Belief: Sacred Scripture and Religious Experience*, ed. Neal E. Lambert (Provo, Utah: BYU Religious Studies Center, 1981), 233–43.

18. Essays I have written on these topics that appear in expanded form in my forthcoming book are "Poetry in the Book of Mormon" and "Book of Mormon Imagery," in *Rediscovering the Book of Mormon*, ed. John L. Sorenson and Melvin J. Thorne (Salt Lake City: Deseret Book, 1991), 100–13, 132–39; and "Book of Mormon Literature," with Donald W. Parry, in *Encyclopedia of Mormonism*, ed. Daniel H. Ludlow (New York: Macmillan, 1992), 1:181–85.

CHAPTER 23

GOOD AND TRUE

JOHN W. WELCH
Professor of Law, Brigham Young University
Editor-in-Chief, BYU Studies

LIKE MOST PEOPLE, I am grateful for good friends who give my life meaningful opportunities for happiness, companionship, compassion, appreciation, and a host of precious feelings and memories. I also like to remember the adventures, explorations, discoveries, challenges, emotions, and many other experiences that life has brought me. For all the same reasons, I am grateful for the Book of Mormon. It has affected me in many ways. I love and respect this book. It is a good and true friend. It has filled my life with purpose, perspective, ideas, values, happiness, adventure, challenges, and frequent sacred experiences. Its truth and goodness are sufficiently evident to me in many ways. Yet, at the same time, I know that I glimpse only a part of all that it has to offer.

I see the Book of Mormon as a true classic. Classics, in my mind, are books that reflect the human condition so accurately that they speak to all humanity, regardless of age, station, or predisposition. A classic is a book that I expect will wear me out long before I will wear it out. This is how it has been for me with the Book of Mormon. Whether as a missionary, graduate student, father, or bishop, I have learned different things at each stage of my life from this book. Its wisdom withstands the passage of time and transcends the compass of individual experience.

Truth may be defined in many ways, and the Book of Mormon is at home with them all. I see its truth manifested by its spirituality; in its internal consistency, accuracy, and coherence; by its astounding complexity, reality, and evidences of antiquity; and through its broad visions of eternity, deep profundity, open clarity, rewarding subtlety, and masterful artistry.

Likewise, goodness may be defined in many ways, and the Book of Mormon welcomes them all. I feel its goodness in all of its various testimonies of Christ, in its practical and prudent wisdom, in its poignant social conscience, dynamic universalism, unrestrained candor, uninhibited idealism, and undeterred optimism.

Since the time I was a young man, I have always felt very satisfied in my testimony of the Book of Mormon. At first, I believed that the book was true with little or no evidence of any kind at all. Perhaps because I never expected to find much in the way of proofs or great evidence for the Book of Mormon, I have been even more richly satisfied by those things I have learned or found.

I believe that many significant insights into the truth and goodness of the Book of Mormon have appeared over the years and that they will continue to do so. Almost every month during the last few years, new discoveries have been made in support of the Book of Mormon; many of these have been reported by my colleagues and me in newsletters, updates, lectures, conferences, papers, books, and other publications. I hesitate to single out any of these in particular, for the same reason that I am reluctant to begin naming the names of friends I like most. But as such evidences or realizations have come to light, I think that they should be pointed out with conviction, care, and caution. I never intend to overstate the case in favor of the Book of Mormon, but I do not want to understate it, either.

I am grateful to two witnesses, a good seminary teacher and a truth-loving Sunday School teacher, whose joint influences prompted me to see the Book of Mormon as a spiritual tutor. With this book, I had my first experience in asking God for wisdom, as James 1:5 challenges, when, as a high school junior, I put Moroni 10:4 on the line, kneeling by my bedside. I cut my spiritual teeth on the Book of

Mormon and learned to recognize the promptings of the spirit. I learned that one of the gifts of the Book of Mormon is that a person can know that it is true without yet knowing everything it contains.

I also learned at that time the limits of logic: that the Holy Ghost is not found at the end of a syllogism, that deductive logic is restricted by its assumptions, and that inductive sciences are limited by lack of agreement on what any given bit of evidence implies. Moreover, as President Benson said, those who try by logic to prove the Book of Mormon either true or false invert the actual process: "We do not have to prove the Book of Mormon is true. The book is its own proof. . . . The Book of Mormon is not on trial—the people of the world, including the members of the Church, are on trial as to what they will do with this second witness for Christ."[1] Thus, it seems clear enough that the Lord does not intend the Book of Mormon to be an open-and-shut case intellectually, either pro or con. If God had intended this, he would have left more concrete evidences one way or the other.

Instead, it seems that the Lord has maintained a careful balance between allowing questions that lead one to wonder about the reputed sources of the book and providing counterweights that lead one to affirm the stated origins of the record. This equilibrium invites the world to approach the Book of Mormon ultimately as a matter of faith and as a modern-day miracle, but at the same time gives people ample grounds to take the book seriously.

The study part of this balance is an important ingredient in my testimony of the Book of Mormon. Although scholarship does not create faith, for me it creates an environment in which faith may thrive. I have found over the years that many intriguing and forceful cases can be made in favor of the Book of Mormon on grounds that combine the resources and faculties of both study and faith. Trying to rely on either faith alone or study alone is like trying to play a violin with only one arm, or to walk with only one leg.

One of my favorite statements in this regard was written by B. H. Roberts in 1909. As he put it, the power of the Holy Ghost

> must ever be the chief source of evidence for the truth of the Book
> of Mormon. All other evidence is secondary to this, the primary and

infallible. No arrangement of evidence, however skillfully ordered; no argument, however adroitly made, can ever take its place.

However, Roberts continued,

> To be known, the truth must be stated and the clearer and more complete the statement is, the better opportunity will [t]he Holy Spirit have for testifying to the souls of men that the work is true. . . . [Moreover,] evidence and argument . . . . in support of truth, like secondary causes in natural phenomena, may be of firstrate importance, and mighty factors in the achievement of God's purposes.[2]

In studying the Book of Mormon, I have found Roberts's description to be correct. Evidence in support of this book's truth invites people to take it seriously, engenders respect, strengthens the impressions it has on us, brings people to contemplate and entertain its claims, and gives the Holy Spirit a better opportunity to testify that the book is true.

For thirty years, I have worked almost continuously on various Book of Mormon research projects. This work has been less of a roaming odyssey than an extended elaboration in pursuit of certain themes. I have especially desired to understand the historical, religious, and intellectual backgrounds of the book, to shed light on what its words originally meant to its ancient authors. Not far in the back of my mind during most of my studies in law, history, philosophy, classical languages, and biblical and Near Eastern studies has always been the prospect of finding information or approaches pertinent to the Book of Mormon text. The results have been rewarding and stimulating, both intellectually and spiritually. I have come to esteem the Book of Mormon as one of the intellectual wonders of the world. It is part of the miracle of the Restoration, "the most singular evidence in support of Joseph Smith's claim to being a spokesman for Almighty God."[3] It is a singular wonder in multiple ways.

The simple fact that the book exists is amazing enough. I have a hard time imagining the task of dictating this book, final copy, without notes, one time through, in something like sixty working days. I was deeply impressed as I gathered copies of all the known documents from 1829 relevant to the translation of the Book of Mormon. My desire was to reconstruct a nearly day-by-day picture of the amazing events in the lives of Joseph Smith and Oliver Cowdery during the months of April, May, and June of that year, when Joseph was translating this substantial volume.[4] A significant number of independent yet consistent historical documents demonstrate that the book as we have it today was dictated, without notes, in very short order. Joseph and Oliver began on April 7, 1829. By May 15 they were up to the passage in 3 Nephi that triggered their inquiry that led to the restoration of the Aaronic Priesthood that day. By the end of June it was finished. This pace allows only a week for all of 1 Nephi and only a day and a half for the speech of King Benjamin, which I regard as one of the masterpieces of religious writing anywhere in world literature. Even more astonishing, this time was neither uninterrupted nor tranquil. Time and energy were lost while Joseph and Oliver looked for odd jobs to earn money for more paper, preached and baptized, moved on buckboard from Harmony to Fayette (more than 100 miles), received sections 3–18 of the Doctrine and Covenants, and took at least one trip from Harmony to Colesville—to say nothing of eating and sleeping. To me it is a wonder and a miracle that out of such a short amount of time could come such an enormous burst of light.

The book is also a wonder in what it contains. The pages of the Book of Mormon reflect ancient culture, language, literature, history, symbolism, doctrine, and other amazing details. I am especially impressed with the authenticity of such texts as the extended allegory of the olive tree in Jacob 5;[5] with King Benjamin's multifaceted speech in Mosiah 1–6;[6] with the enlightened words of Alma on the gospel, conversion, and the plan of salvation in Alma 5, 7, 12–13, 32–33, 36–42; and with the sermons given by Jesus at the temple in Bountiful, particularly in 3 Nephi 11–18.[7] Whoever wrote the text of Jacob 5 knew quite completely the business of raising good olives. Whoever composed Benjamin's speech knew essentially what belonged in an ancient coronation ceremony held in conjunction with a Feast of Tabernacles or the Day of Atonement and a covenant renewal. Whoever wrote the speeches in Alma and 3 Nephi had a comprehensive grasp on the theology of the Atonement, the essence of Christian life, the basic structure of Jewish and Christian temple ideology, and a mature range of religious experience. But the historical, literary, botanical, and other details necessary to produce such texts were not available to Joseph Smith in 1829, and such broad exposure to spiritual life was well beyond his youthful years. Even a few such details or dimensions would impress me that the Book of Mormon is a sign of no ordinary proportions that God's hand was at work in its composition. Yet the book is filled with such features.

For instance, through my study of ancient laws, I have been particularly fascinated by the legal details in the Book of Mormon. One of my favorite examples is found in the execution of Zemnarihah (3 Nephi 4:28–33): the leader of an army of robbers is hung on a tree and then the tree is chopped down—just the punishment the Talmud prescribes, namely, to chop down the tree on which a victim is hanged or displayed.[8] More than one scholar of ancient Judaism has been puzzled by this striking parallel.

Moreover, the execution of Zemnarihah illustrates another significant detail. In ancient Near Eastern laws, a distinction existed between a common thief and a robber. Unlike thieves, robbers in ancient society were outsiders, "outlaws" who lived in bands out in the hills, swearing oaths of loyalty and secrecy, raiding local villages, committing assassinations, and so forth. Robbers like Zemnarihah were dealt with by the military; they received no trials and were usually punished by death. In Anglo-American law and language, the terms "thief" and "robber" are so closely related and nearly synonymous that the King James Version of the Bible uses them interchangeably.[9] But such is not the case in the Book of Mormon. Remarkably, the Gadianton robbers are always called robbers, never thieves, and their behavior and treatment is the same as that of the robbers of the ancient Near East.[10] I remember spending an afternoon at Oxford reading for the first time Bernard Jackson's book on the history of theft in early Jewish law;[11] I could not have been struck more forcefully, both intellectually and spiritually, by the congruence between his historical explanations and the picture I already knew from the Book of Mormon.

Similar ancient legal concepts and elements are to be found in the trials of Abinadi, Nehor, Alma and Amulek, Korihor, Paanchi, and Seantum, and in the backgrounds of many Book of Mormon narratives.

They indicate again that whoever wrote these texts was thoroughly immersed in the social context and jurisprudence of early biblical times—evidence that does not point toward Joseph Smith, but rather invites us to seek elsewhere for the Book of Mormon's authorship.

I have also enjoyed working with several passages in the Book of Mormon that manifest uncommon literary beauty. Although I find elegance and significance in many rhetorical and literary qualities of the book, I will never forget the day I discovered extended chiastic structures in its pages.[12] As a missionary in Regensburg, Germany, in 1967, I had been studying the literary art in the Gospel of Matthew. Very early one morning, I was awakened from a sound sleep with the clear impression that what was evidence of Hebrew style in the Gospel of Matthew had to be evidence of Hebrew style in the Book of Mormon. I stumbled in the dark over to the desk where my companion and I had been reading the night before in the first part of Mosiah. Within a few minutes, some of the very best instances of chiasmus in the Book of Mormon unfolded before me in Mosiah 3:18–19 and 5:10–12. These inverted parallelisms hardly seem to be the result of random dictation; they bespeak developed and polished literary achievement. Perhaps a comment on Alma 36 from David Noel Freedman, whose specialty in early Hebrew poetry is well known, best describes my feelings about the literary content of the Book of Mormon: "Your book," he said, "is very beautiful."

The Book of Mormon is indeed rich. The book makes clear and abundant sense, despite its complexity: records existing inside of other records, later passages quoting and interpreting earlier passages, loose ends all tied together, presupposed backgrounds that make perfect sense, and character traits of individuals that are true to life and consistent from one episode to another. How could any author keep all the historical, geographical, chronological, personal, textual, literary, doctrinal, legal, political, and military details, strands, plots, and subplots concurrently in mind in order to dictate the Book of Mormon one time through without notes or a rough draft? Try as many have to explain by whom and how this book was written, Joseph Smith's explanation is still the most cogent.

Over and over again, the Book of Mormon has impressed me not only with its antiquity and artistry, but also with its wisdom. It is a profound source of knowledge and perspective. This scripture teaches the gospel in doctrinal passages that are crystal clear and uncannily pertinent both to the minutiae of personal life and to the megatrends of world affairs. The Book of Mormon has taught me in quiet moments such things as the essential requirements of God's plan of salvation, the errors of many tendencies in modern society, and the spiritual ills of contention and disputation. I find it quite remarkable that of the myriad arguments written against the Book of Mormon, hardly any have been directed against its ethical positions or religious teachings.

Many of these insights have come when I was least expecting them. On such occasions, I feel a sustaining glow inside my heart and an unexpected quickening of thought. As a bishop, I had one girl ask me: "How can I know I have been forgiven?" Quite unmotivated on my part, the words of Mosiah came clearly to my mind. There, King Benjamin tells his people that they must give to the poor if they would *retain* "a remission of [their] sins from day to day" (Mosiah 4:26). Although rendering acts of charity is usually overlooked when the steps in the repentance process are described, I testify that this is true and wise counsel, and it is known only from the Book of Mormon.

Another day, I was preparing to deliver a lecture on Alma 32. It suddenly dawned on me what this text says we actually learn by planting within ourselves the seed of faith in Christ (Alma 33:22–23). Alma never says that we learn that the seed is true; rather, we learn that the seed is good. Obviously, it is one thing to know what is true—even Hitler knew a great deal of truth. It is quite another thing to know what is good. As I have become more sensitive to this reality, I have become more aware that truth is worthless if it is not conjoined with a value system. Truth, like any other tool, is morally neutral: a hammer can be used either to build up or to tear down. For me, the Book of Mormon thoroughly unites the domains of truth and goodness—even explicitly, in Moroni 10:6: "Whatsoever thing is good is just and true."

I also have come to know that the Book of Mormon is good and true by following it in regular religious practice. For example, every Sunday I enjoy partaking of the sacrament, and I often reflect on the fact that the sacrament prayers—concise and powerfully effective prayers that B. H. Roberts liked to call the "prayers perfect"[13]—were first revealed in this dispensation when the text of Moroni 4–5 was translated. These prayers are directly related to the very words that Jesus himself spoke in 3 Nephi 18 to the Nephites gathered around the temple in Bountiful,[14] and so I like to contemplate the sacrament, not only of the Lord's Supper, but also of the Lord's Appearance—substantial tokens not only of his mortal body, which was broken, but also of his resurrected body, which was made manifest. By pondering the relationships between these sacramental texts and by being willing to do what they ask, I have come to know and appreciate the truth and goodness of these prayers. So it has been for me with all of the religious instructions of the Book of Mormon.

I have found in the Book of Mormon great comfort, for comfort is also an eventual companion of truth. A missionary friend of mine used to call his Book of Mormon his "happiness book." He taught me that whenever I got discouraged or lost touch with the essentials, I would find rejuvenation in the Book of Mormon. Its voices are full of reassurance for the righteous and of hope for the sinful. Over and over again in this book, I learn that the Lord "remembereth every creature of his creating" (Mosiah 27:30), and that he remembers every covenant of his making (1 Nephi 19:15; 3 Nephi 16:11). The Book of Mormon also affirms that God "loveth those who will have him to be their God" (1 Nephi 17:40). I try not to dwell long on the mistakes, the wars, and the occasional violence in the book, but to rejoice with Alma ("Oh, what joy, and what marvelous light," Alma 36:20); be moved with the swelling of the hearts "unto the gushing out of many tears" (3 Nephi 4:33); and be comforted with the words of "peace, peace" to Nephi (Helaman 5:47) and of encouragement at his "unwearyingness" (Helaman 10:4). With this book I never feel alone or lost.

I am ultimately impressed that all the elements of the Book of Mormon work together for one and only one purpose: to stand as a witness of Jesus Christ. The title page of the Book of Mormon announces that its mission is "the convincing" of all people that Jesus is the Christ, the very Eternal God, and all of its features work toward this single end. As a lawyer, I am struck by the many ways in which the Book of Mormon is a credible, convincing witness. Like the speech of all good witnesses, its language is straightforward and clear, direct and cogent, unequivocal and persuasive. It speaks spontaneously and openly, yet reflects a depth of understanding that is embedded with hidden treasures. It gets its facts right. Each prophet bears his own testimony in a personally distinctive and compelling manner.[15] Yet the overall effect is stunningly consistent, both in major themes and in minute details. (Here one may compare, for example, the twenty-one words of Lehi in 1 Nephi 1:8 that are quoted expressly and precisely and hardly accidentally in Alma 36:22.[16]) We live in a day when the message of Christ's Lordship needs to be delivered as much as or more than ever before. Accordingly, I value this good book as a unique and primary witness of Christ.

Finally, an important part of my testimony is that we shall see the Book of Mormon again at the judgment bar of God. As a professor, I watch my students try to figure out what is likely to be on their final exams. Fortunately, the Lord has not left us in the dark on life's final exam. As Moroni closed the book, he wrote: "And I exhort you to remember these things; for the time speedily cometh that ye shall know that I lie not, for ye shall see me at the bar of God; and the Lord God will say unto you: Did I not declare my words unto you, which were written by this man?" (Moroni 10:27). And King Benjamin bore similar testimony that his words "shall stand as a bright testimony against this people, at the judgment day" (Mosiah 3:24). Interestingly, the book is true to its ancient origins, even down to this concluding element, for it is a long-recognized principle of Jewish law that a person cannot be convicted unless he has been warned in advance.

I am glad to have the Book of Mormon. I am deeply grateful for the concerted efforts of the Lord and his prophets in order that we might have the Book of Mormon. I think of the enormous sacrifices of Nephi, risking his life on several occasions, fashioning plates of ore, and tediously writing his reports; of Mormon and Moroni, whose concerns for the suffering and deaths of their wives and children and people must have made it very difficult for them to complete this record; and of Joseph Smith, who endured persecution and eventually sealed his testimony of this book with his blood.

Based on all that I know to be good and true, I gladly testify without hesitation that the Book of Mormon is true and that it is good. I love to read it, teach it, and strive to understand it. To me, this has been a matter of personal urgency. I expect that God will ask one day what we as a people have done with this book. I hope that by then we will have learned enough of its truth and embraced enough of its goodness to give a report worthy of acceptance.

....

NOTES

1. Ezra Taft Benson, in Conference Report, October 1984, 7; or "A New Witness for Christ," *Ensign*, November 1984, 8.

2. B. H. Roberts, *New Witnesses for God*, 3 vols. (Salt Lake City: Deseret News, 1909–11), 2:vi–viii.

3. Ezra Taft Benson, in Conference Report, October 1981, 82; or "Joseph Smith: Prophet to Our Generation," *Ensign*, November 1981, 61.

4. Discussed further in John W. Welch and Tim Rathbone, "The Translation of the Book of Mormon: Basic Historical Information" (Provo, Utah: FARMS, 1986).

5. For extensive analyses of the allegory of Zenos, see *The Allegory of the Olive Tree*, ed. Stephen D. Ricks and John W. Welch (Salt Lake City: Deseret Book and FARMS, 1994).

6. John A. Tvedtnes, "King Benjamin and the Feast of Tabernacles" in *By Study and Also By Faith*, ed. John M. Lundquist and Stephen D. Ricks (Salt Lake City: Deseret Book and FARMS, 1990), 2:197–237; John W. Welch, "King Benjamin's Speech in the Context of Ancient Israelite Festivals" (Provo, Utah: FARMS, 1985).

7. I believe that the Book of Mormon answers the traditional Christian questions about the meaning and mysteries of the Sermon on the Mount. For an extended discussion, see John W. Welch, *The Sermon at the Temple and the Sermon on the Mount* (Salt Lake City: Deseret Book and FARMS, 1990).

8. *Reexploring the Book of Mormon*, ed. John W. Welch (Salt Lake City: Deseret Book and FARMS, 1992), 250–52. This book contains eighty-four FARMS *Updates* from the 1980s.

9. Compare, for example, Jeremiah 7:11, "a den of robbers," with Matthew 21:13, where the King James Version of the New Testament renders this same phrase as "a den of thieves."

10. See further *Reexploring the Book of Mormon*, 248–49.

11. Bernard S. Jackson, *Theft in Early Jewish Law* (Oxford: Oxford University Press, 1972).

12. For several examples, see my initial publication on this subject, "Chiasmus in the Book of Mormon," *BYU Studies* 10 (Autumn 1969): 69–84. For expanded treatments by me and others, see *Chiasmus in Antiquity: Structures, Analyses, Exegesis*, ed. John W. Welch (Hildesheim: Gerstenberg, 1981).

13. See references in Truman G. Madsen, "B. H. Roberts's Final Decade: Statements about the Book of Mormon" (Provo, Utah: FARMS, 1986).

14. *Reexploring the Book of Mormon*, 286–89.

15. I develop this theme further in my article, "Ten Testimonies of Jesus Christ from the Book of Mormon," in *Doctrines of the Book of Mormon*, ed. Bruce A. Van Orden and Brent L. Top (Salt Lake City: Deseret Book, 1992), 223–42.

16. *Reexploring the Book of Mormon*, 21–23.

INDEX

how to live, 76–77; tells how and
not why, 105
Scientific method and religious
experience, 156. *See also*
Enlightenment
Scriptures: learning of, 30; finding
meaning in, 58–59; and philosophy
of men, 62; miraculousness of,
64–65; scholar of, 120–21;
testimony of, requires knowledge
and spiritual confirmation, 121–22;
understanding, requires faith and
obedience, 121–22; doctrinal unity
of, 122–24; latter-day, are more
complete, 124–25; move us to
action, 126; demythologizing of,
145–46; rationalization of
supernatural stories in, 149–50;
could not have been written by
man, 152; selective acceptance of,
156–57; scholarly study of, is not
enough, 184–85; and the Jesus
Seminar, 205–6; acceptance of, is a
spiritual matter, 207–8; blessings of,
207–8
Secular and sacred, balance between,
80–81
"Seeing," 196, 222
Sermon on the Mount, as moral guide,
155
Ships, ancient, 186–88; used to
transport Lehi's family, 188
Signs versus symbols, 38–39
Skepticism of contemporaries, 10–11
Smith, Joseph: on need for personal
spiritual experiences, 41; as
spokesman for God, 65; surpasses
most learned men, 65; on learning
through revelation, 97–98; on
building up of Zion, 136; on his
adversaries, 141–43; consistency of
stories of, 144; never doubted
future of Church, 149–50; on
purpose of life, 151; trustworthi-
ness of stories of, 160–61; testifies
of calling as prophet, 161–63;
misrepresentations in biography of,

162–63; and the Nauvoo Legion,
163–65; expects martyrdom, 164,
168; on human deification, 177;
and study, 185
Smith, Joseph F., on humility versus
ignorance, 99
Social gospel, avoids mention of death
or hereafter, 150
Sorenson, John L., 132
Spirit, characteristics of an individual,
114–16
Spirit of God: learning to recognize,
xii; essential to gaining a testimony,
42–43; influences us constantly,
65–66; aids in scholarly pursuits,
83–85, 97, 200, 228–29
Spiritual and intellectual pursuits,
balance between, 48–50, 53–54
Spiritual experiences: personal nature
of, xii; verified by others who "see,"
222
Spiritual experiments, unaccepted in
secular world, 41
Spirituality and scholarly pursuits:
compatibility of, 7, 14–16, 45–46,
130–31, 156; tips for, 14; achieving
balance between, 14–15, 184–85;
are not of equal importance, 95–96,
100–101
Stace, W. T., 32
Stendahl, Krister, on the Book of
Mormon, 37–38
Stenhouse, T. B. H., 164–68
Stout, Allen J., 164–66
Strupp, Hans, and psychotherapy and
religion, 12
Study of History, A, 31
Sunstone, 141
Supernaturalism, scholars deny, 148–50
Systematic Theology, 39

Taylor, John, on the body as record of
life, 115
Teaching: important in learning truth,
27–28, 30; activism in, versus
rational discourse, 81; sculpture

What Is FARMS?

The Foundation for Ancient Research and Mormon Studies (FARMS) encourages and supports research about the Book of Mormon: Another Testament of Jesus Christ and other ancient scriptures.

FARMS is a nonprofit educational foundation, independent of all other organizations. Its main research interests include ancient history, language, literature, culture, geography, politics, and law relevant to the scriptures. Although such subjects are of secondary importance when compared with the spiritual and eternal messages of the scriptures, solid research and academic perspectives alone can supply certain kinds of useful information, even if only tentatively, concerning many significant and interesting questions about the ancient backgrounds, origins, composition, and meanings of scripture.

The Foundation works to make interim and final reports about this research available widely, promptly, and economically. As a service to teachers and students of the scriptures, research results are distributed in both scholarly and popular formats.

It is hoped that this information will help all interested people to "come unto Christ" (Jacob 1:7) and to understand and take more seriously these ancient witnesses of the atonement of Jesus Christ, the Son of God.

For more information about FARMS, call toll free 1-800-327-6715, or write to FARMS, P.O. Box 7113, University Station, Provo UT 84602.